Living with Colonialism

COLONIALISMS

Jennifer Robertson, General Editor

Living with Colonialism

Nationalism and Culture
in the Anglo-Egyptian Sudan

HEATHER J. SHARKEY

University of California Press

BERKELEY　　LOS ANGELES　　LONDON

University of California Press
Berkeley and Los Angeles, California

University of California Press, Ltd.
London, England

© 2003 by the Regents of the University of California

Library of Congress Cataloging-in-Publication Data

Sharkey, Heather J. (Heather Jane), 1967–.
   Living with colonialism : nationalism and culture in the Anglo-
Egyptian Sudan / Heather J. Sharkey.
      p.   cm. —(Colonialisms)
Revision of the author's thesis (doctoral—Princeton University, 1998)
under title: Colonialism and the culture of nationalism in the Northern
Sudan.
   Includes bibliographical references and index.
   ISBN 0-520-23558-4 (alk. paper).—ISBN 0-520-23559-2 (pbk. : alk.
paper)
      1. Sudan—History—20th century.   2. Britons—Colonization—
Sudan.   3. Great Britain—Colonies—Africa—Cultural policy.
4. Nationalism—Sudan—History—20th century.   5. Postcolonialism—
Sudan.   I. Title.   II. Series.

DT156.7 .S55   2003
962.404—dc21   2002007140

Manufactured in the United States of America
12   11   10   09   08   07   06   05   04   03
10   9   8   7   6   5   4   3   2   1

The paper used in this publication meets the minimum requirements of
ANSI/NISO Z39.48-1992 (R 1997) (Permanence of Paper).♾

Contents

Acknowledgments

The generous support of many institutions made this project possible. In 1990, four years before this research even started, the British Government and Marshall Aid Commemoration Commission granted me the Marshall scholarship that sent me to the University of Durham, where my love for Sudanese history first began to grow. During the 1995–96 academic year, the U.S. Department of Education awarded me a Fulbright–Hays fellowship for research in Egypt, Great Britain, and Norway. Grants from the American–Scandinavian Foundation (Crown Princess Martha Friendship Fund), and from four Princeton University sources—the Council on Regional Studies, the Program in Near Eastern Studies, the Center of International Studies (Boesky and Sternberg Funds), and the Department of History—supported research trips to Norway (1994) and the Sudan (1995). Fellowships from the Mrs. Giles Whiting Foundation, the Josephine De Kármán Trust, the Woodrow Wilson Foundation (Princeton Society of Fellows), and the A. W. Mellon Foundation enabled me to devote the 1996–97 year to writing and completing my dissertation. In 1999 a grant from the Kelly-Douglas Fund at MIT enabled me to undertake a follow-up visit to British archives.

Many individuals read the manuscript at different stages of its development and offered invaluable advice. I owe thanks to Robert L. Tignor, L. Carl Brown, R. S. O'Fahey, M. W. Daly, Abdullahi Ibrahim, Lora Wildenthal, Endre Stiansen, John O. Voll, Lynne Withey, and the readers of the University of California Press. Several colleagues offered insights and suggestions in the course of research, including Peter Woodward, Yoshiko Kurita, Albrecht Hofheinz, Anders Bjørkelo, Robert O. Collins, Fadwa Abd al-Rahman Ali Taha, Robert Kramer, Anita Fabos, and Ahmed Shouk. Many individuals also took the time to share their knowledge in letters, conversations, and interviews. In this regard, I am grateful to Abd al-Rahman Abu

Zayd, Isma'il al-Atabani, Sir Michael Atiyah, Patrick Selim Atiyah, Ahmad Safi al-Din Awad, Muhammad Hashim Awad, Jala' Isma'il al-Azhari, Qasim Badri, Michael Cook, Sir Donald Hawley, Charles Issawi, Muna Shami Jurdak, Sirr al-Khatm al-Khalifa, A. H. M. Kirk-Greene, Phillippa Maghrabi (Mrs. Abd al-Fattah al-Maghrabi), Sadiq al-Mahdi, René Malouf, J. A. Mangan, Yunan Labib Rizq, Maryam Mustafa Salama (Mrs. Isma'il al-Azhari), the late G. N. Sanderson, Amin al-Tum Satti, Abd Allah al-Tayyib, Graham Thomas, and J. O. Udal. Still others facilitated my use of archives and research centers, notably Jane Hogan, Beth Rainey, and Lesley Forbes of the Durham University libraries; Ali Salih Karrar and Muhammad Ibrahim Abu Salim of the National Records Office in Khartoum; Knut Vikør of the Centre for Middle Eastern and Islamic Studies at the University of Bergen; Haydar Ibrahim Ali of the Sudanese Studies Center in Cairo; and staff members of the C.M.S. archives at Birmingham University, the Wellcome Institute in London, and the manuscripts and special collections divisions of Edinburgh University and the School of Oriental and African Studies (SOAS). Librarians at Princeton, MIT, and Trinity College worked wonders in securing Arabic and English books through interlibrary loan. Kate Warne and the staff at the University of California Press guided the manuscript smoothly to completion. I also thank Rosalind Caldecott, who designed the map of the Anglo-Egyptian Sudan that is available to researchers at the Sudan Archive in Durham.

In the Sudan, Batoul Mukhtar Muhammad Taha and Imad Ali Idris showed boundless hospitality in their home in Hillat Hamad, Khartoum North. Through their example, I came to understand why the Sudanese are famous for their dignity and grace. Many others also showed their kindness in Khartoum, including John and Koki Bodourian, Anis Haggar, Fudi Malouf, George and Eleanor Pagoulatos, and the staff of the National Records Office. In Cairo, members of the extended Eveready-Energizer corporate "family" made my stay more comfortable and showed a genuine concern for my well-being. In Durham, the staff of Palace Green Library extended a warm welcome, as did the Hogan family and Alec Cumming-Bruce. In Bergen, I found my place among the affiliated members of the "Senter for Midtausten- og islamske studiar," who introduced me to the beauty and pleasures of Norway while offering keen intellectual companionship. At Princeton, and later at the University of Massachusetts at Amherst, MIT, and most recently, Trinity College, I enjoyed the friendship and encouragement of many colleagues.

While my debts of gratitude are many, I thank my family above all, for their unstinting love and support over the course of so many years. I therefore dedicate this book to my mother and father, Jane and Richard Sharkey; to my five sisters and brother—Donna, Diana, Jill, Joanne, Brian, and Jennifer; to my parents-in-law, T. R. and Jaya Balasubramanian; and to my husband, Vijay Balasubramanian. As my best friend and sidekick, Vijay shared in my adventures throughout the book's creative process, and lived with *Living with Colonialism* almost as much as I did. When this book was nearing completion, our baby boy, Ravi Nicholas Balasubramanian, came into this world and blessed us with great happiness.

To my family

Note on Transliteration, Translation, Spelling, and Dates

In transliterating from Arabic, this book follows the system used in the *International Journal of Middle East Studies*. Diacritical marks are omitted, except for the *ayn* (') and *hamza* (') when they occur in the middle or at the end of words. Exceptions are the terms *mamur* and *ulama*, which appear in *The New Shorter Oxford English Dictionary*, 1993 edition. Note, too, that since the term *mamur* was used widely in British English sources, it is not italicized as a foreign word. Unless otherwise indicated, translations from Arabic into English are the author's own. Moreover, Sudanese place names are spelled according to British usage of the period, as set out in Permanent Committee on Geographical Names for British Official Use, *First List of Names in the Anglo-Egyptian Sudan*, 1927. Finally, in identifying individuals, I have indicated birth and death dates, when they are known.

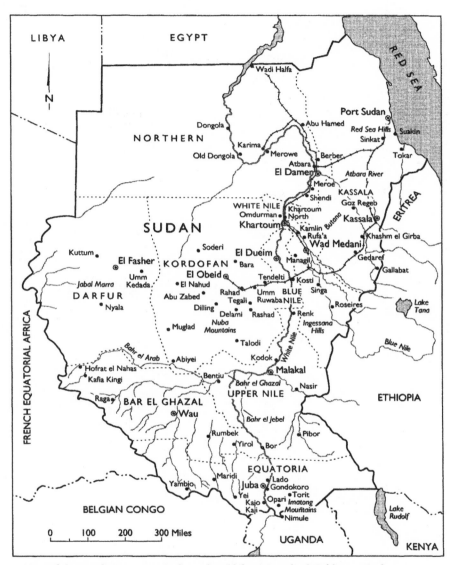

Map of the Anglo-Egyptian Sudan, adapted from Rosalind Caldecott, Sudan
Archive, Durham University Library

1   Living with Colonialism

Writing in 1833 about the British government of India, the historian and parliamentarian Thomas Babington Macaulay declared, "Empire is itself the strangest of all political anomalies. That a handful of adventurers from an island in the Atlantic should have subjugated a vast country divided from the place of their birth by half the globe; a country which at no very distant period was merely the subject of fable to the nations of Europe . . . these are prodigies to which the world has seen nothing similar. Reason is confounded. We interrogate the past in vain."[1]

Macaulay's puzzle—how did the British do it?—contributed to a historical myth-in-the-making: the legend of the lone British ruler in Asia and Africa, drawing upon intelligence, civilization, and character to bring foreign countries and peoples to heel. As compelling and flattering to the British as this myth may have been, the reality was otherwise. Empire worked on the ground because it relied on vast support staffs of clerks, technicians, teachers, and medics who handled the day-to-day tasks of colonialism. As petty employees these individuals produced domination in its most prosaic forms, but as early nationalists they dreamed of displacing imperial power. These were colonialism's intimate enemies, making colonial rule a reality while hoping to see it undone.[2]

In the aftermath of empire, histories have featured conquerors and peasant rebels but have said little of these local functionaries. This book tells their story, explaining the importance of their lives and careers to the operation of the colonial state, the mediation of cultural change, and the elaboration of communal identities. Considering experiences from the Anglo-Egyptian Sudan, the book casts light on three major historical questions:

first, how colonialism worked, not as a system in the abstract, but as a practice of everyday life; second, how nationalism arose in the banal activities and myriad exchanges that occurred on the ground and in print[3]; and third, how the colonial state took shape and evolved into the nation-state, with lasting social consequences.[4]

These questions have living relevance for postcolonial countries as they pursue their search for identity. Indeed, they are more relevant now than they were at decolonization, nearly half a century ago. For, after initially believing themselves liberated from an era of foreign oppression, nationalists and their heirs saw that they were tied more closely to the colonial past than they had originally realized, and that European rule, however brief, had irrevocably altered their societies, economies, and cultures. Hence the need for histories, or more specifically, for usable pasts, that understand the nation in light of the colony that came before it.[5]

EMPIRE AND THE COLONIAL IMPACT

In the late nineteenth and early twentieth centuries, Europe made its last thrust to extend empires in Africa and Asia after four centuries of global expansion. Whether or not this process was the political outgrowth of capitalism, as V. I. Lenin famously argued,[6] imperialism in practice did have an economic ground rule, namely, colonies could not cost more than they paid. Empire, at the very least, had to break even.

The imperial rulers of British Africa and India strove to balance budgets and minimize costs by hiring local recruits for petty administrative jobs. In terms of salary, expatriate Britons were expensive but locals were cheap. To satisfy the need for skilled and literate employees in the lower and middle tiers of the bureaucracy, British regimes established government colleges or patronized Christian missionary institutions. From the Gold Coast to Bengal, such schools groomed young men for clerical, judicial, and technical posts.

By creating new educated classes to serve the regime, Britain addressed the supreme organizational dilemma of the colonial state: controlling vast populations with minute staffs.[7] By the 1930s, the ratio of British ruler to ruled was about 1:28,000 in India and 1:54,000 in Nigeria—but the illusion of mastery remained.[8] Britons may have had weapons, confidence, and competence, but more practically, they had local support staffs, deputized to carry out many of empire's mundane tasks, from filing papers to collecting taxes.[9] At the same time they had a coercive apparatus of locally recruited soldiers and police.[10] Through clever organization of people and resources, colonial regimes conveyed an impression of solidity and thereby secured their "dominance without hegemony."[11]

In the short term, the heavy use of skilled civilian support staffs was a relatively low-cost solution to the personnel problem. By offering salaried jobs and the hope of promotion in return for work well done, the British neutralized opposition among the newly educated—Middle Eastern *effendis*, Indian *babus*, and African "Europeanized natives."[12] However, this stake in the colonial system grew less satisfying with time. Increasingly frustrated by patterns of exclusion that cast them as social inferiors vis-à-vis Britons and restricted their ascent within the bureaucratic system, intellectuals began to develop nationalist ideologies that rested on clear anticolonial foundations.[13] In this way, the nationalist challenge to colonialism arose from within the colonial system and swelled to fill the borders that empire had imposed.

The logistics of empire and its "information order" were conducive to nationalism anyway.[14] The very conditions that enabled the colonial state to consolidate control—conditions created by a host of developing technologies in transport and communications—also favored the rapid movement of people, ideas, and practices. Implications for the colonized were manifold. Daily habits changed, as the new order affected ways people traveled, dressed, conducted business, ate, and treated illnesses. As social contacts with Britons and other expatriates intensified, and as rates of migration rose (particularly toward towns and cities), social groups began to redefine themselves and their relations to others. In addition to communal identities based on religion, sect, language, or clan, a new identity began to form. This was nationalism: the belief that colonial borders enclosed a community of people who shared a heritage and political destiny. In this way, nationalism was an ideological manifestation of compound social changes that colonialism set in motion. It responded not only to the idea of foreign domination, but also, and perhaps more importantly, to political and cultural change.

Nationalism was also a literary undertaking; much like empire itself, it was reliant on the power of the written word to affirm and eventually popularize its values.[15] Cheap printing was essential to its development, because it allowed educated groups not only to read the works of others but to publish journals and sometimes books of their own.[16] In essays, poems, stories, and even, in some regions, novels, nascent nationalists explored and debated ideals. Of course, even as print culture propelled early nationalism, it confirmed its elitism, since advanced literacy was a privilege in African and Asian societies. Readers gained access to a world of ideas, and published writers, political influence.[17]

If nationalism was in fact a "spiritual principle,"[18] as its theorists have sometimes maintained, then it did not emerge from minds full-sprung. It took work to summon up the nation, through efforts, especially in writing, to define its central ideas.[19] Hence the importance of poets and of "the giants of literature lovers,"[20] in general, in propagating early nationalism by evoking lofty ideals capable of giving the nation a soul.

Certain assumptions about colonialism, nationalism, and culture guide the text that follows. *Colonialism* refers to the system of domination that proceeded from the economic and territorial expansion of empires. Colonial systems worked as empire's local proxy within territories (or "colonies") that were acquired by invasion, subject to alien rulers, and dependent on a remote mother country or center.[21] *Nationalism* refers to a collective consciousness among people who imagine shared values, interests, and mutual obligations. While some use the term to describe ideologies that propel movements for political autonomy, the focus here is on nationalism's sentiment, not on its activism or its accoutrements of political parties and unions. Finally, *culture* refers to "the complex of values, customs, beliefs and practices which constitute the way of life of a specific group."[22] As something which is taught, not genetically inherited, culture is flexible and open to change. Culture is also a possible battleground on which political causes can be fought.[23]

In Africa and Asia during the early twentieth century colonialism had strong cultural dimensions because its policies ushered in dramatic economic, political, and social changes and thereby influenced the minutiae of daily life.[24] Its system affected everything from the clothes people wore to the games they played. Although in a colony everyone lived with colonialism, for some—and notably for the new educated classes—the experience was more intimate, and more troubling, than for others.

In short, this book, by drawing upon Sudanese experiences and insights, reconnects early nationalists to the colonial system they shunned but which they helped to create.

COLONIAL SUDAN

The Sudan after 1898 was something of a legal anomaly: a de jure territory of two countries, Great Britain and Egypt. Its unusual situation derived from a nineteenth-century bout of colonialism which preceded the British arrival.

After 1898, Egypt's claims to the Sudan rested on this nineteenth-century colonial history. In 1820–21 armies of the Muhammad Ali dynasty of Egypt had conquered the region, establishing a Turco-Egyptian regime led by military men from the wider Ottoman Empire. By the 1870s, this regime had also begun to draw military administrators from Europe and North America. As Britain's influence mounted in Egypt, Britain, in particular, gained a foothold in the region.

The Turco-Egyptian regime collapsed piecemeal between 1881 and 1885, under the pressure of a popular millenarian *jihad* (holy war) movement led by a Sufi scholar named Muhammad Ahmad (1844–85), who declared himself to be al-Mahdi ("the Rightly Guided One," who had been expected to arrive before the End of Time and Judgment Day). In 1885 the Mahdi's supporters sacked the Turco-Egyptian capital of Khartoum (killing its British commander, General Charles Gordon, in the process) and established a state based on Islamic principles from a capital at nearby Omdurman. Though the Mahdi died later in 1885, the Mahdist state continued to thrive under his *khalifa*, or successor, commonly known as al-Khalifa Abdullahi (1846–99; r. 1885–98.)

Occurring a mere three years after Britain's occupation of Egypt, the Mahdist victory at Khartoum struck a blow at British prestige just as other European powers were beginning to partition the African continent in the rush to expand imperial territories. Responding to the pressures of the "Scramble," Britain launched a campaign against the Mahdist state in 1896 while invoking Egypt's earlier territorial claims. The conquest that culminated in 1898 was extraordinarily violent: Anglo-Egyptian forces used guns and bullets that had greater precision, longer range, and more devastating shrapnel effects than anything used in the region before.[25] Death tolls revealed the technological disparities that enabled Anglo-Egyptian forces to win. At the final battle of Karari (Omdurman), Mahdist casualties included 11,000 dead and 16,000 wounded, compared to 49 dead and 382 wounded on the Anglo-Egyptian side.[26] A young war correspondent named Winston Churchill called it "the most signal triumph ever gained by the arms of science over barbarians."[27]

After the conquest, Britain's Egyptian connections proved useful. By declaring Egypt to be a co-*dominus*, or partner in rule, the British managed to foil French designs on the region. Britain went on to maintain the fiction of Anglo-Egyptian partnership, not only by using the term "Condominium" to refer to the Sudanese regime from 1898 to 1956, but also by placing the territory under Foreign Office (rather than Colonial Office) supervision. To emphasize the Sudan's distinction from other Colonial Office territories, the regime ran a separate Sudan civil service, the British members of which denied the country's colonial status as a badge of professional faith.[28] Writing in 1997, one retired official averred, "We did not regard ourselves as 'Colonists' or 'Colonials' and the Sudan was never a Colony. We rather saw the origin of our presence in the Sudan as strategic and imperial and once there concentrated on working for the advancement of the country and people."[29] To underline the region's legal exceptionalism still further, authorities restricted Sudan representatives to mere observer status at British "imperial" conferences.[30]

In practice, the systematic exclusion of Egypt from power sharing after 1898 made the Sudan a de facto British colony. Having been "occupied" itself in 1882, Egypt spent the Condominium period trying to shake Britain from the Nile Valley even while pressing claims to Egyptian authority over the Sudan.[31] Thus constrained, Egypt remained important in the Sudan mainly as a symbolic counterpoint to the British presence and as a source of encouragement for Sudanese resistance to British colonialism in the Nile Valley. Moreover, Egyptian officials who staffed the middle tiers of the Sudan's administration, especially in the years before 1932, spread ideas about contemporary Arabic literature and about Arab, and Egyptian, nationalism.[32]

Egypt's Sudanese empire in the mid–nineteenth century had been more a sphere of administrative and economic influence than a fixed territory, with its southern reaches supplying a raw materials trade in ivory and slaves. By contrast, the Sudan that emerged after 1898 had a new and definitive shape, its borders set by European policy makers who negotiated British, French, Belgian, and Italian claims in the vicinity. Thus mapped, the Sudan was and is a massive territory of nearly one million square miles. It ranges from desert and semi-desert in the far north, to dry savanna across its central belt, and to moist, wooded savanna, swampland, and pockets of tropical rainforest in the south. Today, the Sudan sits like a great heart at the center of the African continent, surrounded by nine neighbors—Egypt, Eritrea, Ethiopia, Kenya, Uganda, Congo, the Central African Republic, Chad, and Libya—and facing a tenth, Saudi Arabia, across the narrow waters of the Red Sea. During the colonial period, neighboring regimes were British (Kenya and Uganda, and semi-officially, Egypt), Italian (Eritrea and Libya), Belgian (Belgian Congo), French (Ubangi-Shari and Chad), and independent (Abyssinia).

A geographer once claimed that the Sudan had some logic as a territorial entity because of its "significant hydrological unity" in occupying a large part of the Nile basin.[33] The White Nile rises from a source at Lake Victoria and flows through Uganda, while the Blue Nile rises from Lake Tana in Ethiopia. The tributaries meet at Khartoum, flowing as one Nile into Egypt. As a cultural entity, however, the Sudan is much less unified; estimates for the number of languages spoken within its borders range from a few dozen to a few hundred.[34] Although several languages are spoken in the predominantly Muslim northern, eastern, and western regions, Arabic prevails in these areas as either the main language of intellectual discourse or as a lingua franca. Southern Sudan, having today both Christian and Muslim minorities, is even more diverse in languages and religious systems. Sudanese governments of the postcolonial era have struggled to cope with this diversity.

THE EDUCATED SUDANESE

In a country as large and lean in resources as the Sudan, even subsidies from Egypt, penny-pinching on the part of British officials, and judicious use of tax revenues barely met the colonial budget.[35] Hence the British policy of employing Sudanese on low salaries to perform basic government functions, coupled with the gradual elimination of costlier expatriate workers. In waves of "Sudanization" that occurred over the colonial period, Sudanese personnel displaced first Egyptians, later Lebanese, and finally, beginning in the mid-1930s, Britons.

In most of their African territories, the British relied on Christian missionary schools to groom young men for employment. But since British authorities in Northern Sudan were anxious not to offend Muslim public opinion, having recently ousted the staunchly Islamic Mahdist state, they placed the government in charge of education. To address the regime's need for clerks, accountants, teachers, engineers, and *qadis* (Muslim court judges), the British authorities founded Gordon College in 1902. Like kindred institutions elsewhere in Africa—including Sadiqi College in Tunisia, Makerere College in Uganda, École William Ponty in Senegal, and Fourah Bey College in Sierra Leone—Gordon College served as both a training ground for bureaucracy and a crucible for nationalism.[36]

Gordon College took its name from the British general, Charles Gordon, who on his last mission to the Sudan in 1884 to evacuate Turco-Egyptian forces from Khartoum disobeyed orders to withdraw. When the city fell after a long siege in 1885, Gordon died at the hands of Mahdist soldiers and thereafter became a martyr and hero in the British public eye. Years later, his memory fueled popular British support for "Reconquest" and afterwards attracted public donations to the school that bore his name.[37]

British administrators wanted Gordon College to be an elite institution along the lines of a British public school—a kind of "Eton of the Soudan" or "Winchester by the Nile."[38] And so, in recruiting for the school, authorities favored young men of high-status backgrounds. Above all, they enrolled students from Arabic-speaking, Muslim families that claimed Arab genealogies and hailed from the central riverain North.

There were other routes to education in Northern Sudan—for example, by studying the Islamic sciences independently or in small classes with learned *shaykhs*,[39] or by attending a provincial government primary school. Nevertheless, Gordon College offered important advantages that these other sites of learning did not have. It provided direct access to jobs in colonial government, often at the highest level open to Northern Sudanese. It also gave its students a strong literary education in both Arabic and English, and introduced new communications technologies such as typing and printing in classrooms and in extracurricular contexts. Finally, the college promoted an ethos of self-sufficiency and group spirit, on playing fields and in lecture rooms alike. The result was a set of graduates who possessed both the know-how and confidence to articulate and disseminate nationalist ideologies.

Young men with homes in the South could not attend Gordon College, as a matter of British policy. The imaginary line dividing North from South crossed the White Nile somewhere around 12°N latitude, where clumps of water weeds (the *sudd*) had impeded southward navigation in precolonial times.[40] Believing that Southern societies needed to be protected from the Muslim North, whose traders had preyed upon the South in the nineteenth-century slave trade, the British applied isolationist policies. While the colonial government directed educational development in the North, comparatively underfunded Christian missionary groups had free rein over education in the South.[41] And while Arabic remained the main language of instruction and administration in the North, English or local vernaculars served the same purpose in the South. Through these and other policies, British rule helped to reify a North-South divide.[42]

In both the North and the South, educated groups of the colonial era were male. Females had no place at Gordon College, nor was education providing basic literacy easily accessible to girls throughout the colonial period. The conservatism of Northern Sudanese society, which restricted public movement for women of good families, coupled with the reluctance of British officials to spend scarce funds on something as unpopular as girls' schools, stifled the development of girls' education until late in the colonial period.[43]

Three points stand out with regard to the educational legacy of colonialism. First, by selecting students along lines of language, ethnicity, religion, class, and gender, British authorities at Gordon College reinforced rather than reshuffled social power structures of the preconquest period. The

Sudanese example thereby challenges the argument that, for Africa, colonial education "did more to foster social mobility than to entrench old privileged classes."[44] Second, by concentrating government resources on Northern education, and by entrusting Southern education, unsupervised, to missionary groups of limited means, colonial policies pushed the South and Southerners into a deeper rut of underdevelopment vis-à-vis the North and Northerners and made reconciliation at independence in 1956 more difficult. Educational policies, here as in other parts of the British Empire, fostered uneven development among regions and social groups. Finally, by privileging Arabic-speaking, northern riverain Muslims for the most advanced colonial education available, the Sudan's educational policies produced an ethnically specific nationalist elite. This specificity helped to confirm patterns of exclusionary ethnic politics in the postcolonial era.[45]

THE ROOTS OF NATIONALISM

Colonial borders began as arbitrary sketch-lines, but the consolidation of colonial rule made them firm. As a result, colonies provided the framework for new states (administrative structures) and nations (imagined communities of fellow citizens) in the postcolonial era.[46] In Africa, the European powers broke the continent into multiple pieces, producing colonies that account for over fifty "nations" today. In South Asia, this process went to the opposite extreme: there, Britain secured an "India" larger than anything the Mauryas, Guptas, or Mughals had ever known. In the Middle East, the European powers erased the Ottoman Empire after World War I and provided Britain with mandates over "Palestine," "Transjordan," and "Iraq" — three new entities that bore little relation to Ottoman maps.

To integrate colonies politically and economically into larger imperial systems, British regimes built communication and transportation networks within their domains, elaborating them as technology and budgets allowed. Adapted to local use, these networks facilitated the movement of ideas and people on an unprecedented scale. Roads, railways, automobiles, and steamboats; telegraphs, telephones, and postal systems: along these and other channels, conceptions of cultural space and social identity evolved. Before long, new identities formed, reflecting not only nationalisms based on individual territories, but more broadly, perceptions of cultural community on an international scale.[47]

In the Sudan, educated Northerners, and especially Gordon College graduates, were best placed to take advantage of widening communications networks. In the course of government jobs they encountered colonial technologies and traveled widely throughout the territory on transfers or treks of inspection. At the same time, they regularly returned from far-flung postings to the colonial capital at Khartoum, where modernizing developments—tramways, hospitals, streetlights, and so on—were most visible and dynamic. More than any other group within the colonial territory, educated Northerners developed a sense of the Sudan as a unitary whole, with Khartoum as its metropole, and the provinces and districts as its hinterlands. Nationalism's colonial genesis was no accident, for nationalism also filled a psychological need, easing the trauma of colonial subjugation.[48] As government employees, the new educated classes were an intrinsic part of the colonial system, but they bristled at their restriction to the bureaucratic underclass and saw themselves as extrinsic to the regime. Although confident of their skills in state-maintenance, most saw hopes for promotion fall flat. These professional disappointments fed nationalism, an ideology that affirmed local legitimacy (the right to rule, reserved for those who "belonged" to the territory) and authenticity (cultural integrity) in the face of alien control.

Arabic literature gave educated Northerners an outlet for their frustrations as well as space for debating the meaning of "Sudanese" identity. Meanwhile, the moveable-type printing press, which came to the Sudan on the heels of colonial conquest in 1899, gave them the technological means for spreading these ideas among readers. By 1919, a vigorous Arabic print culture was emerging, as locally published and imported books, newspapers, and magazines became more accessible. Though poetry retained its traditional position as the primary medium for political expression, new genres flourished, too, including the prose essay and the short story. Together, these literary works reflected the intellectual mechanics of colonialism: the ways that the educated lived with and struggled against colonialism in their own minds.

Nationalists used literature, however, not just to express anticolonialism. More significantly, they used it to advocate constructive reform. Nationalists became champions of the modern, passionately endorsing social progress based on science and reason and calling for developments in education, health, and technology along Western lines. At the same time they condemned "un-Islamic" or backward customs and superstitions, particularly those maintained by women (such as lip tattooing). But herein lay a problem. Modernity was critical for the nation, but so, too, was tradition—not only with regard to Islam and the Arabic literary heritage, but with regard to something more specifically "Sudanese." And so nationalists struggled to indigenize modernity, to be part of larger global communities—of Arabs,

Muslims, of enlightened people in general—while cultivating the particular and the locally "authentic" on which national identity must rest.[49]

The spread of print culture fortified nationalism, but so, too, did the explosion of visual culture. In the early twentieth century, educated Northerners were among the first to gain exposure to new film media, including the photographically illustrated book, the snapshot and studio portrait, and the moving picture. By enabling educated Northerners to see and imagine the Anglo-Egyptian territory in new ways, visual culture was as important to the development of nationalism as the culture of words.

WHOSE COLONY? WHOSE NATION?

To the educated Northern Sudanese, the colony was Britain's but the nation was their own. Whereas "colonialism," like its analogue "imperialism" (both *isti'mar* in Arabic), evoked despotism and exploitation, "nationalism," like "patriotism" (*wataniyya* or *qawmiyya* in Arabic), conveyed nobility and pride.

Educated Northerners imagined a nation that took its territorial shape from the colony but its cultural shape from themselves. In writings and speeches, they affirmed Arabic and Islam as pillars of the nation. Their nationalism, thus conceived, had serious limitations, especially for the country's non-Muslim or non-Arabic-speaking populations, who occupied the eastern, western, and southern parts of the country.[50] Consequently, after educated Northerners inherited control of the colonial territory at independence, regional power blocs began to form in the eastern and western regions among those who felt alienated or excluded from their agendas. These blocs included Muslim but non-Arabic-speaking communities like the Beja of the northeast and the Fur of the far west.[51]

Grievances were even sharper among Southern groups. Educated Southerners, most of whom were non-Arabic-speaking Christians who had studied in English-medium missionary schools, received only a small fraction of the government jobs that opened during decolonization.[52] Educated Northern Sudanese filled the great bulk of these positions and acquired authority throughout the country at large. At the same time, Northern politicians promoted policies to Arabicize classroom instruction in Southern schools.[53] In 1949 the first Sudanese minister of education declared that "as the Sudan is one country sharing one set of political institutions it is of great importance that there should be one language that is understood by all its citizens. That language could only be Arabic, and Arabic must therefore be taught in all our schools."[54] The civil war that broke out in the South in 1955 signaled an early rejection of this national project on the part of Southern peoples who sensed that the departure of the British was developing into a mere "change of masters" and a new, internal colonialism.[55]

Civil war ravaged the Sudan in the late twentieth century. Caught in this conflict, the Sudanese are still trying to decide, from their varying perspectives, where the colony ends and the nation begins.

APPROACHING THE EVERYDAY HISTORY OF COLONIALISM: A NOTE ON SOURCES

This book tries to recover the daily lives and human encounters that formed the colonial experience.[56] Its sources owe much to the British officials of the Anglo-Egyptian Sudan. Punctilious recordkeepers and zealous organizers, they ran their empire with a strong historical consciousness. They often made copies of official documents and distributed duplicates or triplicates throughout files arranged according to strict rules.[57] Many of these official documents are preserved in British archives, notably at the Public Record Office in London and in the Sudan's national archive, the National Records Office in Khartoum.

Hundreds of personnel files that British officials kept for the regime's Northern Sudanese employees survive today in Khartoum. Containing an average of several hundred folios each, they appear at first glance to be jumbles of miscellany. They contain job applications, confidential work reports by British superiors, pension forms, sick-leave certificates, records of pay, handwritten pleas for promotion, authorizations for reduced train fares for officials' immediate kin, and so on. The documents are handwritten, typed, or carbon-copied, and are mostly in English, with some in Arabic. These files offer insights into the frustrations and workaday concerns of the educated, the intellectual journeys they later took, and the means by which they formed nationalist ideologies.

British officials were often meticulous in preserving their own Sudan-related papers—both official (reports they compiled or received, government memoranda, copies of province handbooks, etc.) and private (letters home, photographs, diaries, and the like).[58] Some of these papers were semi-official, such as confidential letters that they had exchanged regarding particular government policies. After retiring, many British officials published memoirs of Sudan service, while others donated papers to archives.[59]

Photographs taken by British officials in the Sudan, preserved in archives by the thousands, help to redress the limitations of Arabic and English textual sources. Informal snapshots, in particular, provide glimpses into the lives of rural dwellers, non-Muslim or non-Arabic-speaking peoples, and women—groups that can otherwise elude historians of this period, since their lack of education prevented participation in the worlds of print culture and government.[60] Even the silences and gaps in the photographic evidence are revealing. For example, the very Northern Sudanese men whom the British educated and groomed for colonial employment almost never appear in the snapshots taken by Britons in their leisure hours. The near-total absence of these men underlines the social subordination of educated Northerners and confirms the impression gained through Arabic and English memoirs that British relations with the *effendiyya* were strained, inside the office and out.

Fortunately for the historian, educated Northern men were able to speak, or more significantly, publish, for themselves. As a highly literate group, often fluent in English as well as Arabic, Gordon College graduates contributed extensively to literary journals, where they first debated, among other issues, the meaning of Sudanese identity. Printing became so cheap and accessible that some Northern Sudanese of only modest means, by saving from their salaries as government officials or drawing on the support of colleagues and friends, could afford the expense of having their literary studies printed in Cairo or Khartoum.[61] Years later, a number of prominent nationalists published their memoirs in Arabic; like the British, they, too, had a strong historical consciousness. Because of their literacy, their literary bent, and their strong participation in print culture, these men are easily accessible to the historian in ways that other Sudanese groups (such as women, the poor, and the illiterate) are not.

The early nationalists lavished attention on literary endeavors and assigned great value to their literary output at the time of composition and afterwards. Northern Sudanese and Egyptian scholars, writing in Arabic, have followed suit, considering literary trends an integral part of colonial political history.[62] Emphasis on literary accomplishment is especially strong in the genre of Arabic biographical dictionaries, which are similar to "Who's Who" volumes but more anecdotal. Over a dozen such biographies profiling Gordon College graduates and other leading Northern Sudanese men (not women) of the colonial era appeared in the twentieth century. Regardless of the professional fame these subjects may have achieved as nationalist politicians, independence-era Prime Ministers, and so on, the biographical dictionaries inevitably place greater emphasis on their literary production, and on their accomplishments as poets above all.[63]

Historians writing in English have missed the cue that Arabic writings give when they point to literary prowess as an index of social accomplishment and power. Perhaps this oversight in English-language studies relates to the disciplinary boundaries prevailing in European and American universities, where academics have traditionally regarded poetry as appropriate for the realm of literature or language studies, or in the case of oral poetry, for anthropology.[64] By contrast, history, poetry, and politics have coexisted happily in the Arabic-language scholarship, which has recognized poetry not only as a source of history, yielding insights into the intellectual development and concerns of its authors, but also as a force of history, capable of exhorting and arousing audiences through reading or recitation.[65] In the Northern Sudanese context, Arabic poetry was indeed a force in its own right, propelling nationalists in their quest to define Sudanese identity.

History is not merely a study of the past but an ongoing dialogue with it. In this spirit, the following pages engage with and try to build upon a substantial body of Arabic and English scholarship, produced during the past century, that analyzes colonies and nations.

A BRIEF MANIFESTO

The title of this book, *Living with Colonialism*, refers to two fundamental assumptions. The first is that colonialism, as a cultural system, pervaded and affected the entire range of human experience. Colonialism, understood thus, was a day-to-day affair that took shape in "the stretch between the public institutions of the colonial state and the intimate reaches of people's lives."[66] The second is that history, and more specifically, colonial and nationalist history, is not a dead weight from the past but a living force in the present. Actions and interactions of the colonial period continue to affect how people live and relate to each other, and how governments and economies run. Given the postcolonial pervasiveness of colonial legacies, and the desire to understand them, this book pursues "the academic task of revisiting, remembering, and, crucially, interrogating the colonial past."[67]

Because of its relevance for the present in viewing and making sense of the world, historical interpretation must always be a political act. "Kings and leaders vie for it," wrote the fourteenth-century historian Ibn Khaldun, referring to the power inherent in history's narration.[68] At stake, for the history of countries, is the power to define the "nation-state": to assert its languages or religions, its system of law and government, and its division of spoils on the grounds of tradition or precedent.

The struggle to define the Sudanese nation-state, in particular, has been especially brutal, fueling a civil war that since 1983 alone has displaced or killed millions.[69] The Sudanese crisis is so acute that observers wonder if the country is viable within its Anglo-Egyptian borders and whether a Sudanese civil society, based on culturally inclusive notions of national identity and citizenship, could ever emerge to reconcile the people of the North with those of the South and the Nuba Mountains.[70] Finding an answer is easy in theory but harder in practice: living equably within colonial borders will require finding some degree of communal consensus, through interpretations of history and values that accommodate social difference.

Like all other empires in history, the British Empire was a political, economic, and cultural system that spread through hostile takeover. It imposed regimes, extracted wealth, and modified social behaviors. It survived by delegating petty authority to locals and by adapting to each terrain. Providing frameworks for the movement of people and ideas within territories acquired by conquest, it inadvertently transformed corporate identities and established new political and economic structures that outlasted its own presence.[71] To draw out these processes, and to show some striking transregional similarities of the colonial experience, the book considers Sudanese experiences not only in the context of Africa and the Middle East (regions with which it has clear geographic, cultural, and economic affinities), but also relative to India under the Raj and to its contemporary South Asian successors.

The chapters of the book address three implicit questions: How did colonialism work? How did national identity form? And how, and with what consequences, did colonialism and nationalism interact? These questions are approached in sequence by means of identity ("Who were and are the Sudanese?"), education and acculturation ("Who were the early nationalists and how were they formed?"), colonial state mechanics and economics ("How did the system work and change?"), and the tensions of colonial service ("Why and on what terms did nationalists make colonial rule possible?"). The sixth chapter considers the process of defining the nation in theory, during the colonial period, and in practice, after decolonization, and evaluates the impact of the colonial state on its nation-state successor. A brief conclusion sets out broad answers and findings.

This book tells the story of individuals who held the colonial state in place but who were also early nationalists. Performing skilled but petty jobs, they kept empire running but saw themselves as outsiders to its regime. Feelings of exclusion combined with perceptions of new community and a sense of social leadership to fortify their nationalism and their hopes of a new and independent order on some distant horizon. Drawing upon evidence official and personal, poetic and prosaic, these pages show how early nationalists lived with—and tried to live without—colonialism.

2 Being "Black," Being "Sudanese"

Colonial Education, Privilege,
and National Identity

Every country needs a name and a description for its people. In many parts of Africa and Asia where European imperialists imposed borders and named the regions within them, early nationalists modified territorial labels to suit their budding identities. Thus, the early nationalists of India came to regard themselves as "Indians," just as their counterparts in Nigeria came to call themselves "Nigerians." Later, after independence, some nationalist leaders chose new names for nations, to signal their fresh starts. Hence, Gold Coast peoples became "Ghanaians," and Ceylonese became "Sri Lankans"—in both cases evoking ancient kingdoms and a tradition of independence before colonialism. Regardless of their provenance, though, all names for places and peoples came with etymologies and connotations and required elaboration or revision as national epithets.

Some terms came with narrow meanings that nationalists expanded. For example, the term *Algérien*, used by the French after the 1830 conquest to refer to an Algiers resident, evolved in the late nineteenth century to describe European settlers born within Algeria. Members of the Muslim majority, according to the French, were *indigènes*, a term carrying the condescension of the British colonial term *natives*. In the twentieth century, early nationalists asserted that all *indigènes* were also *Algériens*, claiming the term from the settlers. Once linked to the people of a city, *Algérien* thereby grew to serve a wide territory.[1]

In other cases, national names and adjectives bore derogatory overtones and went through a process of ennobling. For example, when a republic emerged in Anatolia in 1923, following the collapse of the Ottoman Empire, its founders called it *Türkiye* ("Turkey"), thereby adapting a name that Europeans, not indigenous peoples, had applied to Anatolia for centuries. At the same time, and following European practice as well, nationalists began to call themselves *Turks*—a term that learned Ottomans, less than fifty years before, would have saved for Turcoman nomads or for boorish Anatolian peasants. This name, once derogatory, became a source of pride, as republican leaders in the 1920s and '30s embraced their "Turkishness" by cultivating knowledge of local history, archaeology, and folklore.[2] Like nationalist leaders elsewhere, their search for authenticity amounted to a search for roots within the nation's cultural and physical landscape.

In the Anglo-Egyptian Sudan, the story of naming the nation is especially dramatic. Once a narrow and derogatory label applied to slaves, the term *sudani*, or "Sudanese," evolved into a badge of national pride, so that its meanings were both expanded and ennobled. This process of redefinition entailed ascribing common values and a fine historical pedigree to the people in the landscape. But close study shows that these values and histories were not manifest—they were chosen or created. The challenge is therefore to understand not only how the early nation was defined, but who had the power to define it and why they made their choices. In the Sudan, this inquiry leads to the colonial educational system, where a small cadre, selected for modern schooling, acquired the power to define early nationalist values.

The discussion below considers how colonial educational privileges shaped nationalist cadres and examines the evolving meanings and conscious re-definitions of the term "Sudanese" as an identity label.

SUDAN, 'SUDANI'

Unlike some territories in colonial Africa for which European rulers coined new names, Sudan had a long history as a name for a place. Early Muslim geographers, writing in Arabic, had called the region south of the Sahara *Bilad al-Sudan*—"Lands of the Blacks." As a geographic concept, Bilad al-Sudan stretched across Africa from the Atlantic Ocean to the Red Sea, roughly including the lands between present-day Senegal and Ethiopia. While the French used the term "Soudan" to refer to one of their West African colonies (known today as Mali), the British and Egyptians applied it further east.

In the northern regions of the Anglo-Egyptian Sudan, where Islam and the Arabic language prevailed, a centuries-old slave trade had bestowed servile connotations on the adjective "Sudanese" (*sudani* in Arabic). To

Northerners, who regarded themselves as Arabs, being "Sudanese" meant being "Black," as the Arabic root of the term denoted,[3] and being "Black," in turn, meant having low social status. Although blackness and low social status usually derived from the condition or heritage of slavery, Northerners sometimes applied the term "Sudanese" to individuals who had come from one of the non-Muslim, non-Arabic-speaking areas that had historically been targeted for slave raids even if those individuals had never been enslaved. For these reasons, around 1900 there existed no generic use of the term "Sudanese" to describe all Sudan inhabitants.

Beginning in the late 1920s, however, some young, educated Northerners began to embrace "Sudanese"—the adjectival form of the colony's name—as a term for nationalist self-reference. To ennoble this term as a badge of identity, they felt obliged to rid it of servile connotations. Their redemption of "Sudanese" as a nationalist label, however, did not destigmatize the heritage of slavery that the term had originally evoked.

At the time Britain took control of the territory, in 1898, slavery or its heritage had placed many members of Northern Sudanese society in positions of low social status. In the Anglo-Egyptian Agreement of 1899 the new regime abolished the slave trade but did not abolish slavery per se. In theory, individuals born after 1899 were deemed free, while those enslaved before then could apply for manumission. In practice, slavery persisted into the 1920s and beyond, tolerated and euphemized by officials as domestic servitude. Moreover, worried that ex-slaves (often called "detribalized Blacks" in official reports[4]) would succumb to laziness and vice once they settled in urban areas, British officials took various social- and labor-control measures—for example, by enacting a law against "vagabonds." With this law, the government signaled that although slaves might migrate to cities, they would not be allowed to loaf. Such policies of ex-slave-labor control had parallels in other parts of British Africa, such as coastal Kenya and Zanzibar.[5]

Although the Sudan government abolished the slave trade and gave limited support to emancipation, it did not promote egalitarianism. On the contrary, British officials respected or absorbed extant status hierarchies and reinforced them through education policies. They did so by favoring males of high social status and self-defined "Arab" ethnicity for the academic educations that would lead to administrative jobs, and by guiding males of low social status and ex-slave backgrounds into army careers or into programs and jobs that stressed manual skills. Such policies had a pragmatic component. By educating and later hiring the sons of business, religious, tribal, and military leaders for colonial service, British authorities sought to co-opt indigenous elites, neutralize potential resistance, and buttress their power.

The British in the Sudan did not create status differentials but fortified existing ones. In favoring precolonial elites for advanced education, British policies cultivated a group of men who went on to develop nationalist ideologies and define the Sudanese nation in their own social image. Working in tandem with an indigenous, deep-rooted legacy of slavery and prejudice, such policies marginalized large groups within the colonial state.

THE BACKGROUND OF "BLACK"

In early-twentieth-century Northern Sudan, use of the term "Black" described more an idea than a color. In short, both "Black" and "Sudanese" were a comment on low social status made by those who claimed a higher status. These terms usually referred to slaves, or to those of slave descent, whose relatives had belonged to a non-Muslim group from the South or from the Nuba Mountains (or possibly from even farther afield, e.g., from Abyssinia). Islam figured in this story of slavery through legal custom: since Islamic law proscribes the enslavement of Muslims, non-Muslims had been historically the targets for enslavement.[6] In the Sudan today, a memory of this connection between Southernness and the stigma of slavery recurs in the term *abid*, meaning "slaves," which Northern Sudanese in the postcolonial period have sometimes used in a derogatory, belittling manner to refer to Southerners.[7]

The history of slavery and the slave trade in the Sudan stretches back to ancient Egyptian times.[8] The early nineteenth century, however, witnessed a burgeoning domestic, as opposed to export, trade in the Muslim northern regions. The stimulus came from the region's new Turco-Egyptian rulers, who sponsored raiding in non-Muslim regions as a way, first, of securing male slaves for their armies, and second, of profiting through the sale of women and children in both internal (Northern Sudanese) and external (Egyptian, Arabian, and Ottoman) markets.[9] Slaves became so plentiful and cheap as a result of this intensified raiding that even the humblest families of the central riverain North were able to purchase a slave or two. This influx of slaves transformed patterns of labor and attitudes toward labor. For example, whereas free cultivators from the region north of the Nile confluence had performed most agricultural work before 1820, by the end of the nineteenth century slaves had come to do virtually all of this labor. According to one historian, slaves accounted for approximately one-third of the Northern population by the time of the 1898 conquest.[10]

In the Sudan, as in northern Nigeria, Zanzibar, and other British African territories, postconquest policies aimed to abolish slave raiding and to transform ex-slaves into wage laborers, who would, in turn, generate tax revenues and stimulate cash-based markets.[11] As slave men and women asserted their freedom (by obtaining manumission papers or simply by fleeing), many migrated from rural areas to the growing urban centers, where they provided important labor (e.g., as construction and sanitation workers) for both the public and private sectors. Although British officials welcomed the transformation of slaves into workers, they nevertheless tolerated or encouraged the continuation of some slavery.[12] They particularly encouraged slave women to remain under or return to the control of their masters, fearing that the women would otherwise slip into prostitution and thence become vectors of vice and venereal disease. By taking such a gradualist policy toward slavery, especially vis-à-vis slave women, officials also hoped to appease and accommodate the slave-owning classes, who were potential allies of the new regime.[13]

Patterns of assimilation were complex for slaves who gained freedom in the Anglo-Egyptian period or in previous generations. Although slaves taken North had routinely converted to Islam and had learned Arabic, it was far easier for them to become Muslims than to become Arabs in the eyes of the slave-owning classes.[14] Moreover, such cultural assimilation on the basis of religion and language rarely entailed a dramatic improvement in status, since low social status stuck to those of servile descent even after manumission.[15] One anthropologist who did fieldwork in the 1960s in a village along the Nile near Merowe, for example, noted that the village's community of slave descendants, still called "slaves" (abid) by landowners, continued to have social obligations toward families who had owned them or their forebears. Since those of higher status frowned upon intermarriage with them, the group had remained largely endogamous.[16]

Slave descent, therefore, "blackened" an individual in social terms. Skin color was no index, since in the years before the nationalist transformation that would make Sudanese-ness acceptable, a person of high status could have had dark skin without being regarded as "Black," or "Sudanese," by his community. Such an individual would most likely have identified himself instead as "Arab," which conveyed not simply his use of the Arabic language, but, more importantly, his claim of distinguished parentage. Good parentage derived from membership in a patrilineally reckoned tribal group (e.g., the Sha'iqiyya or Baqqara) that claimed a distant Arabian progenitor. The father's line was paramount, though high status on the mother's side enhanced social position.

Ultimately, "Arab" and "Black" were both more important to the Northern Sudanese as labels of status and class rather than of ethnicity or color. The British appear to have absorbed some of these attitudes, in the form of an "Arab" / "Black" classification system that easily dovetailed with their own prejudices and notions of race. The system was also reinforced by their partnership with the Egyptians in the Condominium, since Egyptians tended to carry their own racialized stereotypes about Sudanese slavery and servitude.[17] The result, by and large, was the promotion of policies that favored Arabs over Blacks—high status over low—for the finest academic educations and the most lucrative office jobs.

A British soldier, D. C. E. Comyn, provided an insight into this rough classification system in his memoirs, published in 1911. He described his Camel Corps company, at Bara in Kordofan Province, as follows: "Of the 150 men, 50 were pure, straight-haired Arabs; 70 were Kordofan Arabs, who, by intermarriage with the Nubas, etc., have the curly hair of the latter. The remainder were Sudanese."[18]

BRITISH EDUCATION POLICY AND PATRONAGE

Rather than reshuffling this social hierarchy, British authorities reinforced it by setting policies for school enrollment according to gender, region of origin, social status, and religion. Admissions policies for Gordon College, for example, privileged those who were male, Muslim, Arabic-speaking, "Arab," and of high status. Graduates of the college, who were among the first to embrace nationalism, drew upon their own specific social backgrounds for its ideological content. Thus, their new nationalist ideal of "Sudanese"-ness placed great value on Islamic and Arabic culture.

British educational policies were regionally exclusive. Under the leadership of Sir James Currie, director of education from 1900 to 1914, the Education Department concentrated its meager budget on the central riverain North. It left the education of peoples from the non-Muslim South and the Nuba Mountains—the true "Lands of the Blacks" in the view of "Arab" Northerners—to underfunded Christian missionary bodies. In the East, the Muslim but non-Arabic-speaking Beja peoples were left largely to their own devices, although the government opened occasional rural schools with the expansion of elementary education in the 1930s. The same applied to the western province of Darfur, incorporated into the Anglo-Egyptian Sudan in 1916.[19]

Motivated by the need for local colonial bureaucrats, the government channeled its educational budget into schools for boys. Notwithstanding the efforts of the remarkable Babikr Badri (1861–1954), a former Mahdist soldier and merchant who opened a girls' school in Rufa'a in 1907, female education languished. Faced with popular reactions to girls' education in the North that ranged from hostile to apathetic, education officials preferred to channel their limited resources into forms of education that would garner more popular support. Though Christian missionary groups in the North, and notably the Church Missionary Society, offered some schooling for Muslim Northern girls, such schools stressed domestic accomplishments rather than literacy in their programs.[20] The acute underdevelopment of girls' education vis-à-vis boys' education persisted to the end of the colonial period and beyond.[21]

Within the central riverain North itself, officials guided boys and young men into educational programs depending on their social status. Reports show that Currie encouraged Black males to enter government technical or industrial-workshop schools, where they learned to be carpenters, pipe fitters, and the like. (Even among technical-school students, however, the category "Blacks" did not constitute a majority or plurality of students; judging from statistics available for the period up to 1913, many "Berberi" [Nubian], "Arab," and "Mixed" students also attended.[22]) Currie allowed a small number of Black youths to enter into academic programs, "as long as they [did] not bear an excessive percentage to the total number in attendance."[23] Others were admitted to the Khartoum military academy (opened in 1905), an institution that was "intended for Sudanese cadets, prospective officers in the black Battalions," as one government report declared.[24] Until its closure in 1924, this academy offered bright prospects in the Egyptian Army, which included in its ranks many soldiers of slave descent—a legacy of the military slave recruitment policies of the nineteenth century.[25] Still other Blacks entered schools of the American Presbyterian missionaries, who taught manual and agricultural skills to boys and young men from the *dayms* (ex-slave settlements) of Khartoum.[26]

Attitudes toward Blacks in the North found an echo in policies toward Blacks in the South, where British officials encouraged Christian missionary schools to emphasize manual or technical education. In 1904, for example, the Governor-General wrote that the objective of education in Bahr el-Ghazal Province "should be to provide a certain number of trained artisans, carpenters, blacksmiths . . . etc., who in addition to a knowledge of their trade, should also have a moderate knowledge of reading, writing and very simple arithmetic."[27] As in the North, however, British officials made exceptions for those of high status. At the school of the Verona Fathers in Wau, for example, the government encouraged an academic program that would groom the sons of Southern chiefs for government office jobs as clerks in Southern districts. Other boys in the same school went through a technical program. A Verona Father, who was also a historian, mentions that in 1911 one priest called the academic program at Wau "The Princes' College," "for actually 18 of the boarders were children of great chiefs, either sent to Wau as hostages . . . or simply as a token of faithful submission to, and acceptance of, the new government: only five were commoners."[28]

British policy at Wau (perhaps also mirroring Roman Catholic policy) reflected a deep respect for high status combined with a pragmatic concern for co-opting elites. This British educational policy toward Sudan elites in turn inspired Italian colonialists, who in 1911 founded a government school in neighboring Eritrea for the sons of Muslim chiefs and notables.[29] Farther afield, in British India, meanwhile, patterns were much the same; there, schools often favored Brahmins and the sons of princes or big landowners—the counterparts of Sudan Arabs and chiefs' sons.[30]

As a corollary to the policy of channeling low-status Black, or Sudanese, boys into technical schools, British officials actively recruited boys of Arab families for academic and pre-professional programs in the provincial primary-intermediate schools or in Gordon College.[31] When Gordon College first opened in 1902, British officials of the Education Department hand-picked its students. They went one by one to the homes of prominent Muslim families in order to persuade elders to send their sons to school.[32] Initially, parents were reluctant because they feared that the college would try to convert their sons to Christianity.[33] But, in fact, the college hired upright Muslim *shaykhs* as schoolmasters, to teach not only Arabic but the Islamic sciences as well, and devoted part of the college curriculum to the training of *qadis* as judges to staff the Mohammedan Law Courts (i.e., the Shari'a courts). This policy appalled the Church Missionary Society (C.M.S.) and American Presbyterian missionaries, who felt that a school founded in General Gordon's memory should promote the Christian gospel and comprise part of a policy to convert the Muslim population of the North to Christianity.[34]

Although Gordon College catered to Muslim students, in the first twenty years of the regime it did admit a small number of Egyptian Copts, most of whom were the sons of government officials.[35] The college did not admit Christians or others who came from the South, though perhaps not for lack of Southern interest. In 1909, for example, one British official from Upper Nile Province mentioned that "several of the wealthier Dinkas are requesting to have their sons educated at the Gordon College."[36] This Southern barrier stood as late as 1944, when the government sent two talented Christian Southern students for advanced educations, not to Gordon College in Khartoum but to Makerere College in Uganda.[37]

Among the Northerners who initially hesitated in sending their sons to Gordon College were vanquished Mahdist leaders, some of whom still remained in prison or under house arrest. The British were particularly eager to recruit the offspring of these Mahdist soldiers and commanders (*amirs*), even recruiting the sons of the Khalifa Abdullahi, who had ruled the Mahdist state from 1885 to 1898.[38] British policy in this regard reflected not only a favoring of high status but also sheer pragmatism. Using school recruitment, the British sought to quell any anticolonial resistance by giving potential opponents—precolonial elites and their offspring—a stake in the system. British hiring policy mirrored school recruitment policy; the administration employed former Mahdist supporters as clerks, *qadis*, and the like, provided that they declared loyalty to the colonial regime. (Some declared loyalty through letters or petitions,[39] others through *qasidas*, or praise poems, which lauded the British conquerors.[40]) As a result of this dual policy for school recruitment and job hiring, the vanquished Mahdist elite experienced a rapid rehabilitation through their sons, so much so that by 1914 several sons of the Khalifa Abdullahi himself had already risen to hold respectable positions within the colonial administration.[41] The French in West Africa pursued a similar policy by incorporating twenty sons of the empire-builder and resistance leader Samori Ture (c. 1830–1900) into their army.[42]

The British not only incorporated old enemies but also rewarded former allies. Many of the boys they accepted for provincial primary-intermediate schools and for Gordon College, or later for government jobs, had fathers or grandfathers who had shown loyalty to the British. Some of these had been loyal servants of the earlier Turco-Egyptian regime, and some had helped General Charles Gordon prior to the fall of Khartoum in 1885; others had provided intelligence to the British or had cooperated in some way during the Mahdist regime, the "Reconquest," or in the early colonial period.[43]

SEIZING OPPORTUNITIES OR MAKING THEM: EDUCATIONAL SELF-SELECTION

People quickly caught on to the British habit of rewarding loyal supporters and providing jobs and school places to those from prestigious families. Petitioners for jobs, wage increases, and pension supplements made the most of their connections and went out of their way to emphasize a history of family loyalty to the regime.[44] The British considered these histories seriously. For example, Item 7 on the application for the Sub-Mamurs Training Course asked candidates to provide a "Brief note on family history and connections."[45] Good family connections and high social status (with the two usually coming together), and best of all, personal intervention from British provincial governors and district commissioners who knew and liked one's father, made an inestimable difference in securing jobs and school places.[46]

Once the idea of Gordon College and the primary-intermediate schools gained acceptability, Education Department officials had far more candidates than the schools could accept. Parents and sons were well aware of the good job prospects that graduates of these schools would face. By the 1930s candidates were gaining entrance to schools and to jobs through examinations that were becoming increasingly competitive.[47]

In spite of the establishment of competitive entrance examinations and job applications, selection based upon family connection always had a place in the system. One British official, T. R. H. Owen, explained the selection processes for a provincial school:

> In a country where the privileges of position and birth are traditional the barren and mechanical justice of pure competitive examination is neither thinkable nor desirable. An omda, a sheikh of a quarter, a senior official—such men are entitled by prestige and position to some consideration. The Selection Board . . . has to steer a middle course between the granting of such arbitrary priorities and following the results of the entrance test. The method of selection is, in fact, one of Privilege tempered by Examination.[48]

As far as Gordon College was concerned, British officials tried to draw in the "right" sort of students: sons of Muslim notables (be they religious *shaykhs*, tribal *nazirs*, or village *umdas*), of prominent merchants, of former Mahdist commanders or high-ranking Mahdist bureaucrats, and of landowning cultivators. British officials readily lowered their academic standards to admit the sons of such notables.[49] Wealth was not important in their eyes, but prestige and integrity were, as well as an elusive quality regarded by the British as a kind of local authenticity. To enable many poor but worthy boys to attend, school officials offered reduced fees or free places for a large proportion of the students. When the effects of the Depression set in after 1931, college officials lamented that they had had to raise fees and significantly cut the proportion of reduced-fee or free places to a mere 20 percent of total entrants.[50]

British plans to draw in boys of "good" parentage ran awry because in the long run certain Northern groups proved more ready and eager to join the college than others. To the chagrin of British officials, Muslim tribal notables and provincial farmers proved much less enthusiastic than government employees (many of whom, by the early 1930s, were Gordon College alumni themselves) about sending their sons to school.[51] This trend became even more pronounced after 1931, when the Depression caused cutbacks in Gordon College scholarships. With their steady incomes, Northern Sudanese officials, together with merchants, could more easily afford school fees than humble cultivators.[52] During the Depression, families in the so-called Three Towns (Khartoum, Khartoum North, and Omdurman) also had an easier time sending their boys to the school because they could go as day students and avoid paying fees for board.

Similarly, the residents of certain provinces were more ambitious than others to secure places at Gordon College for their boys. Blue Nile Province had a particular enthusiasm for education, thanks in part to the energies of one man, Babikr Badri. In 1903 Babikr Badri opened a boys' school in his small Blue Nile town of Rufa'a; in 1907 he defied convention by opening a girls' school. Although the government had determined to keep education to a minimum on its limited budget in order not to tax people for the purpose, Babikr Badri persuaded officials to apply an education tax in Rufa'a (recognizing that there would otherwise be no school expansion) and promised that no murmur of protest would arise. Meanwhile, in 1913, following a cut in the government education budget, Blue Nile residents agreed to pay triple their earlier education tax in order to maintain their schools. The province governor was amazed, as comments in his annual report show.[53]

Similarly, the parents of some Black students resisted Education Department efforts to channel their sons into technical rather than academic education. When Black students did enter technical schools, their parents often tried to exercise preferences there, too—preferences reflecting concerns of status, not salary. Carpentry was well thought of, for example, but stonemasonry was not, and officials had a hard time filling places for that trade in the early years. A 1907 report on the Omdurman technical school noted, "In spite of the fact that any reasonably competent mason or stone worker in the Sudan earns very high wages, and even the extremely incompetent a good living, many difficulties exist. Popular prejudice is strong against the stone-cutters' craft, as in the Sudan it has always been regarded as suitable employment for the lowest class of slaves only."[54]

Some Black, or Sudanese, boys did manage to gain access to one of the provincial primary-intermediate schools, or to Gordon College, both springboards for prestigious office jobs. The successful included those who displayed the brilliance that enabled them to slip through on the basis of merit. Others were fortunate to have British connections that provided the crucial link of patronage. In 1907, for example, a man named Coutts, of Prisons and Police, started a school, containing about thirty pupils in all, in the

Khartoum area for his prison warders' sons. (The energetic Coutts tried to start a school for his prison warders' daughters in 1908, but the endeavor was so poorly received that he had to drop it by 1909.[55]) It is obvious that Director of Education Currie expected these boys to continue at a technical school. Coutts reported:

> The Director of Education is . . . very kind to us, and has offered me vacancies [for my warders' sons] in the workshops [technical programs]. I regret, however, to say that the boys all seem to prefer the prospects of becoming clerks rather than artisans. I have tried to discourage this idea, but I fancy the parents are to blame.[56]

Although a number of the prison-warders' sons did join technical schools, several of them also made it into Gordon College academic programs in 1907 and 1908.[57] Coutts may have tried to find money to subsidize their educations, since their fathers (who had become prison warders after some years of military service) could not manage alone. In 1907, Coutts noted, "Five of our boys have now passed the test and entered the Gordon College. More, I think, could do so, but I am unable to find money to pay their fees, and the amount required, viz. £4 per annum, is more than the ordinary warder can afford."[58] Coutts took pride in the success of his warders' sons and offered them crucial support.

Over the years, as more people recognized the professional and economic advantages of formal modern education in the colonial context (as opposed to the traditional religious education that relied heavily on rote memorization), residents of the Northern Sudan created their own educational opportunities through the founding of independent schools. In 1912 members of the *ulama* organized a religious institute called the Ma'had al-Ilmi, centered in the Omdurman mosque. The British regime welcomed its founding as a way to divert Northern Sudanese students from al-Azhar, the famous university mosque of Cairo (on which the Ma'had based its curriculum) and thereby reduce Egyptian influence—and the possibility of pan-Islamic or Egyptian nationalist "contamination."[59] The Ma'had received a government subsidy through the Legal Secretariat's Grant-in-Aid to Mosques to pay its staff salaries.[60] But because it was not under government control or supervision, it did not qualify for Education Department funds and was therefore perennially underfunded.[61] Some of the Ma'had's graduates went on to become Shari'a court clerks or teachers in *kuttabs* (elementary vernacular schools) and *khalwas* (schools teaching rudimentary literacy through Qur'an reading and recitation); at least one graduate became a *qadi*.[62]

Meanwhile, after 1926 educated Northerners raised a public appeal for founding an *ahliyya* (people's) primary school for boys, to accommodate the many youth who had not gained entrance into government schools. These schools might have been described using the Arabic terms *watani* or *qawmi*, equivalent in meaning to the English term "national " (as in "National School"), but the Civil Secretary would not allow it; instead, he prescribed the adjective *ahli*, officially translated into English as "native," as in "Native Elementary School."[63] In the ensuing thirty years, *ahliyya* schools developed throughout the North, until they eventually catered to boys and to girls at primary, intermediate, and secondary levels.

KEEPING TRACK OF STUDENTS: FATHERS, PROVINCES, AND "NATIONALITIES"

At Gordon College British educators worried that educational ambition would have an undesirable effect on the social profile of their students. So great was the concern that they listed statistics for "parentage," meaning the occupations of students' fathers, in the annual reports of the college from 1926 to 1944. They did not like the trend of increased representation from the ranks of the urban class of officials and would have instead preferred an influx of sons of rustic provincial *nazirs* or cultivators. Their dislike coincided with the political mood of the late 1920s and 1930s, when Indirect Rule, also known as Native Administration, was in vogue. During this period, British officials tried to bolster the administrative power of village and tribal notables at the expense of the educated Northern Sudanese, who already filled many petty bureaucratic and local administrative jobs. Sir John Maffey, governor-general from 1926 to 1934, helped to set this tone, bringing his contempt for educated "natives"—developed in the course of his career in India—to bear in the Sudan.[64] The 1936 Gordon College report continued in this spirit when it said, "It may be interesting to note that the son of the Government official, and this class now furnishes about 50 per cent. of the total number of pupils, is generally less endowed with brains than the offspring of the illiterate peasant of the provinces or of the townsman following some very humble trade or calling."[65]

In the same reports college officials kept track of students by region. Patterns remained fairly stable from year to year. Khartoum Province always led the way in sending students to the college—a trend not surprising, since the province included the Khartoum conurbation. Blue Nile and Berber Provinces were also front-runners, and Kordofan, Halfa, Dongola, and White Nile Provinces also held strong. Poor showings came from two Northern regions where non-Arabic-speakers predominated, namely the Red Sea Hills in the East and Darfur Province in the West.[66]

From 1925 to 1944, Darfur sent, on average, less than one student a year to the school[67]—a situation that reflected the lack of advanced schooling within Darfur itself.[68] While it is true that Darfur was the last province to be incorporated into the Anglo-Egyptian Sudan, having been formally absorbed through conquest only after 1916, its delayed educational development vis-à-vis other Northern provinces is dramatic. A lack of interest in government, or "infidel," education among Darfurians may have been partly to blame; a fear that government schools were really "a trap to catch boys and send them to the Nile Valley" deterred some parents as well.[69] As one Briton who served in Darfur in the late 1930s recalled, "The problems of education were almost unbelievable. The fathers, from chiefs to peasants, refused flatly to send their children to school, and it required endless persuasion and illustration to make any headway."[70]

Attitudes toward education in Darfur, in the far west, resembled attitudes in the far east among the non-Arabic-speaking, Muslim, nomadic Beja peoples of the Red Sea hinterlands. There, too, government attempts to spread schools among the Beja met with little interest. Since Beja parents were often unwilling to pay school fees and clothing costs for sons sent away to elementary school, the government had helped to establish a special Beja Education Fund, administered by officials and Beja notables, for that purpose. Part of the problem was linguistic: Beja boys had trouble at school because instruction in Arabic was difficult for them.[71] Nomadism compounded the problem. Outside the towns, among some pastoralist communities in the Red Sea region, Darfur, and Kordofan, schools stayed put, but families did not.

Finally, British officials kept track of Gordon College students according to one other category—"Nationality." Early charts (from c. 1907 to 1913) show that Education Department officials divided students into two broad categories of "Nationality"—"Natives" and "Others," with the subcategories "Egyptians" and "Miscellaneous" included under the latter. Gordon College authorities continued this rough classification scheme until the mid-1940s, although by then Egyptians had long disappeared from the school (the result of displacing Egyptians from the administration) and only one or two Abyssinians or Somalis were contributing to each year's "Miscellaneous" tally. The "Natives" category, meanwhile, was further subdivided into four groups, although precise terminology shifted over time.

Roughly, these groups were "Arabs," "Blacks" (or "Sudanese"), "Berberines," and "Muwallads." The "Berberines" were Nubians from the Nile banks of far northern Sudan (bordering Egypt); they came from a group known for having achieved fluency in Arabic even while speaking a Nubian language as their mother tongue.[72] The subcategory "Muwallad" usually referred to those students, of Sudan birth, whose parents were of partial or full Egyptian extraction. The categories of nationality of the education reports therefore conveyed information on origin and ethnicity.

The available statistics for the "nationality" of students categorized as "Natives" at Gordon College show that "Arabs" always had a strong majority. Their proportional size increased with time, perhaps because, in the nature of elite groups, they developed the skill of "perpetuat[ing] their status and privileges by socializing and training their children to succeed them."[73] By contrast, the representation of the Islamized, Arabic-speaking peoples of non-Muslim and possible slave background—variously called "Sudanese," "Blacks," "Negroids," "Southern Sudanese," and "Southern Arabs" in the education reports from circa 1920 to the 1940s—appears to have diminished considerably over time. Whereas "Sudanese," or "Blacks," made up 18.9 percent of the student body of the college's academic programs in 1907, they represented only 7.6 percent by 1913, 4.3 percent by 1926, and 2.2 percent by 1930. This figure remained abysmally low, shrinking even further in the early 1940s. By 1944, the last year for which figures are available, this group represented less than 1.6 percent of the college's student body.[74]

Four factors may explain the dwindling enrollment of Blacks at the college. First, other groups (such as the Northern Arab *effendiyya*, or educated class, consisting of colonial employees) may have been more assertive in pursuing educational opportunities for their sons. Second, from 1924, following anti-British uprisings in which soldiers of Southern or Nuba Mountains origin were active, some British officials began to regard educated "detribalized Blacks" as a potential threat to the colonial order. Authorities may have subsequently discriminated against Black students in college admissions. Third, Black students may have performed weakly in the competitive entrance examinations introduced after 1929, suggesting educational disadvantages that developed in the course of their primary education. In a system of "Privilege tempered by Examination,"[75] Black students lacked the privilege that could compensate for poor performance on tests. Finally, the definition of "Black" may itself have changed, by allowing socially or economically successful individuals to upgrade their status to "Arab."

THE TERM "SUDANESE" IN FLUX

At some point in the colonial period the usage of the term "Sudanese" began to change from that of an ethnic and status label for ex-slaves and their descendants to a label of regional or national identity, meant to be applied to all members of the colonial territory. These meanings of the term varied depending upon the user, so that British administrative officials and self-proclaimed nationalists often intended it to convey slightly different concepts. Although various usages were sometimes circulating concurrently, certain features stand out in the term's evolution.

Colonial authorities were probably the first to employ the term "Sudanese," as an obvious way of distinguishing residents of the Anglo-Egyptian Sudan from residents of other colonies, particularly Egyptians. In at least one case that entailed the keeping of statistics on non-government schools, British officials also used the term to distinguish resident non-Egyptian Muslims from immigrant Christians, such as Greeks or Armenians.[76] By the 1930s, a few educated young men began to adopt "Sudanese" to signify their nationalism (*qawmiyya*, or *wataniyya*), that is, their belief in the integrity of the Sudan as a political and cultural unit. During the colonial period, these different meanings of "Sudanese"—low-status Black, resident of the Sudan territory, non-Egyptian Muslim, or patriot of the Sudan nation—often existed simultaneously, appearing in one guise or another in both English and Arabic accounts of the period.

Colonial personnel files for educated Northern Sudanese employees offer a window into these evolving labels. The files contain a range of documents on individual careers. They include salary, transfer, and pension records; letters of recommendation; job evaluations; annual-leave forms; and the like. In cases where the employee knew English or used it in his job, most of his personnel file documents are in English. For those who knew only Arabic, such as *qadis*, most documents are in Arabic. British supervisors, Syrian and Egyptian clerks, and Northern Sudanese employees added to these files over time, so that the authorship of a single personnel file was mixed. Even a single document could have a mixed authorship. A job application, for example, included information provided by the Northern Sudanese applicant, as well as notes and commentaries written by British officials on the bottom or back of the form.[77]

British authorities routinely demanded certain types of information from employees. Parents' names, place and date of birth of the employee,[78] and educational history and qualifications were standard items. An employee's "Nationality" was also usually listed on the form, although sometimes this information was categorized as "Tribe." In either instance, the Arabic translation on the form for "Nationality" or "Tribe" was the term *"Jins."*[79] In many cases, the query concerning an employee's nationality appears to have elicited a label of local or tribal Northern (in most cases, Arab) ethnicity, such as Ja'li ("Gaali") or Abbasi. Personnel forms also required information on the "nationality" of each applicant's mother and father. Sometimes parental origins differed, although by custom, individuals carried their father's "nationality."

✶ Beginning in the late 1920s some Gordon College students, who were beginning to embrace ideas of nationalism for the Sudan (partly through the inspiration of Egyptian nationalist writings), began to resist government efforts to elicit tribal labels. Khidir Hamad (1907–80) claimed that when he graduated from the college in 1928, he and a few friends vowed to declare themselves "Sudanese" when they were asked to indicate their nationality on government job applications. This was a radical move for the time. He explained,

> When we went to the Financial Secretary's department for employment, the Chief Clerk, namely Issawi Bey,[80] asked our names and then our nationalities (*ajnas*) and when we told him "Sudanese" he insisted on knowing our tribes. We had, however, resolved on the term "Sudanese" and he had to tell us that he was not prepared to appoint us if he did not know our tribes. We said to him, "That's your business, as for us, we don't know tribes, but we are sons of this Sudan, and we do not belong to any other." Finally he wrote [the tribe information] down from old papers. . . . [81]

Indeed, Khidir Hamad's application for government employment lists his "tribe" and his "father's nationality" as "Mahasi," although the sheet listing his record of service says "Sudanese."[82]

In his memoir, Khidir Hamad argues that the British strove to reinforce tribal identities that should have been allowed to disappear.

> They fanned the embers of old tribal grudges that time had caused to die down. If once upon a time one tribe lost its drum to another in war, then the Governor-General would come and present a new drum, addressing them saying that they had lost the old one in such-and-such war with tribe so-and-so. Sudanese, in all their dealings and even in letters, would write with reference to their tribe, saying, "I am so-and-so Mahasi of *jins* and such like, and I present to your Excellency the following." The students in the schools had to recount their tribes, for the word *"Sudani"* was not recognized or respected. How many discussions and arguments broke out between the Ja'li, Mahasi, and so on. In our final year we decided to proclaim the word Sudanese and to deny tribalisms. It wasn't an easy thing to do because we found opposition even among the educated.[83]

In spite of Khidir Hamad's bold and early claims to "Sudanese" identity and his dismissal of tribal identifications, a fellow Northerner would have been able to determine his Arab tribal affiliation just by looking at him, because he wore the pattern of facial scars, *shillukh,* that were typical of a Mahasi.[84] He shares a dialogue that occurred in the Financial Secretary's office with a British inspector named Blackley, who tried to mock Khidir, by this time a stenographer in the office, about his claims to Sudanese identity.[85] It is notable that the two talk past each other insofar as nationality and tribalism, *jins* and *qabaliyya,* are concerned.

BLACKLEY: "Khidir Effendi, what's your nationality?" [*Khidir Effendi, jinsak shinu?*]

KHIDIR: "Sudanese." [*Sudani.*]

BLACKLEY: "I mean, your tribe." [*Aqsid qabilataka.*]

KHIDIR: "I don't recognize these tribalisms." [*La a'tarif bi-hadhihi al-qabaliyyat.*]

BLACKLEY: "Did Gordon College teach you to deny your nationalities?" [*Hal Kulliyat Ghurdun ta'allamakum an tankiru ajnasakum?*]

KHIDIR: "Gordon College has nothing to do with tribes." [*Inna Kulliyat Ghurdun la sha'na laha bil-qaba'il.*]

BLACKLEY: "Fine, so then what are these face scars?" [*Tayyib, al-shillukh di ashan shinu?*]

KHIDIR: "To confirm that I am Sudanese." [*Li-tuthbit annani sudani.*]

Khidir then explains, "He swelled with anger and whispered to another inspector who was with him in the office, and I heard him say the words 'Gordon College boys,' for by that time they had begun to despise Gordon College boys. . . . People take the term Sudanese for granted now, for indeed it became a term of pride, but once upon a time it was attacked from every direction and its users were accused of the most terrible things. Many people shuddered at the thought of calling themselves Sudanese."[86]

Although authorities generally expected to elicit information on local identity or tribe when they asked Northern Sudanese employees about their nationality, in other records they sometimes used the term "Sudanese" for classification purposes, to distinguish the group from Egyptians. This practice dated to the earliest years of the regime. In this sense, Lord Cromer analyzed the nationalities of students at Gordon College in 1904, and wrote, "218 are Egyptians or foreigners of various sorts. The balance of 180 are bona fide Sudanese—Blacks or Arabs."[87] In a single employee's personnel file, therefore, labels frequently vary, between "Sudanese"—here meaning indigenous resident of the Anglo-Egyptian Sudan—and local or tribal labels, such as "Dongolawi." Though terminologies varied with time, the insertion of "Sudanese" alone was becoming increasingly common by the 1940s.

"SUDANESE" ARE NOT "EGYPTIANS"

Usage of the term "Sudanese," in a territorial sense, related to Britain's unease over Egypt, which was supposed to be its official partner in the regime. Beginning in 1919, when a series of nationalist uprisings broke out in the urban centers of Egypt, and intensifying after 1924, when similar uprisings (partly inspired by the Egyptian example) broke out in the Sudan, British authorities hastened to remove Egyptian officials from the country. They began to place great importance on the distinction between "Sudanese," meaning, loosely, a resident of the Sudan, born and raised, and "Egyptian." After 1924, being ethnically Egyptian usually destroyed one's chances of securing an administrative job or a place in Gordon College. The government's use of "Sudanese" to mean "not Egyptian" (in birthplace and parentage) coexisted with the use of tribal labels in official documents for some time. Undoubtedly, this British usage also helped to recast "Sudanese" into a status-neutral term of territorial reference among many people of the North.

The British reified discrete Egyptian and Sudanese (meaning "non-Egyptian") identities, when in fact both terms were quite ambiguous. In the Sudan, "Egyptian" often referred to people of varied ethnic provenance (usually from somewhere within the Ottoman Empire) who had settled in Egypt or entered the service of the Muhammad Ali dynasty.[88] Large numbers of "Egyptians" had come into the Sudan, during the Turco-Egyptian period especially, as administrators, merchants, or teachers. Once in the Sudan, many of these "Egyptians" had married local women or taken slave concubines. Children from these unions often retained family connections and allegiances that transcended the Sudan-Egypt territorial borders of the colonial age. In the early twentieth century, more people emigrated from Egypt in order to find jobs in the colonial administration. Intermarriage among "Egyptians" and "Sudanese" was so common that a word had already come into use in the nineteenth century to describe the offspring of such unions: muwalladin, meaning "those born-in-the-place," or "half-breeds."[89] This term seems to have gone out of vogue sometime around 1929, for in that year the college reports stop listing "Muwallads" and begin listing "Mustawtins," from mustawtinin, meaning "those taken root," or "indigenized natives," for what is obviously the same group.[90]

The British were sometimes reluctant to give school places or jobs to Muwallads. On the one hand, they viewed them as not authentically Sudanese. (Betraying his confusion, Lord Cromer, Consul-General of Egypt, wrote, "I am not sure how to class these [*muwalladin*]. Are they Sudanese born in Egypt, or Egyptians born in the Sudan?"[91]) On the other hand, as literal half-breeds, their political loyalties were unclear. The British knew that many *muwalladin* had family connections in Egypt and feared that they might become conduits for Egyptian nationalist agitation. Hence, they often tried to label Muwallads doubly, as "Egyptians" too, recognizing their *muwallad* ethnicity but insisting that they be assigned their fathers' "Egyptian" nationality. A similar form of ethnic ambiguity surrounded the Masalma, Jews and Christians who had been forced to convert to Islam during the Mahdist period.[92] After 1924, individuals of ethnically ambiguous groups such as the *muwalladin* and the Masalma often went to great lengths to persuade British officials that they were authentically or deservedly "Sudanese" and not "Egyptian." Employment prospects were, after all, much better, in the long run, for the "Sudanese" of the Sudan, although in the early years of the regime, those classified as "Egyptians" had drawn higher salaries.[93]

Personnel files reveal the case of one man who had to fight to be classified as "Sudanese." Born in the Blue Nile town of Wad Medani in 1911 and educated at Gordon College, Yahya al-Fadli was the *muwallad* son of an Egyptian father and a Northern Sudanese Sha'iqiyya mother. (In his later adult years, he became a well-known journalist and politician.) In 1934 a debate ensued among his employers in the Finance Department when the issue of his eligibility for a pension came up. One official wrote, "His father is an Egyptian born in Egypt and domiciled in the Sudan. The fact that his mother is a Sudanese does not alter his Nat.[ionality] which should be his father's Nat., i.e. Egyptian. He should follow his father's Nat." Another wrote, "Yahia Eff. El Fadli is an Egyptian born, educated, appointed and domiciled in the Sudan." Yahya himself wrote to the financial secretary, "Sir, before I sign my Pension Authority, I should like to point out for your consideration the following fact. Having been born of a father of origin Egyptian nationality [*sic*] domiciled in the Sudan, and a pure Sudanese mother from the Shaigia tribe, I think, therefore, I should be rightly recorded as Sudanese, particularly in view of the fact that my father came to the Sudan while he was a child and since then has maintained no home in Egypt. I hope, therefore, the nationality as shown in the pension authority to be altered to that of a Sudanese accordingly." And so it was. His pension forms show a series of crossings-out over his "Nationality" label, with

"Egyptian (domiciled in the Sudan)" replaced by "Muwallad" and eventually by "Sudanese."[94]

Ultimately, Sudanese identities were always negotiable. As far as "Sudanese" meaning "non-Egyptian" was concerned, British officials were flexible. Whether or not they changed an ethnic label for employment, salary, or pension purposes often depended on how much they liked the employee and his work.[95]

Even so, the blurring of the line between the terms "Egyptian" and "Sudanese" concerned some British officials. In 1904 Lord Cromer expressed grave doubts over Currie's policy of permitting so many "Egyptians" and "Muwallads" into Gordon College. Currie had justified this policy on the grounds that "any worthy educational system must stand for the mitigation not the exaggeration of racial differences." Cromer wrote, "I greatly doubt whether racial differences will be mitigated by 'acclimatising' a number of foreign youths, and dubbing them by the name of Sudanese." He added, "It is only human nature that [Education Department officials] should prefer to sow their seed on the intellectually fruitful Egyptian and miscellaneous soil, rather than to scatter it on the relatively unfruitful Black or Arab soil. Nevertheless, it has to be done."[96] Here, the mitigation of race referred to the blending of "Egyptians" and "Sudanese," whereas the bona fide "Sudanese" encompassed "Arabs" and "Blacks" alike.

THE MEANINGS OF "SUDANESE" AND THE NATIONALIST VISION

The term "Sudanese" evolved to have at least four different meanings over the course of the colonial period. Colonial personnel files, education reports, and memoirs (including mainly English materials, but also some Arabic sources) suggest that it was possible for these meanings to circulate concurrently, especially by the late 1920s, when educated Northern males were beginning to articulate ideas on the Sudan as a nation.

From the beginning of the colonial period, the Arabic term *sudani* ("Sudanese," or "Black," in English) could refer to a member of the large population of ex-slaves and their descendants living in the North or to the peoples of the South and of the Nuba Mountains. British official sources also called the Northern group "detribalized Blacks"; less favorably still, some Northerners called them "slaves" (*abid*) in colloquial parlance. Over time, as slavery became less common, *abid* became a disrespectful term used to refer to Southerners especially. Whether called "detribalized Blacks" or "slaves," these "Sudanese" bore social stigmata of slavery and low status.

The term "Sudanese" then came into use as a convenient way to identify inhabitants of the Anglo-Egyptian Sudan. Nationalists later adopted this territorial usage of the term and added an ideological meaning to it. By the 1930s, "Sudanese" had begun to acquire this nationalist significance among some educated Northerners, who assigned to it their own cultural values of Islam and Arabism, and who intended it to imply a transcendence of local and "Arab" tribal identities. In Arabic, the plural term used for the English term "Sudanese" in the territorial and nationalist sense was not *sud*, meaning "blacks" (as a term of color, not status), but rather *sudaniyyin*, which is an abstract pluralization of the singular *sudani*. The nationalist slogan "al-Sudan lil Sudaniyyin" (Sudan for the Sudanese) followed this pattern.[97]

At some point British officials also began to use "Sudanese" in a patrimonial as well as a territorial sense, to imply personal and parental origin in the Sudan and straight descent on both sides from an indigenous Northern ethnic group. Qualified thus, the British intended "Sudanese" to mean "not Egyptian." British authorities used this definition increasingly after 1919, a year of anti-British uprisings in Egypt, to favor Northern Sudanese over "Egyptians" for colonial bureaucratic positions. After the 1924 uprisings in the Sudan, British authorities intensified their efforts to rid the Sudan of Egyptian political and cultural influence. Their formulation of "Sudanese"-ness ultimately had implications not only for job discrimination (favorably, for "Sudanese," and unfavorably, for "Egyptians") but also for Nile Valley politics at large. By causing the *muwalladin*—that is, those Sudan-born men of partial or full Egyptian descent—to scurry to re-define themselves as authentic "Sudanese" for purposes of job security, British authorities muted the identification with Egypt among some residents of the Sudan. The implications were great for Sudanese nationalist politics, since those who were perhaps most inclined to political sympathy with Egypt, namely, the *muwalladin*, emerged from their job experiences with a "Sudanese" identity that they had fought to prove and obtain. As a result, at the time of decolonization, even avowed Unionists supported the proclamation of a Sudanese state independent of Egypt.[98]

As a result of these evolutions in meaning and nuance, "Sudanese" achieved its fourth meaning. It became a term for national, territorial identity among many educated Northerners, but its new use did not necessarily erase the stigma attached to earlier bearers of the term. Indeed, not all "Arab" Northerners took easily to "Sudanese" in its nationalistically revised meaning. One Northern Sudanese historian claimed that the connection between the term "Sudanese" and the taint of slavery was so strong that some educated Northerners, members of the prominent Abu Rawf literary society, "refused, after independence, to apply for passports because they had to register themselves as Sudanese nationals before they could get [one]." To avoid this situation, one member of that society (the historian's uncle) suggested the name "Sennar" rather than "Sudan" for the independent nation, after the Blue Nile capital of the Funj sultanate which had controlled parts of the North from circa 1500 to 1820.[99]

This visceral reaction to the idea of adopting a "Sudanese" identity seems plausible. Around the time of his retirement from the Stores and Ordnance Department in 1949, R. C. Garrett wrote a history of football (soccer) in the Sudan from its first appearance in 1907. In the course of his 260-page narrative, Garrett described an incident that occurred in 1928. At a major tournament staged between teams of government departments, a team made up of Gordon College graduates flatly refused to play against teams that included employees of low social status, including policemen, Sudan Defence Force soldiers, artisans, and paid laborers. Many members of these latter teams were "Blacks," since they were the group most actively recruited for the military, police, and technical and manual trades. "This was a bad start," wrote Garrett, "as it affected the Public Works Department, Stores and Ordnance, Railways, Steamers and the Sudan Light and Power Co. As the Public Works Department were the holders of the Cup[100] (having won it with 8 artizans in the team) there seemed to be no solution to the problem."[101] A year later, the educated Northerners overcame their revulsion and played against the "Blacks" they considered their social inferiors.

If educated Northerners constituted a subaltern elite, privileged vis-à-vis other Sudan inhabitants but subordinate and vulnerable to British officials at work, then the "detribalized Blacks" constituted a straightforward subaltern class.[102] Underrepresented in academic school programs, few "detribalized Blacks" acquired the literacy and connections to secure administrative careers and participate in the new world of journalism. For the historian, therefore, they rarely speak through the sources.[103] Not coincidentally, perhaps, colonial authorities quickly silenced the most politically prominent "Black" Sudanese to emerge in the colonial period—the army officer Ali Abd al-Latif (c. 1892–1948), the son of ex-slave parents of Nuba and Dinka background and a leading figure in the 1924 uprisings. British officials sentenced him to seven years in prison for his role in the 1924 events and then prolonged his sentence indefinitely by consigning him, on dubious grounds, to a mental asylum in Egypt, where he died in 1948.[104]

Among the highly educated, two exceptions stand out. The brothers Muhammad Ashri al-Siddiq and Abd Allah Ashri al-Siddiq were descendants of slaves who came from a group known as "abid al Mawrada"—the slaves of Mawrada—from the Omdurman district of that name, where many ex-slaves had settled.[105] Both attended Gordon College, and both participated actively in the literary salons and journals of the 1930s. (For example, Muhammad contributed an article, "On the Art of Translating," to *al-Fajr*, while his brother Abd Allah published some poetry there.[106]) Abd Allah also attended the American University in Beirut for two years, on his own initiative and with his father's support, in order to pursue studies in botany and zoology.[107]

The personnel file of Abd Allah Ashri al-Siddiq (b. 1910), who worked briefly as a technical assistant to the government entomologist in the mid-1930s, indicates his divergence from the general social pattern of the educated Northern Sudanese. The file lists Abd Allah as having "Shilukawi" nationality through his father (for his mother is listed as a Ja'liyya "Arab").[108] He and his brother were, in fact, the descendants of a military slave, through their grandfather, who was a member of the non-Muslim Shilluk people of the White Nile and who had been recruited into the Egyptian Army.[109]

According to one historian, the Ashri brothers were keenly aware of their slave origins and of their social marginality in the eyes of some peers. Their experiences shaped their political outlook and led them to become staunch advocates of a Sudanese identity that differed from their colleagues' interpretations. In particular, they cherished a vision of Sudanese nationalism that transcended differences of both ethnicity and status, "Arab"-ness and "Black"-ness.[110] Aside from scattered references to the Ashri brothers in studies such as the one mentioned, it is, however, difficult to trace their lives and their ideas through written sources. None of the biographical dictionaries for the period, otherwise such a rich source on the educated Northern Sudanese, includes entries for these two "Sudanese" / "Shilukawi" brothers.[111]

The narrow social construction of the Northern educated elite, whose members later formulated the idea of Sudanese nationalism, was a colonial legacy, the outcome of the colonial state's recruitment policies. It was not, however, an exclusively British legacy. British officials drew in part upon the values of the self-identified "Arab" communities of the North, to whom they looked for colonial cooperation, to set their educational policies and criteria for school admissions. The values of these Northern communities, in turn, derived from an earlier tradition of slavery. Thus, the combined consequences of nineteenth-century indigenous slavery and early-twentieth-century British colonialism bore upon the peoples of the Sudan in the late twentieth century, as they struggled to reach a consensus on what it meant to be "Black," "Arab," and "Sudanese."

Education, Acculturation,
and Nationalist Networks

CULTURE AND EDUCATION IN THE MANDATE TO RULE

According to Lord Lugard, conqueror and later governor-general of Nigeria, the British Empire in Africa had a "dual mandate"—a mission to rule for the mutual advantage of Europe's "own industrial classes, and of the native races in their progress to a higher plane."[1] This claim rested on an ideological principle of imperialism: the belief that economic exploitation (for the benefit of Britain) and social development (for the benefit of the colonies) were compatible. Colonial educational policies were a variation on the theme. The dual mandate of education, in the view of British authorities, consisted of training "natives" to serve colonial regimes, enlightening them in the process.

Education played a critical role in colonial state development. To satisfy the need for skilled and literate employees in the lower and middle tiers of bureaucracy, Britain's colonial regimes founded government institutions or patronized independent colleges that groomed young men for clerical, judicial, and technical posts. The best of these programs used English as the medium of instruction and modeled curricular and extracurricular life on British public schools. Throughout Africa and Asia, the products of such schools constituted a "modern" elite and shared a common culture, manifestations of which included fluency in English as a second language, the wearing of European clothes to demonstrate Western ways, a history of colonial government professional employment, and a budding or growing commitment to nationalist ideals.

Gordon College in the Sudan was a classic example of the government school-cum-training ground. Like comparable institutions in India, it was a "machine for turning out clerks and officials."[2] In the view of British authorities, it also aimed to build character, that is, to promote the moral uplift that justified the imperial enterprise.

The following pages discuss the ways in which Gordon College socialized its students and produced a shared culture—meaning an outlook and lifestyle based on achievements, interests, and assumptions. This acculturation occurred consciously, through policies to train men for and attune them to government service, and inadvertently, as the school affected not only *what* students learned and saw, but *how* they did so, and how, too, they behaved. To illustrate this process, these pages examine culture as it developed—at school, through physical training and discipline, dress and appearance, verbal exchange (in speech and in print), and visual imagery; and after school—within the networks of graduates who served the colonial state. The goal is to show how, without the intention or cognizance of British officials, and in many ways contrary to their aims, schools like Gordon College primed students for nationalism as much as for government service.

The emphasis here is on the *acculturation* rather than the *formation* of an educated elite, and the distinction is significant. "Elite formation" was a prime concern of postcolonial and national studies from the 1950s on.[3] Its frame of inquiry hinged on decolonization, a process that had turned petty employees of colonial states into statesmen of free "nations." Wanting to understand these "new men" after independence, political analysts examined their social backgrounds and asked, "How did they get power?"[4]

By contrast, the emphasis on elite acculturation responds to two historical developments of the 1980s and '90s, namely cultural and globalization studies. Cultural studies was the offspring of new alliances between history, anthropology, and literature.[5] Under its influence, scholars began to reevaluate culture in colonial and national contexts, defining it not as a "heavy weight of tradition" but as "a set of understandings and a consciousness under active construction"[6]; not as "a placid realm of Apollonian gentility" but as a political and ideological "battleground."[7] Globalization studies, meanwhile, responded to the sense of "global compression in which the world [is] increasingly regarded as 'one place.'"[8] Globalization studies lurched ahead with the advent of the internet, a technology some hailed as the start of a communications revolution, as profound in its transformative impact as literacy (the technology of writing) and the printing press had been before. Prompted partly by the World Wide Web to consider networks of exchange, scholars began to question, first, the relevance of national borders in delineating social identities and economic interests, and second, the distinction between cultures high and low, global and local.[9]

Equipped with insights from cultural and globalization studies, one can fruitfully ask a new question about colonial educated elites, including Gordon College graduates and their counterparts in the wider empire. This question goes beyond the refrain of elite formation—"How did this group gain power?"—to encompass a broader context—"How did this group develop a common worldview, and with what consequences for the nation and state?" Thus framed, the inquiry turns to issues of job training and acculturation at school. Groomed for colonial state service and sent afield at graduation, the students and "Old Boys" of Gordon College developed certain conceptions of their own place in the Sudan and of Sudan's place in the wider world.

Geography classes, a basic part of the curriculum, helped students to imagine place and space in practical ways. Every year, students studied different aspects of the Anglo-Egyptian Sudan (such as its flora and fauna, climates, and "principal towns, races, and tribes"), as well as the geography of neighboring territories, the Nile Valley, and Africa, Asia, and Europe at large.[10] Geography classes were just one way that Gordon College enabled students to form a conceptual map of the nation by identifying a people (the Sudanese) with a place (the Anglo-Egyptian Sudan) and an ethos ("a spiritual principle"[11]) that was distinguished, in the students' view, by the Arabic language and Islamic faith.

If power (who had it, who lacked it, who sought it, and who lost it) has been the central drama of colonial and postcolonial studies, then culture has been its lead player. Reflecting on the British in India, one historian suggests, "Colonial conquest was not just the result of the power of superior arms, military organization, political power, or economic wealth—as important as these things were. Colonialism was made possible, and then sustained and strengthened, as much by cultural technologies of rule as it was by the more obvious and brutal modes of conquest that first established power on foreign shores."[12] Schools like Gordon College were certainly cultural mechanisms of rule, producing skilled labor for the regime. Yet, ultimately they weakened the colonial state, by emboldening graduates to claim its domain as their nation. Their nation and the colonial state came together at decolonization when Britain ceded its mandate to rule.

GORDON COLLEGE AND THE SCHOOL REGIME

The Sudan is an ideal test case for the study of colonial education, administration, and nationalism. Unlike India, where several colleges and (after 1857) universities provided advanced English-medium educations to students of varied mother tongues (e.g., Bengali, Marathi, Tamil), the Sudan had a single dominant institution catering to a single (Arabic) linguistic group. This institution was the Gordon Memorial College, opened in Khartoum in 1902 and carefully regulated by British government authorities until decolonization.

Located on the banks of the Blue Nile, a few blocks from the governor-general's palace, Gordon College had a prime location in the layout of the colonial capital. It occupied a grand, double-winged, Gothic-arched building, newly constructed for its purposes out of red brick. Built initially on a bare, dusty plot, its grounds grew increasingly elaborate over the years with the laying out of lawns and flowerbeds, tennis courts and playing fields, dormitories and staff houses.[13] For many years, the college also hosted two affiliated educational programs—the Instructional Workshops (operative from 1904 to 1932) for training artisans and technicians, and the Khartoum Military Academy (operative from 1905 to 1924), which trained Northern Sudanese officers for the Egyptian Army in the Sudan[14]—as well as several government research organizations, including, for example, the Wellcome Tropical Research Laboratories and the Antiquities Service.

The elaborate grounds of the college, together with the prestige of its educational and research programs, made the place a showcase for government. Indeed, it became a standard part of any tourist expedition to the Sudan and earned mention in travel accounts from the period.[15] For years the college also was featured in the Khartoum section of Baedeker's *Egypt and the Sudan: Handbook for Travellers.*[16] More significantly, the college awed students who came to it, with its piped water, dining hall to seat hundreds, and landscaped fields of green (so striking amid the dust and dryness of Khartoum). Applicants coming from the provinces were even more impressed by its amenities.[17]

In these surroundings, students knew that they were special—not only because so many of them had come to the school handpicked from the most eminent Muslim families in the land, but also because their studies put them at the center of the new regime. As one writer noted, "The students could, almost every day, see the Director of Education, the Sudan Government, come and go. To them the Gordon College was more than just a college, it was the Government in person. No wonder . . . [they] expected to find government employment after finishing their studies."[18]

British officials modeled Gordon College on their own alma maters but placed extra emphasis, in the colonial context, on the inculcation of values. In the words of Sir Francis Reginald Wingate, governor-general from 1899 to 1916, the college's goal was "to regenerate the Sudan" through character training, thereby "engendering the English public school code of honour amongst the youth of the country."[19] Discipline and the playing of "games" would contribute to Britain's civilizing mission in the Sudan and provide an antidote for the "slovenliness" of Sudanese homes.[20] For this reason, character-building activities—sports first, and literary and social activities second—took up almost as much of the daily schedule as did classes, notwithstanding the college's job-preparatory goal. The intensity and rigor of these shared experiences meant that students experienced a similar school culture, regardless of what they studied.

British authorities tried to structure the school with lessons from the wider empire in mind, drawing particularly on historical memories of the 1857 Indian Mutiny and the 1881 Urabi revolt in Egypt. Lord Cromer, who as consul-general of Egypt (1883–1907) supervised the early construction of the Anglo-Egyptian regime, worried that "modern" schools—in Egypt as in India (and by extension, in the Sudan)—would manufacture nationalist malcontents and rabble-rousers out of aspiring government employees.[21] In 1925, a Foreign Office official, anxious to obtain a full report on Gordon College, echoed such sentiments by remarking, "It is the tragedy of British rule in India that, with the best intentions in the world, we have ruined many a young man by our education, i.e., by unsuitable instruction which did not build up character."[22]

Britons who worked at Gordon College variously called it "The Eton of the Soudan" or "Winchester by the Nile."[23] Students at the school became acquainted with the world of prefects and dormitories, soccer matches and slide shows. But Anglicization had its limits. In the 1920s, as theories of indirect rule (inspired by Lord Lugard) came into vogue among policy setters, British authorities made a conscious effort to preserve the cultural authenticity of its students, to avoid creating individuals like the Bengali "Babus" or African "Europeanized natives."[24] College rules now required students to wear "traditional" Sudanese clothes, and to be true to their origins in appearance. This contradiction in the college agenda—which now sought to both change and preserve the culture of its students—epitomized the paradox of the British colonial enterprise.

Gordon College was a vocational school in the sense that it educated students to fill specific jobs in the regime. Yet, in its incarnation as a school in the British "public" style, the college also trained students "for life." It attempted to make out of each student the jack-of-all-trades, the sportsman, the man of strong character and code of service—in other words, an individual fitting the ideal of the British district commissioner. With this training, Gordon College served as a laboratory for colonial service and nationalist activity alike, imbuing graduates with a leadership mentality that exceeded the bounds of their jobs.

SPORTS CULTURE

The British ruling classes—those who served in the Indian Civil, Sudan Political, and Colonial Administrative Services—emerged from their public school and university educations infused with a strong "games ethic," a belief that sport was a field of endeavor where men cultivated and asserted both strength and character. Given this faith in athleticism as moral exercise, the British viewed physical education as a boon for schools in the wider empire, and made sports a "chief spiritual export."[25] Among students, however, sports forged an esprit de corps that unified early nationalists as a team against the British.

To reform what Wingate had called the "slack habits" of life in the Sudan,[26] and at the same time to promote moral and social uplift, Gordon College authorities established a disciplinary regime that drew upon military traditions. It was therefore no accident that the college "savoured strongly of the barracks," as a Lebanese official who had taught at the school in the 1920s reflected critically years later.[27]

Until the early 1930s, when a new generation of British educators began to emphasize the importance of adventure rather than discipline in learning, life at Gordon College was highly regimented. The college's 1929 timetable had students beginning their day when the bell rang at 5:30 A.M., and ending it with lights out at 9:00 P.M. After taking their required 5:45 A.M. baths, students lined up in the college quadrangle for the morning roll call and parade of inspection, where, in keeping with the public school tradition, student prefects, or "officers" (who were deputed to handle petty discipline cases), could whack their juniors with sticks.[28] Regular exercise drills, modeled on the Egyptian Army system and taught by Sudanese army sergeants, heightened the martial atmosphere. Class time fell between 8:00 A.M. and 1:30 P.M., when students attended six academic sessions of fifty minutes each. After classes, they had designated times for sports and physical training, "preparation" (evening study hours), and on Thursdays, Fridays, and holidays, more afternoon parading.[29]

Conditions at the school were spartan. Students slept in large dormitories on "native beds" (*angarebs*) and were required to make their beds, sweep the floors, and wash their own clothes. They ate communal meals of lentils, bread, meat, and rice—simple Sudanese fare.[30] They had to do other chores, too, such as weeding the playing fields on one afternoon a week.[31] Corporal punishment—a routine practice in Northern Sudanese schools of the period[32]—was occasionally applied. At Gordon college, this entailed flogging, before 1937, and caning thereafter.[33]

"Games" were intrinsic to the Gordon College regime. Afternoon schedules included football (soccer) in winter, and rounders in summer, supplemented by track-and-field events. Competitive matches and sports meets, formalized by the regalia of trophies and prizes, promoted values of team spirit but also encouraged students to seek individual distinction. College authorities tried to make games less authoritarian and more fun in the early 1930s, when, against the gloom of the Depression, they introduced recreational activities such as Ping-Pong, lawn tennis, and volleyball.[34]

Scouting was also central to the college regime. Founded in Britain in 1908 by Lieutenant-General Robert Baden-Powell (a veteran of India and South Africa) to instill virtues of manliness and obedience in young men,[35] the Boy Scout movement spread throughout the British Empire and arrived in the Sudan by 1917.[36] Atbara, a city based around the railway headquarters, had the first Sudanese scouting troop; nevertheless, Gordon College assumed the central place in Sudanese scouting when Imperial Scouting Headquarters in London appointed the college warden as its chief commissioner for the country.[37] Photographs show that Gordon College students had their own colonially authenticized scouting uniforms: along with khaki shirts and shorts, they wore turbans, to which student leaders affixed their badge.[38] Scouts learned first aid, tying knots, setting up bivouacs, and other tasks suited to the good citizen and outdoorsman; they also endeavored to perform good deeds, such as surveying streets to report stray dogs.[39] Amin al-Tum (who became a minister of defense in later years) was one scouting success story. He remembered proudly, "At Gordon College I was among the first Scout leaders. Later I became deputy to the Chief Scout for an *Ahliyya* [independent school] scouting troop. One day during our troop's travels along the White Nile I saved the life of a youth from certain drowning . . . and I am happy with the memory of that day."[40]

After leaving Gordon College, most graduates never did another drill exercise again. Nevertheless, British-style sports became a way of life, on the job and off. Some played games for the sake of their careers, for as one Briton acknowledged, "A confidential report which contained a reference to enthusiasm for polo could help a man's career be he British or Sudanese."[41] But some played for the love of sport.

Football, in particular, became a favorite pastime for graduates, who participated either as players or spectators. In the big towns, graduates often competed on a governmental department basis—teachers from the Education Department, for example, versus accountants from Finance—suggesting, in yet another way, the pervasive influence of government employment on leisure activities.[42] But unlike tennis and polo, which were sports of the elite, football was a game that even the humble could play. After all, from the earliest years of the regime, it had been introduced not only to Gordon College males but to men in the army, police corps, artisanal programs, and Christian missionary schools, many of whom went on to form local teams of their own. In the early 1950s, by which time football in the North had acquired a mass following, Gordon College graduates assumed leadership roles in the council of the Sudan Football Association.[43] Their engagement with organized football was, in some sense, an early exercise in mass politics and popular government.

In the Northern Sudan before the twentieth century, games had been for children.[44] The British came, however, and introduced games as a sport for men—a hybrid of martial training and play. At Gordon College, this brand of sport promoted the team spirit that later invigorated the early nationalists.

CLOTHING CULTURE

"It would seem natural," mused one Bengali, "that in the interest of their own empire [the British] would welcome all trends towards Westernization ... [,] but this was the last thing they were prepared to do. They were violently repelled by English in our mouths, and even more violently by English clothes on our backs."[45] A Gordon College graduate might have observed the same. In the Sudan, as in India, clothing was a cultural battlefield where nationalists asserted their claims to modernity or tradition.

The phenomenon of British revulsion in the face of Westernized dress by "natives" was by no means specific to India's *babus*; the Westernized educated elites of Africa and the Middle East encountered the same British repugnance. Drawing upon his Nigerian experience, Lord Lugard used medical arguments to convey disapproval for the "native" in Western dress. He wrote, "The Europeanised African differs not merely in mental outlook from the other [African] groups, but also in physique. Doctors and dentists tell us that he has become less fertile, more susceptible to lung-trouble and to other diseases, and to defective dentition—disabilities which have probably arisen from in-breeding among a very limited class, and to the adoption of European dress, which writers in the native press say is enervating and inimical to the health of the African."[46]

British dislike for the suit-wearing *babu*, *effendi*, or Europeanized African arose from a sense of threat. By donning suit and tie, hat and shoes, local educated elites implicitly shook the foundations of imperial dominion, which were based on notions of difference. Analyzing the empire in India, one historian points out, "Behind this condescension [toward the Indian *babu*] lay unvoiced, anxious fears. By his mimicry of English manners, the babu reminded the British of a similarity they sought always to disavow; and, steeped in English liberalism, he posed by implication, if not by outright assertion, a challenge to the legitimacy of the Raj."[47] By emulating their British superiors in dress, *babus* and their trans-imperial counterparts could aspire to inclusion in the British social order. It was a short step from there to demanding a political voice on British terms—a short step, in other words, to nationalism—espousing the right of local peoples to serve as "the ultimate source of political authority."[48]

British authorities in the Sudan knew that the *effendis*—distinguished by their modern education, Western clothes, and government employment—posed a latent nationalist challenge. Their fears were confirmed in 1919, a year marked in Egypt by popular anti-British revolts, and again in 1924, a year marked by the same in the Sudan. To treat this *effendi* problem, and to restrict the spread of "office-wallahs" (to use the Raj-inspired terminology of one Education Department official)[49], the Sudan government attacked the symptom of Westernized dress, starting with government schools. Hence, new policy now required humble *kuttab* (primary-school) teachers to wear "sheikh's robes," however much they may have dreamed of "aping the European"[50]; at the same time, the new policy also barred Gordon College students from wearing Western dress. In setting these policies in the Sudan, Britons drew upon a reservoir of imperial experience; in India, and especially in Bengal, debates over "natives" in European attire (whether they could wear shoes and dispense with "traditional" Mughal-era garb) went back to the 1850s.[51]

Of course, Gordon College had always had a dress code, but it evolved to suit changing British attitudes toward cultural tradition. In the college's first decade, British authorities had posed no barriers to Western dress and had even encouraged it. Al-Dardiri Muhammad Uthman, who arrived at the college in 1906, observed in his memoir, "The students in those days tended to wear Western clothes topped by the *tarbush* (Fez)."[52] Pictures support his claims: a postcard of the new college shows young boys lined up wearing jackets, trousers, and red-tinted tarbushes,[53] while a class photograph from 1912 shows about sixty students, all but eight or so in suits and ties.[54] The exceptions were student *qadis*, who wore the *jibbas* (outer cloaks), caftans, and silk belts that were—or arguably, were made by the British to be—a mark of their profession.[55] Upon leaving the school and entering Shari'a courts, the *qadis* would retain their robes and turbans—a policy which not only satisfied British fantasies of traditionalism, but sought, more pragmatically, to affirm the government's respect for Islamic custom and continuity.[56]

The Gordon College dress code changed dramatically in the 1920s, when the concept of indirect rule—an imperial philosophy that responded to threats of incipient nationalist organization by favoring the preservation or invention of tradition—gained momentum among British authorities.[57] In 1925, Geoffrey Archer, governor-general from 1924 to 1926, expressed the hope that "under moral suasion [from British officials], these Sudanese youths [will] cast off their shoddy European clothes and tarbush and revert to national dress," thereby resisting the temptation to join the ranks of the effendiyya. "Natives endeavouring to emulate Europeans in their manner and mode of dress," he added, "are always a sorry sight."[58]

Sanctioned by policy, British officials applied dress codes to students with rigor. At age 62, Yusuf Badri still remembered the trauma of an incident in 1924 when he had been twelve years old and a student at his father's kuttab school in Rufa'a (before his years at Gordon College.) The British district commissioner met Yusuf, wearing European shoes that his brother had bought for him in a shop, on the street in Rufa'a. "He sent me back in a furious temper to change my shoes and put on my marcoub, the native shoes. By the time I got back to school, I found the whole school paraded and Mr. Richardson was inspecting the shoes of the pupils. Every boy wearing European shoes was sent home to change into Sudanese shoes."[59] The D.C. had acted by the book; government regulations for kuttabs (as set out in the code of 1929) stipulated that "European shoes and socks shall not be worn by the natives."[60]

At Gordon College, too, "native" dress became school uniform in the 1920s. By 1930, a large group photograph of the Gordon College student body showed a sea of white cotton jallabiyyas (robes) and immas (turbans), with not a suit or tarbush in sight.[61] By this time, Egyptians were for the most part no longer welcome at the college, and the muwalladin, Sudan-born males of full or partial Egyptian descent, were finding it wiser to play up the Sudanese side of their identity by dressing for the role.

The authorities had less control over graduates' attire, although some British officials after 1924 did encourage Northern Sudanese employees to revert from suit and tie to the traditional robe and turban—to transform themselves, in other words, from effendis into shaykhs. Some Northern Sudanese officials, like the schoolteacher Ahmad Muhammad Salih (1894–1973), consciously resisted British persuasion by refusing to wear the robe and turban in place of the modern suit. But others did the opposite, showing just how ambiguous resistance through clothing could be.[62] For example, the translators Farah Abd al-Rahman Hamid (b. 1907) and Abd Allah Waqi Allah rejected the suit and tie of the colonizers and affirmed their indigenous Muslim identity by donning the *jallabiyya* anew.[63] Years later, in the 1930s and '40s, some took this pro-*jallabiyya* attitude to its logical conclusion by promoting a local industry in weaving Sudanese cotton cloth (*dammur*), as a Gandhi-inspired exercise in self-sufficiency and non-cooperation.[64] These exceptions aside, most *effendis* asserted their right to wear suits and ties instead of *jallabiyyas*, and wool and silk instead of cotton, regardless of the sniffs, sidelong glances, or under-the-breath remarks that their clothing inspired in Britons.[65]

Though trousers and shirts were proscribed for students after about 1920, they definitely had cachet in society at large. For many, European clothes symbolized an escape from manual labor or from low social status. Such clothing evoked modernity, education, and an office job—what British officials sniffed at as "Effendyism."[66] Indeed, because they were so desirable, Western clothes were a common article for theft in the Anglo-Egyptian period. For example, a monthly report for the Eastern and Central Districts of Darfur Province lists two cases of clothing theft for May 1934 alone, the victims being a wireless engineer and a Greek merchant.[67] In the same year, one British official explained to his mother that his house in Singa had been burglarized and that clothes had been stolen, including the trousers of his green pajamas and the coat of his blue pajamas. "It would not have mattered much if he had taken a pair," he wrote, " [but] as it stands he has ruined two pairs." Police detectives later caught the culprit near Karkoj. He was found wearing the Briton's "best shirt and trousers and giving himself out to be a veterinary officer."[68]

As a primary symbol of modernity in the eyes of the colonized, Western clothes were a marker of professional progress and achievement.[69] This point eluded, frustrated, or simply bemused British officials. One noted wryly in his memoirs, "During the war many Sudanese NCOs became officers but, in order to qualify, they had to pass a relatively simple exam in English, which was taught from the intermediate school upwards. The question set in one of these exams was 'Assess the progress made in the Sudan since the Reoccupation.' The *pièce de résistance* of one aspirant's essay was 'Look at the clothes your father wore. Look at the clothes you wear. Bloody marvellous.'"[70] Certainly, Gordon College graduates were proud of their European clothes, which simultaneously set them apart from "co-nationalists," defied British social exclusivity, buttressed their claims to colonial succession and national leadership, and affirmed their place among the "modern" classes worldwide.[71]

THE CULTURE OF WORDS

Just as Napoleon's conquest of Egypt in 1798 led to transformations in the Arabic literary culture of the region, so did Britain's conquest do to the Sudan a century later. A literary historian summarized the process by writing, "Out of the fruitful meeting of the indigenous Arabic literary tradition and the cultural forces of the West modern Arabic literature was born."[72] European genres and styles were not the sole stimulus behind modern Arabic literature, however, since the printing press, by publishing poetic and prose works intended solely for private reading (and not recitation), also guided its birth. Introduced to Egypt by Napoleon and to the Sudan by the British, the moveable-type printing press stimulated the rise of Arabic journalism, promoted literary experimentation, and ultimately fostered the development of early nationalism through the medium of print culture.[73] At the same time, it stimulated a sense of Arabic renaissance (*nahda*), comparable in its literary genesis, content, and agenda to the contemporary Bengal renaissance (*nabajagaran*) in Calcutta.[74]

Gordon College was the focal point of these developments in the Sudan. Its graduates went on to become leading Northern Sudanese literati who experimented boldly with new poetic forms and literary genres such as the play, the short story, and the critical essay. The same graduates played leading roles in the development of the Sudanese Arabic press. Their efforts led to two pathbreaking journals of the 1930s, *al-Fajr* and *al-Nahda*, which simultaneously championed Sudanese literature and nationalism. It helped that from 1933 Gordon College students were able to get firsthand experience in periodical publishing by producing a school literary magazine that targeted alumni subscribers.[75]

As the primary purveyor of English education in the Sudan, Gordon College initiated its students into a wider Anglophone culture. Classes in English language and literature exposed students directly to prominent English authors from Shakespeare to Kipling.[76] Meanwhile, classes in English grammar and composition exposed students to new models of prose, which they later adapted to Arabic. For instance, according to one scholar and alumnus, the "controversial essay," a staple of Gordon College English classes, resurfaced as the Arabic political essay among early nationalists.[77] From as early as 1907, classes also incorporated study of English short stories and newspaper articles.[78] Although relatively few Gordon College graduates (scholars excepted) wrote in English outside their jobs, many nevertheless continued to read English extensively. Since English was also the language of many radicals and of educated elites throughout the empire,

English literacy had subversive potential. Command of English opened the door, for example, to the nationalist and anticolonial writings of Nehru and Gandhi, whose thoughts on self-government and self-sufficiency inspired many Gordon College graduates in the 1930s and '40s.[79]

Gordon College was also a premier center for Arabic education. Its Arabic teachers not only taught literature but composed and published poems and essays of their own, thereby serving as literary role models to students. Influenced by intellectual currents emanating from Egypt and Greater Syria, many of these teachers conveyed to students their belief in a modern Arabic revival (*nahda*) that could draw on the glorious Arab Islamic past. They thereby nurtured the Arabism (*uruba*) that became central to Northern Sudanese nationalism. Recognizing this debt years later, Gordon College graduates hailed their great Egyptian and Levantine Arabic teachers, singling out men like the Syrian Fu'ad al-Khatib (c. 1878–1956), an inspiring poet who during World War I wrote odes in praise of the Arab Revolt, then left Gordon College in 1920 to support Faysal ibn al-Sharif Husayn in his failed bid for an Arab Syrian kingdom, and later served the Hashimites in the Hijaz and Transjordan.[80]

Gordon College integrated its students into an Arabic and English print culture inside the classroom and out. Unlike the Northern Sudan's traditional *khalwas* (Qur'an schools), the college was rich in books. Already in 1904, when books were still relatively rare in the Sudan because mass printing was so new, the shelves of the school library contained "rows and rows of the stirring tales of Defoe, Scott, Dickens, Henty, Ballantine, and Rider Haggard."[81] By encouraging students to use this library, authorities inducted them into the practice of reading for pleasure. By the late 1920s, books had become so cheap, and journals so accessible, that many students were reading outside the classroom and library, for example, by sharing copies of Egyptian journals that had been banned on the grounds of their anti-British sentiment.[82] Their reading habits contributed to the growth of a local Arabic periodical press, which in years to come would offer the most important ground for nationalist literary debate.

With the abundance of books came new modes of thought. Whereas traditional *khalwas* had emphasized learning orally and by rote (a necessity when books were scarce), Gordon College stressed learning by reading and mental synthesis. During examinations, British teachers expected students to demonstrate mastery of class material, not by repeating it verbatim but by combining the content of books and lectures with personal insights.[83] As college reports show, this approach did not come easily to students whose early educations had impressed upon them the value of memorization. The head English instructor noted in 1929 that Gordon College students had difficulty composing extemporaneous essays on any given subject although their "oral English" reached a high standard. Furthermore, he observed, "Most of the boys still prefer to learn their History notes by heart and, if possible, reproduce them word for word. This was shown clearly in the History examination, when no less than 30 boys failed in the Third Year. The boys are keenly interested in this subject, but they need to learn to think for themselves." Similarly, in chemistry and physics classes, students foundered when it came time to apply their mathematical knowledge to chemical and physical problems as opposed to recounting formulae.[84]

Gordon College promoted free-thinking in another venue, namely, the college's Literary and Debating Society, which became the most popular literary activity at the college after its debut in 1933. The society sponsored lectures and debates in English and Arabic, often inviting former graduates and current teachers (who were, by that time, exclusively British or Northern Sudanese) to participate. These debates maintained a link between alumni and current students and presented a rare opportunity for sparring with Britons.[85] Emphasizing oral communication and rhetoric, the debating society cultivated skills that proved especially valuable after 1938, when graduates entered the arena of organized nationalist politics.

Sirr al-Khatm al-Khalifa, distinguished in later life as an educator and later prime minister of Sudan, recalled that debate topics had direct relevance to the Sudan and were based around such questions as "Is it better to spend more money on elementary education or higher education?" "Should women be allowed to work outside their homes?" and "Should the Sudan emphasize agriculture or industry?"[86] A quintessentially colonial topic, reflecting British concerns, appeared in the form of the statement: "A little learning is a dangerous thing."[87] College debates were something that even the British wrote home about. E. A. Balfour, a young Assistant District Commissioner seconded to the Education Department, wrote to his mother in 1936: "This evening I have got to deliver a speech in the Literary and Debating Society. I am opposing the motion 'That this house views with satisfaction the replacement of the camel by the motor car throughout the Sudan.' I have really not had time to prepare my speech but I mean it to be a virulent attack on modern inventions and a plea to keep the Sudan as it is." Much to his delight, rising to the defense of the camel, Balfour and his side swayed the house and defeated the motion.[88]

Another popular debating society event was Hat Night. Members wrote topics on scraps of paper and put them into a hat, whereupon each person selected a paper and spoke extemporaneously on the topic they had chosen.

Amin al-Tum wrote, "I remember that I was participating once in one of these evenings and took out my paper, and what should be written on it but 'What would you do if you found yourself with four legs and no hands?' It shook me. . . . It was impossible for anyone to think about such a topic . . . but after a few moments I gathered my strength. . . . My response was a very long and fiery discourse and at the end of the applause the appointed time for speech had ended."[89] Other typical Hat Night subjects were "Our Place in the Arab World," and "Our Civic Duties towards Our Town."[90] These were the very topics that interested the budding Gordon College nationalists, who went on to emphasize Arabism and modernity (meaning social and technological progress), in addition to Islam, as platforms of national identity.

The Gordon College debating society had such an impact on its participants that they tried to reenact it after graduation. When the future newspaper publisher Isma'il al-Atabani (b. 1910) was posted as a government accountant to Wad Medani in the early 1930s, he introduced Hat Night to the town's Graduates' Club, which was the social center for Northern Sudanese government officials like him. He and his friends at the club also began a literary circle, with lectures and discussions. It is perhaps no accident that the members of this Wad Medani literary circle—Gordon College graduates who were well read in Nehru—later claimed the credit for suggesting a Graduates' General Congress modeled on the lines of the Indian National Congress.[91] Founded in 1938, the Sudanese Graduates Congress gave rise to political parties and functioned as the precursor to the National Assembly.

Most of the students who participated so actively in the debating society also joined the college's Social Service Committee, out of a commitment to ideals of progress—social, political, and scientific—that contact with Britain and Egypt had stimulated. This idealism had strong literary antecedents. In the closing years of the nineteenth century and the opening years of the twentieth, pathbreaking Egyptian literati had begun to use poetry as a tool for social reform.[92] By the 1920s, Gordon College students and graduates were following these cues by composing poems and essays that called, among other things, for the expansion of education (controversially, for girls as well as boys); the development of health services; and the extension of public works.[93] These debates over social reform—over how (not if) the Sudan should modernize—were central to the nationalist enterprise.

Students and graduates applied the ideals they voiced in poetry through several social projects, which confirmed the sense of public service and civic duty that propelled the nationalist mission. At Gordon College the Social

Service Committee started a literacy night school for adult male artisans and staged fundraising plays in collaboration with the college dramatic society. For example, the goal of one of these student–graduate theatricals, staged in 1932, was to raise money for extending the city's piped water system and for building a rest house in the Mawrada district of Omdurman.[94] Students and graduates also worked together to raise funds for an orphanage trade school called Malja' al-Qirsh ("Piastre House," named for the mode of collecting contributions in the local currency, piastre by piastre) and for building non-government independent schools.[95] The latter goal reached fruition with the opening of the Ahliyya and Ahfad Schools, which introduced primary (and later intermediate and secondary) programs (originally for boys, later for girls as well) that met a growing demand for modern education which the government could not meet. The legacy of these independent schools endures today in two private universities that bear their names, Ahfad University for Women and Omdurman Ahlia University.[96]

At Gordon College the culture of words was a culture of speech and print. Although oral communication remained important in lectures, debates, in the recitation of poems, and in face-to-face conversations, print became increasingly important as the colonial period progressed. The result was that, unlike their elders who had reached adulthood before the 1898 conquest, Gordon College men constituted a "print generation," for whom books were a source of edification and entertainment alike. Journalism also played a growing role in their formation, keeping them together, as readers and contributors, as job transfers sent them far afield. Regardless of the distances between them, Old Boys maintained conversations in print, thereby creating the community spirit that was the essence of the nationalist movement.

VISUAL CULTURE

Gordon College also taught its students new ways of seeing. By introducing them to the media of still photography and the moving picture, the school made images of people, places, and objects a part of daily life. This pictorial proliferation led to a revolutionary transformation in Northern Sudanese visual culture. In the riverain North, after all, in an effort to suppress idolatrous or polytheistic practices, local Muslim norms had hitherto discouraged the representation of animate beings. (The visual context of Sudanese was therefore radically different from that of Britons, for whom photography evolved out of traditional artistic conventions of figurative painting and portraiture.[97]) In the Anglo-Egyptian era, however, photography (understood as the product of chemicals reacting with light, and therefore of natural laws), faced no objections from leading religious scholars, which helps to explain its enthusiastic reception among the cognoscenti. Indeed, it was so well received that in 1921 Fu'ad al-Khatib (a popular teacher at Gordon College) delivered an ode in praise of photography at a party in Khartoum.[98]

In the Sudan as elsewhere in Africa, photography had made its first showing in the late nineteenth century as a tool of European exploration and conquest.[99] In the 1870s at least one photographer-explorer—the Austrian Richard Buchta—had traveled the length of the Nile Valley from Egypt to Lado (near the current Sudan–Congo border), capturing the Sudan in film. His early photographs of pyramids, peoples, and landscapes visually mapped out the region and (converted to drawings) graced the pages of travel accounts.[100] Twenty years later, photographers arrived with the troops of Anglo-Egyptian conquest, shooting cameras rather than guns,[101] and taking pictures of the Mahdi's bomb-blasted tomb as a war trophy.[102] Transported to Britain, images of the Sudanese "Reconquest" stimulated popular imperialism and jingoism, as pictures of the South African or Boer War were to do a few years later.[103] Images of the Sudan also fed popular imperial science at a time when the Darwinian classification of peoples into racial types was a major field of endeavor.[104]

Gordon College served as photography's first point of transfer to Sudanese (as opposed to European) audiences. The college exposed students to a range of film media, including photographically illustrated books, snapshots and studio portraits, magic lanterns (glass-plate slides used to project black-and-white or hand-tinted images onto a screen), and narrative (cinematic) film. Because photographs and pictures enabled the boys and Old Boys of Gordon College to see and hence to imagine the world, the British Empire, and the Sudan in new ways, visual culture was as important to the development of nationalism as the culture of words.

When Gordon College opened in 1902, the technological conditions of photography were ideal for the growth of visual culture. The cumbersome camera equipment of the late nineteenth century had given way to cheap handheld and pocket cameras which were making photography accessible and affordable to British officials across the pay scale. From 1906, if not before, British educators started taking "snapshots" of Gordon College students.[105] Students also encountered professional photography when they posed for class pictures before cameras on tripods.[106] Placed in government jobs after graduation, Old Boys continued to pose for group photographs as members of departments or district staffs.[107]

Gordon College students and graduates soon became so comfortable with photographic rituals that they were incorporating them into their private lives. By the early 1920s it had become common for educated males—both *effendis* and *shaykhs* (including eminent men of the older generation and leading members of the *ulama*)—to go to studio photographers to have their portraits taken.[108] Many such portraits made the transition to print, appearing, for example, as biographical illustrations in *Shuʿara al-Sudan* (c. 1923), one of the first Arabic printed books to appear in the Northern Sudan, devoted to local poets and their work.[109] Images and words began to appear in print together, and the literate were reading both.[110] By the late Anglo-Egyptian period, this familiarity with pictures had extended to cartoons and caricatures, which began to be featured in locally produced Arabic periodicals and monographs.[111]

Gordon College students also encountered photography through the magic lantern, the glass-slide projector that predated the moving picture.[112] At the college, just as in a British school, lectures accompanied the slides, thereby making the magic lantern a potential medium for instruction, entertainment, and propaganda. In 1915, for example, one government official delivered a lantern slide lecture to the students about the origins and causes of World War I—an important maneuver for stating the British case and buttressing colonial loyalties in wartime.[113]

In 1911 (sixteen years after the birth of cinematography in Paris) the moving picture debuted in the Sudan. The occasion was the visit of King George V and Queen Mary, who stopped briefly in Port Sudan and Sinkat on their way back from the Royal Durbar in India. As a surprise for the Northern Sudanese notables who had been gathered for the occasion, British authorities had the festivities filmed and used the occasion of the opening of a new rail line to the West to present this spectacle a few days later. With the notables now assembled in El Obeid (the speed of their journey from east to west having been itself a technological wonder), British authorities waited till nightfall. Sir Stewart Symes, then assistant director of intelligence but later governor-general, recalled:

> Hardly any one had remarked a large white sheet of cloth, strung taut on a wooden framework, until as the light faded a square patch of light illuminated it. Silence fell on the crowd as a dark object moved across the patch of light, and interest became general as from its side appeared a narrow ladder with figures in uniform ascending it and descending. Some one recognised an individual figure; and as various scenes of the arrival of H.M.S. *Medina,* the reception of Their Majesties and presentations of Sudanese notables were thrown on the screen, popular clamour increased in loud gusts of applause and laughter. It was like the sound of a crowd at critical moments in a football cup tie. Above the din I heard several of my recent clients shouting to their entourages,

"There, see for yourselves: you thought we were liars; it was just as we told you. W'Allahi—praise be to God." It was Lord Kitchener's idea to organise this first cinema performance ever given in the Sudan. It was a great success!"[114]

This event showed how, in years to come, photography would help to unify the Sudan in a single visual field. Members of an audience in El Obeid could see themselves in Port Sudan moving in action, not frozen in time, thereby eliciting the sense of simultaneity across distances that is so important to the imagining of national communities.[115]

In the 1920s Gordon College served as the premier center of cinema for Northern Sudanese audiences. In 1920 the school was able to buy its own "cinema machine" (at a time when the only other machine in Khartoum was owned by the YMCA) and to show movies once a fortnight. Within a year, it had screenings once a week.[116] In 1929 a college report noted that "cinema performances or Magic Lantern lectures were given every Friday evening and afforded keen enjoyment to large audiences, not composed exclusively of school boys"[117]—suggesting that the school helped to induct the wider community into its visual culture.

Greek businessmen began to build the first commercial cinema in Khartoum in 1929, just as Hollywood was perfecting the "talkie," the movie with synchronized sound.[118] In the 1930s and '40s the city had two cinemas that showed British and American (English-language) films especially, but also Egyptian Arabic and, by the late 1940s, Indian films, too.[119] It apparently took some time for graduates to overcome their embarrassment about sitting in the cinema among Europeans, people "of different color, language, and creed."[120] But Gordon College graduates soon became such enthusiastic movie-goers that the journal al-Fajr created a regular film review column called "The Silver Screen" (al-shasa al-baydaʾ, lit. "the white screen"). John Wayne, Basil Rathbone, Claudette Colbert, and even Snow White made their appearances,[121] but the real luminary was Greta Garbo, the subject of two reviews and even an Arabic praise poem, entitled "Greta: Radiant Star of the World."[122] Cinema was influencing not only journalistic prose (through film reviews) and poetry, but narrative fiction as well. Its romantic themes and moods surfaced in short stories, as shown by one tale, "Catastrophe!: A Modern Tragedy," published in the literary journal al-Nahda in 1931 and signed by "Rudolf Valentino" at Gordon College.[123]

In the Sudan as in other colonies, British authorities were worried that the cinema might expose some of Britain's weak spots, by illustrating British poverty or crime, or its vulnerability in war, and thereby incite impressionable local audiences to challenge colonial authority.[124] Commercial cinema, after all, was for the most part not designed as a vehicle for British propaganda.

In the end, however, cinema appears to have posed a greater challenge to traditional Northern Sudanese society for a very different reason. Namely, Hollywood visions of strong-minded women leading public lives, finding romance, and securing happy-ending marriages prompted many young men to painfully reconsider their ideals of women and wives. Their concerns surfaced in writings on marriage that appeared in *al-Nahda* in 1931; there, educated Northern Sudanese men hotly debated the idea of the modern woman through their letters to the editor.

This debate about marriage and womanhood surfaced most poignantly in a short story, printed in *al-Nahda* that same year. Called "The Defeat of Hope," it featured a young *effendi*, an avid reader and cinema-goer named Hasanayn Effendi, from Khartoum, who dreams of finding an educated, progressive Northern Sudanese bride. He wants a woman with "the allure of Clara Bow, the enchantment of Greta Garbo, and the smile of Lillian Gish," a woman who "would give him a morning kiss on the cheek when he left for the office, and an afternoon kiss on the mouth when he returned." He makes a list of forty girls' names, but crosses many out.

> The first one would be useless as a wife in any case because the midwife's razor played with her cheeks, gashing and scarring them. The sole defect of the second is the coloration of her lips with this indigo dye which made her a display for the mockery of foreigners and the jeers of friends.

. . . and so on. Eventually, Hasanayn has five names left. Before making his final choice, he develops elaborate plans in his head that might enable him to catch a glimpse of the likely candidates.

> Every one of them could read and write, and none of them had any deformity or scarring, and their circumcision had not been of the Pharaonic kind, which damages women and destroys their silence during childbirth.[125]

Ultimately, his dreams wither when his father marries him, by proxy, to his eldest cousin, a farm girl strong enough to "pull the waterwheel herself, if any harm befell the bull."[126]

Gordon College graduates belonged to a new "print generation" in the Sudan; they also belonged to a generation that had firsthand experiences with photographs and film. The explosion of visual culture had several effects. Through pictures, students and graduates were stimulated to think about the wider world and their place in it. Pictures presented images of modernity in the Western mode and challenged attitudes toward male-female relations in particular. At the same time they promoted forms of intellectual globalization, by making the world seem both a bigger and a smaller place. Finally, photographs of the territory promoted the imagination of a people in a place—in this case, of the "Sudanese" in the "Sudan"—and helped graduates to envision the colony as a nation.

LIFE AFTER COLLEGE

The day came when Gordon College students finished their courses of study and faced the employment for which they were groomed. Before 1930, new Old Boys received, rather than applied for, their first government jobs. The director of education or the college warden simply wrote letters to the appropriate departments to place new college graduates in suitable entry-level positions.[127] After 1930, the administrative cutbacks of the Depression compelled graduates to compete for places by taking a civil service examination.[128] Even then, however, the government continued to employ most graduates—a trend that persisted into the late 1960s, more than a decade beyond independence and years after the college had evolved into Khartoum University.[129]

Launched in their careers, graduates found themselves in new and often wholly alien environments. Some went to small towns or remote district centers, where, as clerks, teachers, or qadis, they found their main or even sole source of companionship among fellow district staff members. Others, the envy of all graduates, got posted to Khartoum or another big town, where they could enjoy a rich and varied social life and a host of urban amenities. Of course, few spent their careers in one place; regular transfers, every few years, kept employees on the move.

Even when scattered far and wide, graduates retained their group cohesion, partly because they continued to socialize in common milieux. The government aided or patronized their interaction in three social settings: Old Boys reunions, employees clubs, and graduates clubs. All three venues promoted the social and intellectual contacts through which nationalism took shape.

Gordon College played a direct role in maintaining links among graduates, beginning in 1913, when the school sponsored an Old Boys reunion, at which Wingate gave an address.[130] Hosted annually thereafter, reunions were so popular that they drew graduates by the hundreds every year. Consisting of football matches (graduates vs. students), theatrical performances, film showings, and formal garden tea parties, the festivities enabled Old Boys to re-live some of their happier school experiences.[131] Newspaper coverage ensured that those too far away to attend could participate through print.[132] Over the years, governor-generals and other high-placed Britons regularly attended reunion events, thereby affirming the graduates' importance to the colonial state and further consolidating their sense of confidence and capability.

The government also facilitated relations among graduates in towns and rural district centers by supporting employees clubs, which typically consisted of an outdoor café and a tennis court or two.[133] While the authorities wanted to keep employees happy (knowing that a desperately lonely or homesick worker would not be most productive), they also wanted to keep them in check, that is, to gather them in one place under light surveillance. A Northern Sudanese writer reflected that during the tenure of one particular British D.C. in Wad Medani in the late 1930s, the club "resembled the palace of Louis XVI because it was full of small intrigues." If news reached the D.C. that an employee had been unexpectedly absent from the club, the D.C. might summon him for an explanation. "After that our friend would live in a state of continuing fear, full of doubt about all the members," wondering which one had informed on him.[134]

Though some officials went to the clubs simply to chat, play cards, and pass the time, others, notably those who went on to play leading roles in the nationalist movement and the Graduates Congress, went for intellectual exercise. Clubs, indeed, often doubled as literary societies, where employees read and discussed books and periodicals and composed and delivered poems (many with oblique nationalist themes). After the advent of the government-run radio station in 1941, employees also went to the club to listen to and discuss news from Radio Omdurman, the BBC, and Cairo Radio.[135]

In addition to employees clubs there were a few graduates clubs (also supervised by British authorities), the first and most important having been formed in 1919 in Omdurman, which was the main bedroom community for Khartoum employees. Located in urban centers, graduates clubs catered to Muslim Northern Sudanese men, not to Egyptian or Lebanese expatriates (many of whom frequented provincial employees' clubs). By their very names, graduates clubs sought to emphasize the educational and intellectual attainments of members, who had graduated from Gordon College or one of the provincial intermediate schools.[136]

During the interwar years, the Omdurman Graduates Club, in particular, became the center of organized nationalism. Of course, to avoid government disfavor and to keep their jobs, graduates could not broach politics directly.

Literature and social debates (e.g., about the reform of family life) were therefore "safe" for discussion, whereas the nature of the regime and of Sudanese-Egyptian relations was not. These restrictions notwithstanding, the club provided graduates with valuable political experience. Permitted by authorities to hold elections among members, the Omdurman club formed a proto-governmental committee which "legislated" to the best of its abilities. In the words of a founding member, this committee set principles "to supervise the personal behavior of the graduates and to guide deviators," by evaluating them according to "(1) Religion; (2) Community Spirit [ijtima'iyyat]; and (3) Patriotism [wataniyya]." The ultimate goal was to promote the development of the upstanding national citizen (muwatin).[137]

The Omdurman Graduates Club was a precursor of organized nationalism in another sense: its members soon displayed the tendency toward factionalism that became a feature of Sudanese party politics and later of self-rule.[138] This factionalism followed the Muslim sectarian divide between affiliates of the Khatmiyya Sufi order (who tended to favor cultural or political unity with Egypt) and the neo-Mahdists (descendants of those who had supported the Mahdist movement in the late nineteenth century and who emphasized the Sudan's cultural and political autonomy). Ultimately, sectarian factionalism remained in check until the end of the Anglo-Egyptian period only because the graduates shared a common enemy—the British—and faced constraints on political expression and organization.

Through their various activities the Graduates Clubs also helped to refine the ideologies of nationalism. In 1926, for example, the Omdurman club hosted a competition which, in its topics and format, echoed Gordon College debates. This contest featured four lectures, three open only to those whose jobs fell into specific government job categories (teachers, engineers, qadis), and the fourth open to all. Among teachers, the winner was Abd al-Rahman Ali Taha (1901–1969), who later became the Sudan's first minister of education. Addressing a topic deemed modern by its very newness, he called for reforms in prenatal and early childhood care and urged parents both to instill self-reliance in their children and to teach them national sentiment, by explaining, for example, how birds yearn for home after their migrations.[139] The engineers competed by answering the question, "What is the best way, in terms of economics and sanitation, to improve domestic buildings in the provinces according to the peoples' financial state and to environmental conditions?" Their answers, in effect, had to reach beyond Khartoum to prescribe policies for the wider Sudan. The qadis were asked to speculate on the practice in Islamic law of divorce by oath, on its prevalence in the Sudan, and on its social disadvantages—a topic that, again, brought family life under scrutiny. Finally, the general category appealed to all of the educated graduates, by asking, "When, how, and by what routes did the Arabs enter the Sudan, and what were the results of their entry?" Among the educated members, these lectures affirmed a belief in Arab ethnicity, Islamic ethics, and social progress (in public and private life), all core values of the developing nationalist movement. So memorable was this competition that, years later, it earned a chapter in a cultural chronicle of the early nationalist movement, under the heading, "The Graduates Plan Society."[140]

THE NATION, THE STATE, AND THE INFORMATION ORDER

Meeting face-to-face at clubs and reunions was not the only way that graduates came together. Increasingly, they gathered on the printed page, turning to the nascent Arabic periodical press to exchange ideas in poems, essays, and stories. Graduates were able to engage in these conversations across great distances because they had the skill and the know-how to tap into the "information order"[141]—the communication and transportation network that was the outcome of colonial state development. What they had not learned about this order at school, they learned at work—for example, travelling by new means such as the railway and later automobile to reach their posts, or gaining familiarity with new technologies such as the telephone in their offices.[142] (In 1936 about twenty thousand telephone calls were being made in the Sudan daily;[143] by this stage, the educated Northern Sudanese were gaining exposure to "telephonic conversation" themselves.[144])

The postal system was particularly important to nationalist exchange because it allowed the cheap and increasingly quick distribution of books, periodicals, and letters. Since British officials ached for mail from home, they made regular deliveries—to even the remotest of areas—a development priority.[145] As time went on, old standbys like camel postmen were supplemented by mail delivery via steamers and trains, later by cars, and finally, after 1935, by airplanes, all of which connected the Sudan to Europe and to other parts of Africa.[146] The load of mail became so heavy that, in 1939 alone, the Sudanese postal system delivered over twenty million items.[147]

The educated Northern Sudanese used the mail extensively. In the hours after work, many drafted poems and other compositions and sent them off for publication in journals, which they could themselves get by subscription. The turnaround time for transmitting, typesetting, and publishing a text was short. In 1927, for example, one sub-mamur in Managil, Blue Nile

Province, wrote some essays, sent them to a newspaper in Khartoum (a hundred miles away), and had them printed within six days of their completion.[148] The post was sufficiently reliable, too, that officials could get books by mail order. One Khartoum shop, ready to ship books anywhere within the Sudan, stocked dozens of works, including texts by influential Arabic writers such as the Egyptians Muhammad Husayn Haykal (1888–1956) and Ibrahim Abd al-Qadir al-Mazini (1889–1949) and the Druze Shakib Arslan (1869–1946).[149]

By delivering both periodicals and books, the postal system enabled the educated Northern Sudanese to tap into intellectual currents emanating from Egypt, the Levant, Europe, and further afield. This ability to participate in local and global print cultures from remote regions played an important part in the construction of nationalist ideologies. Indeed, although most officials craved for jobs in Khartoum, it helped the nationalist movement that they were scattered far and wide. Writing from all corners of the Sudan territory, and often describing distant places in their poems, graduates could more easily imagine the Anglo-Egyptian Sudan as a nation and a place.[150]

In the earliest days of the regime government posts were often so remote that the officials in charge, including Britons, Egyptians, and Sudanese, frequently possessed a high degree of autonomy within their jobs. They were cut off from the administrative center of Khartoum—and from each other—by sheer distance, and in parts of the South by the perennial flooding or drying up of rivers and swamps. Not for nothing were many British officials in the South known as the "bog barons."[151] There were parallels among Northern Sudanese. As late as 1933, for example, one mamur in the Nuba Mountains, Muhammad Abd al-Raziq, was responsible for a hilly tsetse fly–infected area "the size of an English county . . . including 50,000 irascible people." With his British D.C. based a hundred miles away, this mamur had to take charge in dealing with frequent cases of tax-evasion, murder, and cattle raiding.[152] Gradually, posts in the South, the Nuba Mountains, and elsewhere became less remote as a result of steady improvements in transport and communications.

The implications of these changes for the colonial and postcolonial state were profound. The far corners of the Sudan became accessible by plane, train, and automobile as they had never been before. A Foreign Office official summed up the possibilities in 1930, when he traveled from London on an Air Force plane to take a two-week tour of the Sudan.[153] During that time he stopped in nine provinces and covered six thousand miles. In thirty-five minutes, he flew from Kadugli to Talodi in the Nuba Mountains—a journey that took two-and-a-half days overland during the rainy season. In Darfur, he covered in a day what it would have taken two weeks for a camel to cover. By the middle of the colonial period, these developments were allowing a degree of central state control that had never before been imaginable.

CONCLUSION

British officials generally mistrusted the *effendi* "type": the petty official, "aping the European," who was a potential political hothead or "nationalist."[154] Paradoxically, the British in the Sudan designed Gordon College as a virtual *effendi* machine that would produce modern men who had sufficient familiarity with British ways and objectives to perform jobs in an "Anglo" regime. This familiarity was not simply a question of knowing how to speak English, how to play tennis, or how to behave toward a Briton and his wife at a garden tea party—although these skills helped in many jobs. It was also a question of knowing how to think, how to keep records, and how to organize information according to a British order of things—a method, in other words, "of grouping and isolating, of analysing, of matching and pigeonholing" according to a particular worldview.[155] It involved, moreover, a habit of managing time, of living by the clock, with office hours (like school schedules) carefully prescribed.[156]

In its capacity as an *effendi* machine, training students as bureaucrats, Gordon College also propelled nationalism. In a manner that ultimately worked against British interests, the school convinced its students and graduates that they were, or would be, leaders among Sudanese. For a start, the school picked students from eminent families, installed them in grand buildings at the heart of the capital, provided them with an education unlike anything else available, and groomed them for state service. These policies alone were enough to build students' self-esteem. The college also worked on their character, molding students according to the British image of the good sportsman, scout, citizen, and team leader, all the while encouraging independent thought, for example, by insisting that students interpret rather than memorize history. The expectation was that graduates would need initiative and pluck to shoulder varied responsibilities, especially in remote districts. Finally, the school introduced its students to modern ways and devices, by placing them first in line among Sudanese peoples to see, use, or experience such things as suits and ties, cinema shows, indoor plumbing, printing, and photography. Students emerged from this school regime with a shared culture that had a global reach; they were likely to know not only the latest trends in the Sudan and Egypt, but also those in Britain and farther afield. Believing that this very modernity and worldliness set them above other Sudanese groups (including, significantly, their fathers), the products of Gordon College went on to describe themselves as a new generation (*jil*), engaged in a dual liberation struggle against both foreign colonialism and home-grown backwardness.[157]

4 The Mechanics of Colonial Rule

Bureaucracies produce domination in its most prosaic forms and leave little room for history in the heroic mode. Nevertheless, the colonial bureaucracies of the British Empire warrant study because they illuminate three major facets of the colonial state: first, its mode of operation (the nuts and bolts, or mechanics, of rule); second, its adaptive responses and strategies in the face of wider economic and political forces; and third and most importantly, its role in providing territorial and administrative structures for nationalism. By its very practice of hiring and promoting local recruits as a cost-cutting measure, colonial bureaucracies integrated educated elites into local states, ensuring that, upon decolonization, administrative power would pass to them.

The following pages trace the process that gave local recruits progressively more responsible jobs in the colonial regime by examining "Sudanization" in the Anglo-Egyptian Sudan. The details of this process were unique to each territory, but the general contours were the same throughout the British Empire.

In Africa and Asia, Britain maintained empire on the cheap by keeping British staff at a minimum. The men on the spot compensated for the thinness of their ranks in three major ways. First, they maintained a coercive apparatus of hi-tech guns and paid armies, kept in reserve for the selective application of violence.[1] Occasionally, they staged shows of their force, for example, by "route marching through a tribe in a perfectly peaceable manner."[2] Second, realizing that treaty and collaboration would be cheaper and more effective than conquest, they forged alliances with local potentates and, where possible, brought them into the colonial state as ruling intermediaries.[3] Third, they promoted an impression of mastery and control. Whereas Belgians in the Congo welcomed the local sobriquet of Bula Matari ("Rock Crusher") for their colonial state,[4] the British in Africa and India cultivated an image of benign rule through popular acquiescence. One veteran of the Indian Civil Service went so far as to say that the British official "really was at heart what the villagers called him in their petitions, the father and mother of his people."[5]

In Britain, the romance of empire made colonial service highly desirable and prestigious. Yet the British government's commitment to scaling down costs guaranteed that the corps of colonial service would be small. Entry into the ruling cadres was therefore competitive, and primarily benefited sons of the professional classes (sometimes described as the "upper-middle" classes).[6] Educated, for the most part, in "public" schools, and later at university in Oxford, Cambridge, or London, the British elites of colonial service arrived in their assigned territories imbued with a sense of character, rooted in a code of discipline, self-reliance, sportsmanship, and national and cultural pride.[7] This confident ethos translated into the self-image of the lone District Commissioner, who could "single-handedly" run an area the size of Yorkshire or Switzerland, or a population as large as Denmark's.[8] It also translated into the racial arrogance that piqued early nationalists.

Reflecting on Britain's success at keeping empire cheap, one historian described British rule in Africa as "a great confidence-trick, a huge game of white man's bluff."[9] Historians of India have acknowledged the same. "India was held more by bluff than by force," wrote one, especially considering that Indians typically outnumbered British district officials a million to one.[10] In such a context, British officials could show no fear, and the stiff upper lip became a real necessity, not a figure of speech. Still, the display of confidence and sangfroid on the part of the "lone D.C." and others was as much for internal as for external consumption. George Orwell grasped this point when, as a police officer in Burma in the early 1920s, he found himself shooting an elephant for the sake of appearances—needing to prove his authority not just to the Burmese crowd, but to himself.[11]

Colonial rule had many elements of trickery and bluff. One of its greatest sleights of hand was in downplaying a major foundation of rule: extensive use of low-salaried, non-British staff. British regimes were able to rule territories on a shoestring not merely because they had advantages of competence, coercion, and co-optation,[12] but because they deputized thousands of others to work in the bureaucracy. This pattern was the same throughout the British Empire. Since it was cheaper to hire locals for petty administrative jobs than to hire Britons and other foreign expatriates, recruitment occurred on the spot.

In India, this process of "native" hiring started in the late eighteenth and early nineteenth centuries, the era of Company rule, when the East India Company established state structures (notably, a tax collection system and a judiciary) with the approval of the British government.[13] In Africa, "native" hiring followed on the heels of colonial conquest, from around 1900 (with precise timing varying by territory), giving rise to what a Nigerian historian called the "Age of the Clerks."[14] The African exception—and the Indian parallel—was coastal West Africa, where, from the second half of the nineteenth century, decades before the imposition of formal British colonial rule, educated creoles from the Gold Coast and freed slave descendants from Sierra Leone worked for the British navy or for British commercial organizations, which were precursors of colonial states.[15]

Colonial bureaucracy and education expanded together. Requiring a small corps of workers who could stand in for Britons—almost—and communicate with them as well, colonial states patronized select colleges that provided a British-style education, and instruction in English. The nature of these schools varied by territory and region. Some, like Gordon College, were government-sponsored, others were Christian-missionary-run, a few were independent. Some offered programs modeled on British secondary schools; others aimed for university standards. Grooming students for government service, these elite institutions stressed literacy and skills appropriate to bureaucracy's demands.[16]

Supplied with salaries, pensions, and other perquisites, graduates gained a stake in the colonial system. But it was not enough. Confident of their skills and eager to assume progressively greater responsibility, educated "natives" found promotion blocked: they could move so far, and no further, in a system dominated by Britons. Bureaucratic exclusion mirrored social exclusion: Britons treated them as underlings, not as equals, and regarded the *effendis*, *babus*, and "Europeanized natives" with contempt. Many shared the plight of Dr. Aziz in E. M. Forster's *A Passage to India*, who approached his British superior with trepidation "not because his soul was servile but because his feelings—the sensitive edges of him—feared a gross snub."[17] Stung by petty humiliations, and frustrated by jobs that hemmed them in, the educated classes developed ideologies of self-rule to challenge the prevailing order. They issued their demands for a devolution of power under the banner of nationalism, continuing, in the meantime, to work for the regime.

The grievances of colonial government service fed the growth of nationalism in British India and Africa alike. Indeed, a sense of professional failure among government employees may have been just as critical to the nationalisms of nineteenth-century Europe.[18] In a copious literature on the post-

Mughal bureaucracy, historians of India emphasize that the exclusion of Indians from the higher echelons of government service stimulated calls for an "Indianization" of jobs and thereby gave shape to early nationalist agitation.[19] Historians of Africa, by contrast, have seldom drawn connections between colonial employment and nationalism, because a "resistance" paradigm has been so influential in the field.[20] Although African historical trends have changed over the past twenty years, so that the complexities of the colonial encounter have come under increasing scrutiny,[21] studies of colonial administration have continued to privilege Europeans. In the long run, this omission of African bureaucrats in histories of colonial administration has enabled the imperial myth of the "lone D.C." to flourish in the history books along with the mystique of British rule. It is important to correct this picture by recovering the participation of colonized peoples in their own administration.

Government jobs also gave structure to budding ideologies of nationalism by incorporating the educated classes into a system of rule that claimed authority within clear territorial borders. By sending employees on professional pilgrimage—the result of regular job transfers throughout the territory—the educated were able, in their minds, to connect the government to the land.[22] From here, it was a short step to seeing the territory and administration as a unitary nation and state, grounded in native soil. For this reason, too, it is essential to understand the growth of the colonial bureaucracy.

Despite the exceptionalism of the Anglo-Egyptian Sudan as a two-country colony on a double (Middle Eastern–African) frontier, the career of its colonial state followed a pattern common to imperial Africa and Asia. This pattern went as follows: Constrained by its own ground rule—that the colony must pay its own way—and by political circumstances (such as the two World Wars), the colonial state educated, trained, and hired local men, and unwittingly gave nationalism an institutional framework. Granted authority, at first in petty administrative jobs, these local intellectuals, able to organize ideas and people alike, desired greater responsibilities. The colonial regime had a clear economic incentive to accede to some of their wishes. In the end, the colonial state's transfer of power in the lower and middle tiers of the bureaucracy compelled a transfer of power at the top.

COLONIAL SERVICE IN THE SUDAN

Because of the Sudan's anomalous legal status as an Anglo-Egyptian condominium, it had its own elite British corps, the Sudan Political Service. Supplying District and Assistant District Commissioners and province

Governors, the S.P.S. was the counterpart of the I.C.S. (Indian Civil Service) and the Colonial Service. According to one estimate (intended to show their elitism and level of mastery), S.P.S. officials rarely numbered more than 125 at any one time, spread thinly over nearly a million square miles.[23] But they were hardly alone. Several hundred less-exalted Britons, employed in high-level clerical, technical, and military capacities, bolstered the British presence in Khartoum, the large Northern towns, and army installations.[24] More substantially, thousands of literate and skilled non-Britons—including many Egyptian and Lebanese ("Syrian") expatriates—also worked in the bureaucracy on pensioned service. The scope of non-British employment increased over time with the expansion, consolidation, and retraction of the colonial state, and in the wake of economic trends on global, imperial, and regional scales.

To rein in the budget while expanding government services, the regime recruited skilled Northern Sudanese to replace first Egyptian and later Lebanese and British personnel at lower cost. Political factors also had a bearing on employment patterns. Eager to suppress Egyptian influence in the Sudan, and to stave off Egypt's claims to power-sharing (as per the 1899 Condominium agreement), British officials expedited the hiring of Northern Sudanese in the place of Egyptians. But if Egypt's political influence was odious to Britain, its economic role was indispensable: as late as 1941 the Sudan government relied heavily on Egyptian loans and subventions. This arrangement allowed Britain to shoulder the power, but shrug off the costs, of Sudan administration, leaving Egypt some token claim to Condominium partnership.[25]

Gordon College graduates were the major beneficiaries of Sudanese hirings, filling the most responsible jobs available to Sudanese in any period. However, their numbers were small (with total enrollments at the college hovering in the 300–400 range in the years from 1902 to 1938). As the colonial educational system expanded at the primary level, Gordon College graduates constituted a dwindling portion of the Northern Sudan's literate population.[26]

British authorities carefully regulated the number of Gordon College graduates so as not to exceed the regime's demand for employees. By minimizing student numbers, they also hoped to forestall political intrigue. Experiences in Egypt and India had shown that those educated along "modern" lines could deploy Britain's rhetoric of civilization and political enlightenment to challenge the British presence. In the *Journal of the African Society*, in 1934, one professor recognized the attitude shared by many British authorities in the Sudan when he wrote that "even the best officials find the educated African a nuisance." Writing in the language of the Raj, he paraphrased the sentiment of British authorities as, "Let us have a real pukka African [instead]," and analyzed concerns over the "civilised African [who] must be more like a European than like his brother from the bush."[27]

Politicized or not, Gordon College graduates were crucial to the regime, since their skills and services met the demands of so many departments, having been tailored for specific jobs. Indeed, from its founding in 1902 until its evolution into a university college in 1951, Gordon College offered programs that became steadily more specialized and advanced, according to the needs of the government. Since the production of general clerical workers was the administration's first priority upon the school's opening in 1902, the early curriculum stressed basic skills: Arabic and English (including grammar, dictation, composition, penmanship, and translation), arithmetic, and geography. More specialized programs trained students as teachers and *qadis*, the latter to serve in the Mohammedan Law Courts (to which the regime delegated personal and family law). A few years later, in 1905, the college responded to the needs of the Irrigation and Public Works departments by starting a small civil engineering course, which emphasized practical training.[28] Student engineers learned how to draw and construct bridges and brick kilns, using cheap local materials, and how to plan hydraulic systems using pipes and channels.[29] In 1912 the college added specializations to clerical training, instituting a program at the secondary-school level for translation, penmanship, and typewriting.[30] Accountancy later became a separate secondary program; later still, after the opening of the Kitchener School of Medicine in 1924, the college started teaching biology, chemistry, and physics to potential medical school entrants or laboratory technicians.

By 1929, more than 96 percent of living alumni from the Gordon College secondary school were in government service.[31] But notwithstanding the attractive terms of their service—steady pay, prestige in the public eye, and chances for promotion—many of them found their government careers demoralizing. Some of them also resented that their educations had been vocational, and regretted that their learning had not been for learning's sake alone. Khidir Hamad, a self-avowed nationalist who spent years as a clerk, reflected years later that, after nationalism, "the most important thing that occupied our minds in our final year at Gordon College . . . was our feeling that our education was curtailed [*qasir*] and that colonialism only wanted us as employees to push through the rush of routine." As a young man, Khidir Hamad believed that he and his peers deserved a better, and a grander, fate, and that nationalism would help them to attain it.[32]

The timeline of Sudanese nationalism has no clear beginning, since the idea of the Sudan as a nation evolved slowly in the minds of the educated Northern Sudanese. Some historians, writing in the postcolonial era, traced the roots of nationalism as far back as the Mahdist movement of the 1880s, an earlier episode of anticolonialism, or "primary resistance," which followed sixty years of Turco-Egyptian rule. Yet it was only after the conquest of 1898, when the region gained fixed borders as the Anglo-Egyptian Sudan, that a self-conscious nationalism, centered around the notion of a "Sudanese" identity, emerged. The first few decades of the twentieth century witnessed the slow growth of nationalism along these lines.

Although Sudanese nationalism was slow in the making, some trace its formal debut as an organized political movement to 1938, when over a thousand educated males met in Omdurman to establish the Graduates' General Congress. Inspired by the Indian National Congress, its organizers established this body as an elective assembly, restricted to holders of secondary- or intermediate- school diplomas, and dedicated vaguely to national welfare. The Sudan government acceded to the formation of the Graduates Congress, viewing it as a means to co-opt budding nationalists and to forestall Egyptian influence (particularly in light of the 1936 Anglo-Egyptian Agreement). Much to the regime's dismay, however, the Congress became a center of agitation, and in 1942 issued a memorandum calling for Sudanese self-determination after the war. Writes one historian, "The quick transformation of the Congress from the hope of the government to its bane is striking: so deep was the government's misunderstanding of its junior civil servants."[33]

After 1938, as nationalists became more organized, the Sudan government modified its employment policies to conciliate them. At the same time, the start of the Second World War obligated the Sudan government to appease the educated classes ever more, as a way of ensuring their continued cooperation and loyalty. By the early 1940s, the Civil Secretary was calling for the "dilution" of British staff by Sudanese as a (tentative) step toward (distant) self-government. Called "Sudanization," this policy prevailed during the next ten years, reaching its peak in the final rush of decolonization, from 1953 to 1955. Like Indianization, Nigerianization, and Kenyanization (its analogues in other British colonies), Sudanization routinized the transfer of power.[34]

Sudanization was an official policy of the 1940s and '50s. But as a term for a bureaucratic process, it can describe the entire colonial period. Thus extended, "Sudanization" can refer to the waves of hiring and promotion that displaced Egyptians, Lebanese, and Britons from the conquest to withdrawal. Taken in this broader sense, Sudanization proceeded in several rough stages.[35] In the years before 1924, Northern Sudanese men increasingly filled low-level administrative posts as clerks, telegraphists, medical assistants, and so on. Between 1924 and 1932, they displaced Egyptian and Lebanese staff from middle-level posts, as doctors, mamurs, school inspectors, and more. After 1935, job prospects brightened for those who had attended Gordon College before the Depression in 1929. But for those who came of age after 1929, entry into the college and into government positions became more competitive. (Indeed, a new chapter opened for the college in 1930, when the government reduced the size of incoming classes and required parents or guardians to sign statements acknowledging that the government would be under no obligation to employ graduates.[36]) Later, in the years after World War II, Sudanization affected British posts, as highly educated Northern Sudanese moved into positions with greater authority. In the years from 1953 to 1955, a period of self-government that preceded formal independence in 1956, Northern Sudanese supplanted the British authorities who had once towered over the administration. These employment patterns—affected by educational developments, economic and political crises, and changes in leadership—are explored in greater detail below.

THE FIRST PHASE, 1898–1919:
THE RISE OF A SUDANESE BUREAUCRACY

A year passed after the colonial conquest before the regime began to systematize its administration.[37] From 1900, James Currie, the new Director of Education, declared the need for training "a small administrative class, capable of filling many Government posts."[38] In 1902, to meet this demand, authorities opened Gordon College, along with a few primary schools in the Northern provincial centers.

Within two years, Gordon College was able to supply the government with a dozen or so young men, trained as surveyors and clerks.[39] By 1906, Gordon College and the provincial primary schools were able to supply dozens more, as qadis for the Legal Department, railway employees, kuttab-school teachers, surveyors, and clerks (in postal and telegraphic capacities especially).[40] Although the regime had already hired some men from an older generation of educated Northern Sudanese, including many who had served the Mahdist or Turco-Egyptian regimes before, these hirings marked the rise of a younger generation of educated Northern Sudanese who were coming of age against a context of colonial education and employment.[41]

Throughout this early period, government services were expanding quickly and the schools were unable to keep up with demands for staff. In December 1918, for instance, when government departments asked for thirty Gordon College boys to fill openings, the school could supply only ten. The Director of Education commented on this shortfall by drawing attention to the urgent need for more "type-writing machines," without which the college could not expand its clerical training section.[42] World War I only intensified staff shortages, as many military officials seconded to the regime, including both Britons and Egyptians in the Egyptian Army, left to serve farther afield.

For many years, to fill middle-level posts that required advanced, "modern" training, the regime hired highly educated Egyptians and Lebanese. Egyptians supplied most of the schoolteachers and accountants in the period before 1919, and were prominent in the Railways and Posts and Telegraphs departments especially. Lebanese men, many of whom were graduates of the American University in Beirut (known as the Syrian Protestant College from 1866 to 1919), and who were highly literate in both Arabic and English, filled many of the highest positions that a non-Briton could attain in the regime. Lebanese served, for example, as *bashkatibs* (head clerks), intelligence officers, and finance officials. Lebanese were also prominent as doctors, and some became specialists in endemic diseases of the Southern Sudan, such as sleeping sickness and leprosy.

Egyptians and Lebanese were more expensive to hire than Sudanese. Their salaries had to take into account their high qualifications and the discomfort of living in a climate as hot as the Sudan's. In other words, Egyptian and Lebanese salaries, like British salaries, included the incentive of an expatriation bonus. Egyptians in the Sudan commanded 150 percent of the salary that they would have earned at home, and sometimes more.[43] According to the Director of Education, who faced a shortage of teachers at Gordon College in 1907, especially good Egyptian candidates would not come to the Sudan for less than 250 percent of their normal pay.[44] The meagerness of the Sudan government's budget and the need to save money at every turn pushed the drive to train Sudanese candidates who could fill these posts instead.

Saving through Sudanization was already evident by 1905. The Financial Secretary reported, "I understand that the number of employés at the present moment in the Government service, who have been taken from Sudan Schools, is about 80. These are in receipt of £E3½ per mensem each at an average against a minimum salary of £E.7 per head if they had to be brought from Egypt. There is therefore already a savings of about £E.4,000 per annum to the Government."[45] In 1908, meanwhile, the Director of Education pointed out that by hiring a Northern Sudanese *qadi* trained at Gordon College, rather than an Egyptian *qadi*, the regime was saving £E.100 per year.[46] Savings incentives led the regime to replace Egyptian *qadis* with Northern Sudanese; by 1912, twelve district qadis and twenty-two assistant *qadis* were Gordon College graduates.[47] The same considerations prompted the Surveys Department to cease recruiting Egyptians after 1909 and to appoint only Gordon College graduates for new plane-tabling positions.[48] Cost-cutting continued to drive Sudanization until the end of the colonial period.

THE SECOND PHASE, 1919–1924: POLITICAL TURMOIL AND EGYPT

Two political crises framed the second period in Sudanization. These were the 1919 uprisings in Egypt and their 1924 counterparts in the Sudan, both of which challenged the British imperial presence in the Nile Valley. The educated Northern Sudanese lost favor among the British for participating in anticolonial activities during these years. Many nevertheless benefited from the crises in the long run, by stepping into the higher positions of Egyptian employees who were expelled on grounds of sedition, real or potential, after 1924.

In 1919 a broad spectrum of the Egyptian population, including students, workers, and civil servants, took to the streets of Cairo and other large towns in Egypt to protest the British occupation of their country. The frustrations that drew them together had developed after years of wartime requisitioning and hardships and broken promises of independence.[49] While investigating the causes of the 1919 uprisings and their effects on the Sudan, Britain reevaluated Egypt's role in the Sudan administration. These investigations resulted in the Keown-Boyd report of 1920 and the Milner Report of 1921, the latter anticipating Britain's unilateral declaration of Egyptian independence in 1922. The Keown-Boyd report advised the gradual elimination of Egyptian military and civilian personnel from the Sudan and their replacement by trained Sudanese.[50] The Milner Report went one step further, advising not only the replacement of Egyptians by Sudanese personnel, but also investing greater administrative responsibility in the hands of Sudanese "native authorities" in outlying districts.[51]

The Milner Report reflected a growing distrust of educated groups that found expression in policies of indirect rule, also known as "native administration."[52] The major ideologue of this administrative philosophy was Lord Lugard, governor of Nigeria from 1907 to 1919, who expounded his ideas in a 1922 treatise entitled *The Dual Mandate*. Lugardian indirect rule advocated enhanced administrative roles for "traditional" local authorities, such as chiefs and village headmen, as a way of avoiding reliance on educated "natives." The Milner Report and *The Dual Mandate* registered both the growing presence of local educated elites in the colonial administrations of British Africa and the challenge that they posed to British imperial authority.

The Milner Report made the removal of educated Egyptians a first priority in the Sudan's administrative reshuffling, though British authorities had been working toward this goal for years. In 1922 there were already 1,800 Gordon College alumni in government service.[53] By this time, they had established a strong presence in departments that were once Egyptian strongholds, such as Post and Telegraphs. The manpower shortages of the World War I years had allowed Northern Sudanese to move even more quickly into positions as sub-mamurs (officials in charge of police). Open to Northern Sudanese civilians for the first time in 1915, sub-mamur positions included seventy-six Northern Sudanese civilians, or 55 percent of the total number, by 1924.[54]

Egypt's 1919 uprisings reinforced the British conviction that Egyptians were a corrupting force in the Sudan. The British feared that Egyptians were able to exploit cultural ties of language and religion to spur anticolonial sentiment and incipient nationalism among Sudanese, through contacts built on the job in civilian, but especially in military, capacities. The extent and nature of the links between the Egyptian uprisings in 1919 and the Sudanese uprisings in 1924 remain a subject of debate. It is nevertheless clear that Egyptian employees in the Sudan, intellectuals publishing in Egyptian journals, and even Egypt's own Wafd Party, offered a degree of support or inspiration for the clandestine anti-British societies which appeared in the early 1920s.[55] The most politically significant of these proved to be the White Flag League, founded in 1923, which supported some form of unity within the Nile Valley and steered the uprisings of 1924.

The Sudanese 1924 uprisings consisted of urban demonstrations, the distribution of seditious circulars, and army mutinies.[56] Their events took place in the northern urban centers of Khartoum, Omdurman, Port Sudan, Shendi, and Atbara, as well as in military battalions as far south as Malakal and Wau. Although many participants voiced admiration for and solidarity with Egyptians, the grievances that propelled the uprisings had roots in economic hardships being experienced by urban artisan and working classes (as salaries failed to keep up with rising prices), job dissatisfaction (over promotions and salaries) for Sudanese military and civilian personnel, and generational conflict between the young educated classes and their elders.[57]

The British response to the uprisings was harsh and swift. Authorities held trials, fined or imprisoned participants, and exiled ringleaders. In November 1924, the assassination of the Sudan's governor-general, Sir Lee Stack, in Cairo, led to immediate reprisals against Egyptians, whom the British regarded as nationalist agitators. British authorities in the Sudan demanded the eviction of Egyptian troops, along with many Egyptian schoolteachers, mamurs, and others. These deportations, in turn, sparked a mutiny among some Sudanese soldiers in Khartoum. Bloody conflict followed, prompting the execution of a few mutineers by firing squad.[58]

Sudanese writers usually call the uprisings of 1924 a *thawra*, or revolution, and regard them as an early manifestation of *wataniyya*, or nationalism.[59] Postcolonial Sudanese historians have regarded 1924 as a defining moment of the Anglo-Egyptian period, a landmark in the development of anticolonial nationalism.[60] However, the uprisings brought neither the change of revolution nor the mass appeal or ideological coherence of a nationalist program. Although they drew together a remarkable array of the Sudanese urban population—uniting Gordon College graduates, army subalterns, butchers, and tailors under a shared banner[61]—they had little appeal for the rural populace, the religious and land-owning notables of the provinces, and the established merchant classes of the towns, many of whom proved their loyalty to the British with petitions of support.[62]

British officials blamed two groups for whipping up trouble in 1924: Egyptian officials and "detribalized Blacks."[63] (The latter group consisted of those whose families had originated in one of the societies of the Southern Sudan or Nuba Mountains, and who had been absorbed into the Muslim, Arabic-speaking cultures of the Sudan or Egypt through domestic slavery or military service.) British officials dealt with the first group by expelling all Egyptian military personnel from the Sudan and by evicting 118 Egyptian civilian officials—including many schoolteachers and mamurs—as well.[64] They dealt with the second group by dismantling Sudanese battalions of the Egyptian Army, in which "detribalized Blacks" had been particularly prominent, and by establishing a "Sudan Defence Force," with locally-recruited and -based contingents, in January 1925.[65] At the same time, they singled out for punishment key figures of the White Flag League, and notably Ali Abd al-Latif (c. 1892–1948), an Egyptian Army officer and "detribalized Black" of mixed Nuba and Dinka descent, a prize-winning graduate of the Khartoum Military School, and a onetime military sub-mamur.

Without a doubt, participants in the 1924 uprisings were remarkably young, with very few of those arrested for participation in demonstrations being more than twenty-five years old.[66] Unlike their fathers and grandfathers who harbored bitter memories of the Turco-Egyptians in the Sudan, it appears that this young generation found Egypt appealing, and inspiring, for its strident resistance to the British occupation.[67]

Yet, rather than acknowledge the broad appeal of the uprisings to members of the younger urban generation, Intelligence Department officials stressed a theme of class conflict and pointed a finger of blame at men of low status, and especially of slave origins, as rabble-rousers. Far more significant than men like Ali Abd al-Latif in the uprisings were males of high-status families, whose fathers were among the regime's most loyal supporters. Many of these youths were graduates of Gordon College and employees in colonial administration who later rose to high positions as independence neared.[68] However, authorities often avoided prosecuting these youths for the sake of their fathers, many of whom, as eminent *shaykhs*, had remained key supporters of the British before and during the troubles. Their lack of retaliation was therefore an exercise in the "politics of collaboration."[69]

Such was the case with Shaykh Salih Jibril (1853–1938), whom the Director of Intelligence, C. A. Willis, described as "a scout for Lord Kitchener's expedition [i.e., for the colonial conquest] and later contractor for camels to the Egyptian Army, and a man of tried and proven loyalty." Willis went on to say, "His sons have all been brought up at Government expense and every assistance given them to make a career for themselves."[70] Paternity and patronage notwithstanding, Shaykh Salih's two sons caused trouble. One son, Muhammad Salih Jibril (1883/84 [A.H.1301]–1937), a Camel Corps officer, was arrested in 1924 for political subversion: he had been spreading pro-Egyptian propaganda in Kordofan and was reportedly in contact with the Egyptian nationalist, Saʻd Zaghlul.[71] He later pursued a career with the Egyptian Army in Egypt and rose to the rank of *Qaʼim-maqam* (Lieutenant-Colonel).[72] Another son, Tawfiq Salih Jibril (1897–1966), a well-known poet, managed to cling to his job as a sub-mamur, in spite of frequent grumblings over the years by British superiors who were dissatisfied with his work.[73]

Other Gordon College graduates from eminent families were implicated in the 1924 events, much to the chagrin of their fathers or guardians, who sometimes disowned them for it. For example, when Shaykh Muddaththir Ibrahim al-Hajjaz (1886/87–1937), a historian who had served as personal secretary to the Khalifa Abdullahi during the Mahdist period,[74] learned of his son Ahmad's role in White Flag League activities, he threw him out of the house.[75] Ahmad was later sentenced to six months in prison for involvement in the League,[76] though his brother, Hasan Muddaththir Ibrahim, eventually rose to become Grand Qadi of the Sudan. Similarly, Babikr Badri, an Education Department inspector and Mahdist army veteran, was upset about the doings of his nephew and ward, Ibrahim Badri, and forbade him from attending White Flag League meetings.[77] In spite of that involvement, Ibrahim Badri went on to have a long career as a mamur in the Southern Sudan. Indeed, in 1946, Ibrahim Badri became an Assistant District Commissioner—a post previously reserved for Britons.[78] Family connections probably rescued many a Gordon College participant in the White Flag League from prison or professional ruin.

As these differences between elders and youths suggest, generational conflict was a strong feature of the 1924 events. At a time when the intense social and economic changes of the colonial era were straining norms of paternal authority and filial obedience, clashes of ideology often occurred within single families. This trend applied not only to the educated classes, but to farming communities as well, where sons were known to describe the tyranny of their fathers as "colonialism" (*isti'mar*). Contemplating, in the 1980s, his youth during the 1930s, one farmer observed that the communications barrier between fathers and sons was so high that "we did not mix with them enough to even know what they talked about."[79]

Indeed, while the graduates of Gordon College agitated against the British in the early 1920s, their fathers were signing petitions of support. Both Babikr Badri and Shaykh Salih Jibril, for example, were among the Omdurman notables who signed a petition of loyalty to the regime in June 1924.[80] The British turn toward indirect rule in some sense marked a preference for this older generation over their sons. This policy shift was, moreover, a conscious maneuver. Amid the troubles of 1924, the Sudan government sent a deputy on an overland trek to Nigeria—Lugard's laboratory— to investigate practices of native administration for adaptation to the Sudan.[81] Indirect rule became the watchword for the decade that followed, as elder *umdas, shaykhs,* and *nazirs* gained prestige among Britons at the expense of Gordon College graduates.

THE THIRD PHASE, 1924–1935: INDIRECT RULE TO THE WORLD DEPRESSION

The political crisis of 1924 signaled the start of the third phase of Sudanization, characterized by indirect rule, while the conclusion of an economic crisis signaled its closure by 1935. The latter date marked the end of a series of staff and salary cuts which occurred between 1930 and 1935, as effects of the world Depression wrought havoc on Sudanese budgets.

In the heyday of indirect rule, after 1924, graduates of Gordon College fell out of favor among British officials and lost ground vis-à-vis rural notables. The disappearance of nearly all non-British staff from the government's quarterly staff lists in this period symbolized their fall from favor.[82] So did the Powers of Sheikhs Ordinance of 1927, which formalized the legal authority of tribal or regional *shaykhs* over the administration of newly constituted Tribal Courts.[83] In Northern and Southern districts alike, *shaykhs*, or chiefs, also gained authority over local police forces that enforced "customary" law.[84] Where chiefs were gaining powers, mamurs (who had until that time been mostly Egyptians) were losing them; in 1922, for example, the regime had stripped mamurs of their Third Class magistrate's status, which had allowed them to impose up to fifteen days' imprisonment and small fines.[85] Further restructuring occurred as the regime consolidated districts under "traditional" authorities, often cutting out posts for sub-mamurs, mamurs, and clerks.[86] One British supporter of indirect rule, the district commissioner and later government archaeologist A. J. Arkell, praised these administrative rearrangements as part of a "definite policy . . . of making the Sudan safe for autocracy."[87]

"Southern Policy," inaugurated in 1930, also worked to the disadvantage of the educated Northern Sudanese. This policy sought to isolate the South administratively and culturally from the North, in order to minimize the southward spread of Islam and of "subversive" (i.e., anticolonial) ideas like those that prevailed during the 1924 uprisings. The line between "North" and "South" became subject to border control, as authorities required Northerners to secure visas if they wished to cross it.[88] As a result of "Southern Policy," Northern Sudanese officials began to lose Southern jobs to Southern Sudanese graduates of Christian missionary schools or to Southern chiefs. For Gordon College graduates, these losses in job opportunities in the South, where Southern Policy came into effect, and in the North, where indirect rule prevailed, added to their sense of malaise.

Sir John Maffey, governor-general of the Sudan from 1926 to 1934, helped to set the tone of this period in which high-ranking British officials regarded the graduates of Gordon College with heightened distrust. Maffey's career in the North-West Provinces of India had instilled in him a contempt for *babus* and *effendis* alike, although his comments suggest that he regarded the Sudanese as more intellectually and culturally backward than Indians. Though impressed with the good physical development of Gordon College students, he privately felt that "[it] was very much open to doubt as to how far the Sudanese students could rise to the top of any profession. . . . Another very difficult point was to place a Sudanese student in a position of authority."[89]

Under Maffey, the educated Northern Sudanese were sure to suffer professional setbacks. But one thing ameliorated their position: British authorities were anxious to minimize Egypt's role in the Condominium and consequently welcomed the Sudanization of Egyptian posts.[90] The result was that some educated Northern Sudanese were able to step into middle-ranking jobs (as schoolmasters, postmasters, etc.) that Egyptians had previously held. Perhaps most significantly, the position of the mamur, whose responsibilities in district administration included everything from tax collection to locust control, opened to Gordon College graduates once Egyptians were expelled from the post en masse in 1924.[91] A government report noted that "whereas in 1924 there were only 7 Sudanese Mamurs, there are now [in 1930] five times that number." As a result of the "Sudanization" of Egyptian jobs, the number of "classified Sudanese staff" (i.e., permanent and pensionable employees, made up almost exclusively of Northern graduates of Gordon College, the primary-intermediate schools, and the technical schools) rose from 1,823 in 1924 to 2,756 in 1930—an increase of more than 50 percent.[92]

In the immediate post-1924 period there were also two positive educational developments, which, though benefiting few, offered hope to Gordon College graduates and budding nationalists who were eager to acquire more advanced education and training. The first of these entailed the opening in 1924 of the Kitchener School of Medicine, founded in Khartoum in memory of Lord Kitchener, conqueror of the Sudan. The Kitchener School of Medicine drew students from Gordon College, which introduced classes in biology, chemistry, and physics to prepare suitable candidates for entry.[93] In 1927 it graduated its first class of seven doctors, and in the years up to 1938 it continued to produce about seven graduates a year.[94] Slowly, these young Sudanese doctors replaced the Egyptians and Lebanese who had previously held the bulk of medical posts.[95]

The second development of the post-1924 years entailed sending several talented Gordon College graduates to pursue advanced degrees at the American University in Beirut—a policy that continued through the interwar years.[96] Ironically, these Northern Sudanese men pursued degrees in Lebanon so that they could return to replace Lebanese officials at lower salaries. For example, Yusuf Badri, son of the redoubtable Babikr Badri, trained as a pharmaceutical chemist and returned from AUB to replace a Lebanese as dispenser at Omdurman Civil Hospital.[97] Another graduate, Abd al-Fattah al-Maghribi, gained a B.A. in mathematics. When he returned to the Sudan in 1928, the Education Department cancelled the contract of a Lebanese so that Abd al-Fattah could fill a teaching post at Gordon College.

Although Abd al-Fattah received a pay raise when he took this post (from £E168 to £E180), the Lebanese whom he replaced, George Abu Shahin, had been making £E324.[98] The Sudanization of this one post saved the government £E144 per year.

As late as 1929, Gordon College was unable to meet the regime's demands for trained personnel—suggesting that neither indirect rule nor British contempt stifled the need for highly literate Northern Sudanese personnel. In his report for 1929 the Director of Education was still envisioning an expansion in the size and offerings of Gordon College, in order to meet demands not only of the government, but also of commercial firms—something the school had not done before.[99] The world Depression put an end to these plans for educational growth.

When the effects of the Depression hit after 1929, the regime had to cut jobs, through dismissals and early retirements, in a process that continued until 1932. Lebanese, many of whom held relatively high positions in the regime, were proportionally hardest hit. Their numbers fell by 181, entailing a drop of 65 percent in their ranks.[100] Egyptian numbers fell dramatically as well. At the beginning of 1932, there were still 1,148 Egyptians in the bureaucracy (down from 4,250 in 1925[101]). In the course of 1932, the regime released 395 Egyptians, or 34 percent of remaining Egyptian staff, leaving only 753 by 1933. Even British numbers fell. In 1932, 183 Britons (or 19 percent of the remaining British staff) lost their jobs, adding to the 92 already released in 1931.[102]

Retrenchment affected Sudanese more modestly. All but 5 percent of established Sudanese employees kept their jobs. As a result of these cuts, Sudanese employees (including Northerners and Southerners) were holding 58.4 percent of all classified government posts by March 1932.[103]

Sudanese employees suffered most in salary loss, through "abatements" applied to all employees of the regime, which persisted from 1932 until 1935.[104] Officials also lost other benefits, such as the "climate allowance," a bonus for serving in the South, below the 12th parallel.[105] Some British officials privately reflected on the unfairness of the cuts, noting that a British district commissioner and a much lower paid Northern Sudanese clerk would both have the same 7.5 percent skimmed off their salaries. One Briton wrote to his mother, pointing out that "a miserable 4th rate clerk getting £5 monthly loses the same percentage as I do who am getting £660, and I lose the same as does Reid who is getting £1500 or £1600. It ain't fair dealing really."[106]

Although the salaries of most Northern Sudanese went down by 7.5 percent, the pay of those just entering government service went down more.

Maffey, the governor-general, proposed reducing the salaries of new Gordon College graduates from £E96 (£E8 per month) to £E66 (£E5½ per month)— a drop of 31.25 percent. He justified the cuts by asking why a young Northern Sudanese graduate deserved a starting pay of £E96 per year. "Certainly not because it costs him that to live reasonably. Some spent the money in undesirable extravagance. Others used it to support family barnacles, who increased in numbers and in power of adhesion with each further [salary] increase."[107] Gordon College students disagreed and protested in 1931 by organizing a school strike—a learning experience for the development of an organized Sudanese nationalist movement in later years.[108] One graduate, who participated in the strike as a first-year student at the college, recalled that the strikers saw the cuts as part of much larger grievances. "Everything discussed in speeches was not about salaries at all. All of the discussion was about tyranny, imperialism, and autocracy."[109]

In the end, Maffey compromised slightly, but not because the strikers persuaded him to do so.[110] Rather, it was Foreign Office intervention, prompted by James Currie (the Sudan's director of education from 1900 to 1914) that changed his mind. Currie had warned the Foreign Office in London that if the Sudan government went forward with its plan to reduce the salary of Gordon College graduates "to no more than the pay of a Berberine [Nubian] cook," then the graduates would have "a genuine and well-founded grievance."[111]

Yet despite a raise in starting salaries by one pound to £E6½ per month (£E78 per year), new Gordon College graduates ultimately suffered a salary drop of 18.75 percent—still a dramatic decrease. Maffey protested that British officials would suffer much more from their salary cuts, for unlike the Sudanese, with their cheap style of living, Britons had wives and children to support back home. Maffey argued that a province governor, making £E1,500 per year, might even have to give up a house in England.[112]

With their low salaries compared to expatriates, Sudanese personnel stood to benefit from the 1931–32 staff cuts, as hiring for middle- and lower-tier jobs resumed in the ensuing years. In particular, the promotion of Sudanese doctors, clerks, and schoolteachers in 1932 is directly linked to the disappearance of high-ranking Lebanese as a result of the economic crisis.[113] The *Quarterly List of the Sudan Government* for October 1, 1933 marked this change by allowing a Northern Sudanese (a Gordon College graduate) to creep onto the list. This was Muhammad Salih al-Shinqiti, a one-time mamur who now became District Judge (2nd grade) in Omdurman, taking over from a Lebanese Druze, Yusuf Bey Najjar.[114]

Staff cuts in the period 1930–32 also restructured province administration. Sometimes entire districts were "economized." In 1932, for example, the government shut down the district office at al-Rahad, in Kordofan, leaving only an accountant and a thirteen-man police force at that remote post.[115] Late in 1930, when John Winder took up a post as assistant district commissioner, he was sent to Opari, the southernmost district of the Sudan on the Uganda border. He later recalled,

> My District staff [in Opari] consisted of two northern Sudanese, a Clerk and an Accountant. Both were first class men, and thoroughly reliable. I could pass through Opari, throw them letters to write and send off, and carry on elsewhere. However the economic depression was upon us and, after a few months, these 'expensive' officials were withdrawn, and I received, as replacements, two [of] what were termed 'Bog Boys' (i.e. boys trained at the Roman Catholic Mission in Wau, Bahr el Ghazal Province, who were considered as just able to do a clerk's and an accountant's job.) In fact they were unable to perform either of these duties, and I had, actually, to see that letters were put into the right envelopes, and leave the accountant with only just enough money in his safe for immediate needs, while keeping the rest of the cash under my own lock and key. The accounts were invariably wrong and needed going through each time I came to the office. They did their best, but were not really ready for the responsibility thrust upon them, and District work suffered a good deal in consequence.

Like these Southern Sudanese officials, Winder found himself thrust into a position for which he was not suitably trained. The regime put him in charge of coffee cultivation, an experimental cash crop of which he knew nothing, after the British coffee officer had been "economized."[116]

Economically driven Sudanization worked on two levels in the years after 1930. In the North, it led to the replacement of Egyptian, Lebanese, and even British officials with Northern Sudanese (and especially Gordon College graduates). In the South, it brought a partial replacement of Northern Sudanese with Southern Sudanese educated in mission schools. Both forms of Sudanization brought budgetary relief.

THE FOURTH PHASE, 1935–38:
THE RISE OF THE GRADUATES

The years between 1935 and 1938 marked the peak of colonial state development, years of administrative consolidation before the start of World War II. Whereas in previous years the educated Northern Sudanese had taken over Egyptian and Lebanese positions, now they began to edge toward British jobs. In 1935, when the government stopped the salary abatements of the Depression years, the first Northern Sudanese officials became "sub-inspectors," a newly created position ranking between the mamur and the assistant district commissioner. By 1938, Sudanization of British posts was well underway, while nationalist politics was taking organizational shape.

The status of the educated Sudanese improved after the selection of Sir Stewart Symes as governor-general in 1934.[117] Symes had been the resident at Aden and governor of Tanganyika. He also had prior Sudan experience, having served in the Egyptian Army in the Sudan from 1906 to 1909, as assistant director of intelligence from 1909 to 1912, and as private secretary to the governor-general from 1913 to 1916. Symes sympathized with the aspirations of the educated Sudanese more than his predecessors had, and began to reverse some aspects of the indirect rule policies that had started in the 1920s. He favored "decentralization," or what he also called "provincial self-government," a policy emphasizing administration at the provincial rather than central (Khartoum-based) level. Symes also pushed for the acceleration of Sudanese hiring in responsible posts. Though his policies were decisive, his philosophy of administration and his vision for the colonial future were less clear, as his memoirs, published in 1946, suggest.[118] Moreover, his policies enjoyed limited support within the higher echelons of the administration. Many S.P.S. men hated his policies, realizing that the reduction of provinces and the Sudanization of jobs threatened British employment prospects.[119]

Symes persisted anyway. In June 1934, the Sudan's civil secretary, Angus Gillan, issued a memorandum on the governor-general's behalf. Its very title, "Substitution of British A.D.C.s by Natives," suggested a new and in some sense revolutionary direction in the colonial regime.

> I feel that the time has now come to take a definite step forward in increasing the sphere of responsibility and improving the prospects of the best of the Mamur class. This policy appears to be in accord with Section 4(d) of Your Excellency's Note on Administrative Policy of 5.3.34.
>
> I believe there are a few who are already fit for the assumption of increased responsibility, and it is the declared policy of the Government to fill more responsible posts with Sudanese who are qualified for them.
>
> To be effective, practically and politically, we must go for some form of definite substitution of British by native officials.
>
> The Doctors are ready to do it now. Certain other Departments are making steady progress in the same direction. The politico-administrative side cannot afford to lag behind with consequent loss of prestige.[120]

To implement this proposal, the regime created the position of sub-inspector, and appointed two mamurs in this capacity at the start of 1935.[121] This job was something of a reinvention, since the title "sub-inspector" had in fact been used before 1922, to refer to British province officials who later became known as assistant district commissioners. Symes and his supporters hoped that once new sub-inspectors settled into their posts, it would be possible to eliminate British A.D.C.'s in that locale, thereby saving money through lower salaries. Eventually, this did occur in some areas.[122]

The scope of the sub-inspector was unclear. Assigned a purposely vague job title, the sub-inspector was expected to share in responsibilities of the A.D.C. but not in his stature, and to take rank junior to a British A.D.C. irrespective of pay.[123] Moreover, he did not gain access to the secret memoranda distributed from Khartoum to high-ranking province administrators—these were for British eyes only.[124] For these reasons, the sub-inspector's position combined aspects of the mamur and A.D.C. The mamur had been the jack-of-all-trades of petty administration on the district (sub-province) level, collecting taxes, trying minor cases, investigating crimes, reporting on crop blights, supervising construction of government buildings or digging wells, and so on. The assistant district commissioner had been the young British probationer in colonial administration, trying more serious cases, checking account-books and making sure that district finances were in order, going on trek to villages, and issuing reports to the province governor. The sub-inspector stood somewhere between. According to one district report, "A Sub Inspector . . . should be out on trek more than a probationer [British] A.D.C. (who should get down to office work), and there is also the danger of a Sub Inspector reverting to the Mamur [sic] if he is not given enough scope outside."[125] Symes did not expect the sub-inspectors to have the discretionary powers of a British A.D.C., but he did expect an upgrade in their work from mere "bottle-washing."[126]

Sub-inspectorships did not open floodgates of opportunity for the educated Northern Sudanese because the number of positions remained so small. By 1939, there were only five sub-inspectors, handpicked for their strong records as mamurs and for fluency in English, and averaging 43 years in age. (One of these five was a rare Egyptian, who had cut his ties to the Egyptian Army after 1924 in order to remain a career mamur for the Sudan government.[127]) Plans were afoot to hire four more sub-inspectors by 1941, so that they would account for one-tenth of the number of British A.D.C.'s and D.C.'s combined.[128]

Their small number notwithstanding, the sub-inspectors had symbolic importance. Their promotion signaled an increasing tempo for the Sudanization of British jobs and a reversal of the policies of the 1920s, which had demoted the *effendiyya* in pursuit of indirect rule. With these changes in mind, one Briton objected to this measure in a 1934 memorandum, writing:

> Once a man becomes a Sub-Inspector, he is bound to feel that he has
> put his foot on the ladder of the Political Service [to which upper-level
> British administrators belonged] and the goal to which his eyes (and
> those of his juniors and of the educated class as a whole) will be turned
> is not that of becoming executive officer to a Native State [i.e., of a dis-
> trict administered by indirect rule], but rather that of becoming Gover-
> nor of a Province—and that is the beginning of the end. We have not
> gone too far yet, but if we go one step further, we are lost.[129]

In fact, over the years to come the regime would go several steps further.
Already by the middle of 1935 the Governor-General had appointed a commission to evaluate the professional advancement of Northern Sudanese
over the previous ten years and to "advise, and wherever possible make specific recommendations, as to whether this process of Sudanese dilution can be
accelerated, economically and without undue risks to the public service."[130]

In the years that followed, when job mobility improved for the educated Northern Sudanese, a particular generation of Gordon College graduates benefited, namely, those who had attended the college before the
economic crunch of 1929. Born between 1881 (the rise of the Mahdist
movement) and 1915 (in the midst of World War I), they were the ones
who had gained sufficient experience on the job to step in for Egyptians,
Lebanese, and later Britons in the various waves of Sudanization. The sub-
inspectors chosen between 1935 and 1939 fit this trend: most were born in
the 1890s. These men were able to progress because they were at the right
place at the right time.

For those who entered Gordon College secondary school after the financial crunch of 1929, opportunities were not as rich. Budgetary and staff cuts
in all fields led to a sudden shrinking of job opportunities in government
service. The annual reports of the college show that the Education Department steadily decreased enrollment in the school, from a high of 510 boys
in 1929, to a low of 291 in 1936. Entry became increasingly competitive. So
did appointment to a government department or province, no longer
assured as it had been for Gordon College alumni of the pre-1929 period.
Proof of this change exists in a 1936 issue of the Khartoum newspaper *al-
Nil*, which included a congratulatory article on the fifty-five students who
had passed the civil service examination that year. These included twenty-
one from the college's engineering section and thirty-four from the clerical
section.[131] One British official wrote home to his father about his invigila-
tion at the 1937 examination, explaining that about one hundred young
men had competed for only thirty or so jobs.[132] By the time successful candidates entered government service, Sudanese officials were numerically far

surpassing Britons. Of classified government staff, 62.7 percent were Sudanese by 1933; this figure rose to 75 percent by 1938.[133]

Meanwhile, in the late 1930s, education authorities began to advocate important structural changes to Gordon College, in order to meet the regime's need for ever more specialized officials. The arrival of the Lord De La Warr Commission, sent by the British government to East Africa and the Sudan in 1937, marked a move in this direction.[134] The De La Warr Commission drew a blueprint for the expansion of Sudanese education at all levels. It encouraged the government to revise its educational agenda by preparing students actively for private-sector employment (and not only for government jobs).[135] It also advised transforming Gordon College from a secondary school into a university college.

Although World War II slowed the pace of change, educators acted on some suggestions of the De La Warr Commission by implementing programs for advanced professional training at Gordon College, beginning in 1939.[136] These programs, or "Higher Schools," offered postsecondary study in law, administration, arts, agriculture, and veterinary science, in addition to extant programs in medicine (at Kitchener School of Medicine) and engineering (constituted at a separate postsecondary institution in 1936).[137] By 1942, there were already 138 students in these Higher Schools.[138] Men of the generation born between 1881 and 1915 were the beneficiaries of these Higher Schools, and changed careers accordingly. Isma'il al-Atabani (b. 1909), for example, a well-known literary salonist and journalist (and proprietor of the Sudanese newspaper *al-Ra'y al-Amm* from 1945 to 1970), graduated from the Gordon College secondary program in 1930, worked as an accountant for ten years, and then joined the Law program in 1940.[139]

The creation of a Higher School for Administration signaled a dramatic turnaround for mamurs and sub-mamurs. Beleaguered during the years of indirect rule, their numbers had dwindled, from 196 in 1924, to 80 in 1935.[140] The Sub-Mamur's Training School, opened in 1919, and scrapped after the 1924 uprisings, only resumed operation in Omdurman in 1936. The program was soon absorbed into the new Higher School, which was open to Northern Sudanese officials, of about 25 to 30 years of age, with approximately five years of government service.[141] Administration students attended lectures given by Northern Sudanese and British officials. Describing a lecture he gave to trainees in 1937, one British official wrote:

I'm having to give a course of lectures to the young Mamurs . . . on the subject of Native Administration and its various aspects, and, after the natural nervousness of the first lecture, find it rather fun. They are an extremely intelligent and able set of young men, and after about 40 minutes of lecture, we have a 'question time' for 20 minutes which always keeps me hopping. I can feel what it must be to be a cabinet minister, and no longer blame everyone who gives evasive answers or burkes questions when in a hole![142]

The openness which characterized these sessions, especially with regard to a topic like native administration (indirect rule), was something new.

The late 1930s witnessed another innovation, as the regime began to send small numbers of educated Northern Sudanese officials to Britain for short stints of advanced professional training. The Lebanese Edward Atiyah, who was serving as intelligence officer at this time, advocated this policy of Britain-visiting as a way of wooing educated Northerners and diverting their political sympathies from Egypt.[143] Abd al-Salam Abd Allah, the mamur of Renk, was among the first to participate in this program. In 1937 he went to England to attend the coronation of King George VI and then accompanied his district commissioner, J. G. S. MacPhail, on a tour of Scotland. The visit was a public relations success. MacPhail later wrote to his mother, "[The mamur] was very grateful for his visit to Scotland. It caused quite a stir in the Sudan. Quite a number of native officials have thanked me for having him to stay with us. It was apparently considered a very kind act that I should have asked him to stay in the same house as you!"[144]

In the interwar years, specially selected Northern Sudanese had gone to Beirut to study before "Sudanizing" Lebanese posts. In the same way, from the late 1930s and until decolonization, educated Northerners went to Britain for short-term training before "Sudanizing" British posts. The doctors Ali Badri and Husayn Ahmad Husayn, for example, went on a medical training course to England in 1937, after they were appointed as medical sub-inspectors in place of British doctors.[145] In 1947 the civil court judges al-Dardiri Muhammad Uthman (1896–1977) and Muhammad Salih al-Shinqiti (1896–1966) went to England to observe proceedings of local, criminal, juvenile, and appeals courts; this experience figured into their promotion.[146] In 1948 the medical doctor al-Tijani Muhammad al-Mahi (1908–70) went to the University of London for a one-year course in psychological medicine[147]—until that time, medical specialization among Northern Sudanese doctors was unknown. Such study trips to Britain became increasingly common in the years before independence.

Finally, the year 1937 saw "Sudanization" occur in contributions to *Sudan Notes and Records*, the government's scholarly journal. In the next few years, Gordon College graduates such as the engineer Ibrahim Ahmad (1898–1989) and the mamur Ibrahim Badri (1897–1962) began to contribute scholarly articles of their own.[148] Significantly, *Sudan Notes and Records* even ran a review of *Sudan Courtesy Customs*, a book of etiquette in Anglo-Sudanese relations written by V. L. Griffiths and Abd al-Rahman Ali Taha. The mere publication of this book, in 1936, confirmed a slight blurring in social and professional boundaries between Britons and the "sophisticated Arabic-speaking population of the Northern Sudan."[149] Following the rise of the Graduates Congress in 1938, the need for diplomacy between the regime and educated Northerners became more urgent still.

WINDING DOWN: SUDANIZATION AND DECOLONIZATION, 1938–1956

World War II put British imperialism in reverse. The process began slowly and accelerated, culminating in decolonization. India started the trend in Asia by gaining independence in 1947; the Sudan moved British decolonization to Africa when it got independence in 1956. In trying to explain the wartime and postwar conditions that prompted this shift in the British Empire, historians cite several factors: pressure from the two emergent superpowers, the United States and the Soviet Union, which endorsed decolonization for idealistic or self-serving motives; economic strains that compelled Britain to focus on domestic reconstruction; anticolonial sentiment emanating from leftists (including Labour Party supporters) at home; and, in the colonies, pressure from nationalist movements and the erosion of collaborative support. In the end, buffeted by these challenges and plagued by ethical doubts about war and imperialism, Britain lost heart.[150]

World War II affected nationalists in several ways. First, it heightened their awareness of European schisms and weakness, and dispelled some of Britain's mystique. Second, it sharpened their confidence in administration. Wartime exigencies had called many Britons away, resulting in staff shortages that pushed many Northern Sudanese officials into "British" jobs.[151] Some gained responsibilities that they had never had before, though job titles and salaries did not reflect the change. (The case of Ibrahim Badri is illustrative: as a mamur from 1941 to 1944, for example, he found himself in charge of the sub-district of Renk, without a British D.C. or A.D.C. above him.[152]) Finally, the Atlantic Charter of 1941, enshrining principles of self-determination, also gave nationalists a boost.[153] In the Sudan, this confidence found voice in the Graduates Congress memorandum of 1942, which demanded Sudanese self-rule after the war. In issuing their statement, Northern Sudanese nationalists did not expect the regime to comply with their bid for self-rule. They did, however, want to deliver the message that nationalists felt prepared for political change and for the assumption of much greater responsibility.

As war drew to an end, many British officials saw decolonization on the horizon but still believed that it was a good way off.[154] In 1944, Douglas Newbold, the civil secretary, suggested a plan to province governors for "dilution" of British administrative posts—a plan which he described as "Sudanisation." Like his colleagues, Newbold expected a very gradual thinning, though individuals envisaged different time scales. One governor, for example, foresaw no reduction in British staff for twenty years (until 1964); another thought that forty or fifty years were necessary. The 1948 "Sudanisation Committee" confirmed a horizon in the twenty-year range, projecting that by 1962 only 55 percent of highest-ranking administrative officers would be Sudanese.[155]

Already by 1946, new British recruits to the Sudan came on non-pensioned contracts.[156] One Briton, starting in 1951, received a twenty-year contract with a promise for £20,000 in severance pay upon earlier loss of office. He recalled, "With the offer of a post came a letter from the Governor-General Sir Robert Howe saying that our principal job was to prepare the Sudan for self-government. Anyone out of sympathy with this objective was told that he should not accept the appointment."[157] Decolonization, when it finally occurred, was quick and sudden. One Briton later observed, "When it came time the end was undramatic—a telegram suggesting that I should hand over to the Sudanese Assistant District Commissioner and catch the next plane to Khartoum. There was no time even for the customary tea party."[158]

To the last, the future role of Egypt and the quality of North-South relations remained open-ended questions. At the 1947 Juba Conference, British officials and Northern Sudanese nationalists had ascertained that the Sudan would gain independence as a single unit, with North and South together, but Southerners had had no say in this decision and some said prospects for harmony were grim. Egypt's claims to the Sudan went unresolved until 1953, when the Anglo-Egyptian Agreement laid the framework for a transfer of power in which the Sudan would decide its own future position vis-à-vis Egypt. From 1953 until independence on the 1st of January, 1956, Sudanization rushed forward, as Britons of the Sudan Political Service left the country, and their posts, to the charge of former underlings. One historian could have been thinking of the Sudan when he remarked that while divide-and-rule had been the motto of the colonial period in its prime, unite-and-quit was the byword of decolonization.[159]

Exhilarating to the educated Northern Sudanese, the Sudanization of the late 1940s and early '50s was traumatic to Britons of the S.P.S. old guard, who were passing authority to the very *effendis* whom they had long disdained. In 1943, J. W. Robertston, deputy civil secretary, privately maintained that "the Sudanese should not be encouraged to believe that their culture and civilisation is equal to British civilisation which has been built up in two thousand years of development and has past and present achievements to its credit to which the Sudanese are now becoming the heirs." The greatest fear of the old guard was that their work would be undone. Robertson voiced this fear obliquely, explaining that a major source of British disdain for the educated Sudanese was the poor way they treated common folk who came to district offices, to post offices, or to hospitals, for consideration or service. Robertson worried about the fate of the common people once the *effendis* had control.[160]

The younger generation of British officials was relatively more sympathetic toward the educated Northern Sudanese, their abilities, aspirations, frustrations, and "growing pains."[161] Yet, these Britons were worried for their own futures. Many of the Egyptians and Lebanese who lost their jobs in the regime in the 1924–1932 period were fortunate in having reached a reasonable retirement age by the time their contracts lapsed. (By 1925, the retirement age for pensionable Egyptian officials was 48 or 50.[162]) In contrast, Britons who entered the Sudan Political Service after 1933 found themselves out of jobs by the early 1950s, when they were in their thirties and forties. Too young to retire, these "fallen angels," as they called themselves, struggled to find new careers at home.[163] As one recalled, "Retirement from the Sudan at the age of 40 after 17 years service was a great blow to me: I liked the Sudanese immensely and loved the job and was hoping that one day I might be promoted to provincial Governor."[164]

Meanwhile, Northern Sudanese officials moved up on the career ladder. Rural chiefs and "traditional" notables had had their day; now it was the turn of the "modern," educated town-dwellers. In 1954 a publicity photograph showed a Northern Sudanese mamur neatly clad in a white shirt and pith helmet. The caption explained that this was "Sudanese Mamour, Khalid Hamed, an important local Government official with a large territory to cover. The job of Mamour is equivalent to that of an Assistant District Commissioner."[165] No more sub-inspector as intermediary: by this stage, the British assistant district commissioner was a figure of the past.

Even Gordon College made its move to independence. Having started as a primary school in 1902, it had developed several specialized secondary-school programs by the 1920s. It had reached new levels of specialization in the late 1930s and early '40s with the founding of various postgraduate

"Higher Schools." In 1945, anticipating decolonization, these Higher Schools were officially renamed Gordon College, while the secondary-school component merged into the Omdurman Secondary School.[166] Later, in 1951, the college became University College Khartoum, affiliated with the University of London and granting subsidiary degrees. In 1956 the school made its final metamorphosis into Khartoum University. Appropriately, the former Gordon College achieved independence along with the colony itself.

From the earliest days of the Anglo-Egyptian Sudan, the regime had educated Northern Sudanese to fill positions in the administration. Even when their posts were low-ranking (in the years before 1919, especially), these officials were essential to the functioning of the system. The most significant of these employees were the pre-1929 alumni of Gordon College, the vast majority of whom were serving in government jobs.[167] These men were the most important beneficiaries of the Sudanization that occurred in waves over the duration of the colonial period. They moved slowly up the ladder of authority, until finally, at independence, their professional rank and stature made them first heirs to national leadership. Mamurs became province governors, accountants became finance ministers, engineers became diplomats, and schoolteachers became prime ministers.

5 Life and the Regime
The Terms of Cooperation

COLONIAL NATIONALISTS

As government employees, the *effendis*, *babus*, and "Europeanized Natives" of Britain's African and Asian territories had intimate but tense relations with the colonial state. Comprising an elite vis-à-vis local populations but a subaltern class as low-ranking employees within the government hierarchy, these men struggled to cope with their marginal inclusion in the ruling system. It made matters worse that while the colonial state inspired them to think of the territory as a nation—or rather, as "their" nation—it denied them leadership in it. These vexations made the psychology of their service and the terms of their cooperation exceedingly complex.

The Sudanese experience illuminates these points. In the Anglo-Egyptian Sudan, Britain maintained control by enlisting large numbers of educated Northern Sudanese to work for the regime. These employees collected taxes, translated and publicized government ordinances and memoranda, and even, on occasion, joined in military reprisals to suppress rural uprisings. With their help, the colonial system stayed in place for more than fifty years. Nevertheless, the same educated group developed nationalist ideologies to challenge Britain's presence on political and cultural grounds. After independence in 1956, these men gained a place in Sudanese national history books for their heroism as anticolonial figures.

Why did nationalist heroes prop up the colonial systems that they yearned to overthrow? The question seems to be a contradiction in terms. To appreciate its relevance, one must first understand why it was not posed in the historical dialogue of the past century.

THE COLONIAL RELATIONSHIP IN
HISTORICAL PERSPECTIVE

As Britain's "colonial moment" in Africa and Asia came, went, and receded, evaluations of its character and impact changed.[1] Whereas colonial-era accounts highlighted the participation and cooperation of "natives" in government, narratives in the early independence era focused on their resistance.[2] Each approach—the one imperial, the other national—upheld a different claim to political legitimacy. The imperial approach emphasized the collaboration of chiefs, *shaykhs*, maharajas, and other authority figures, and thereby endorsed Britain's claim to rule by consent. The national approach, by contrast, stressed widespread resistance to colonialism on the part of peasants and politicians alike, and served three related purposes. First, it enabled newly decolonized countries to claim a tradition of national heroism and cohesion within colonial borders. Second, it asserted psychological as well as political liberation from the recent past. And third, it bolstered the ideal of a civil society in which national citizenship could transcend primordial ethnic loyalties, on the one hand, and differences of educational attainment and wealth, on the other. Since both approaches posited exclusive categories of supporters and rebels to satisfy their respective agendas, neither asked, "Why were the collaborators also resisters?"

By the 1970s, the heroism of the early nationalist, anticolonial movements was starting to lose its shine. As a new generation reached maturity without having observed colonialism or the independence struggle firsthand, some began to question the extent of repression, corruption, and mismanagement in independent governments.[3] Disillusionment grew particularly sharp in countries where parliamentary government had collapsed into military dictatorship or one-party rule, or where civil war had shattered illusions of national rule by consent. Meanwhile, as the euphoria of independence faded and the challenges of widespread poverty loomed, critics reexamined colonialism's economic foundations. While the question of the colonial heyday had been, "How has Europe developed and benefited its colonies?," the question in its aftermath became instead, "How did Europe underdevelop and exploit them?"[4] In spite of the dashed hopes underlying this criticism, the assumption remained that the nation-state had integrity and legitimacy within its borders and that it was discrete in essence (if not in history) from the colony that begat it. Influenced by this assumption, few were ready to blur the line between colonialism and nationalism by considering the colonial employment history of the early nationalists.

In the last quarter of the twentieth century, the distance gained from decolonization enabled some reconciliation to occur between imperial (Britain-focused) history and its colonial and national (African- and Asian-focused) counterparts. Increasingly convinced that the nation-state, as colonialism's major legacy, was at times a "burden" and at times a "curse,"[5] historians of Africa, the Middle East, and South Asia began to interrogate colonialism and nationalism not as unrelated entities, but as twins.

In India, the major critical development of the past quarter century emerged in the "subaltern studies" movement.[6] Like Saleem Sinai in Salman Rushdie's *Midnight's Children,* its scholars felt that independence in 1947 had left Indians "handcuffed to history," with the terms of the colonial encounter dictating the course, and discourse, of the country.[7] Frustrated with "the aggravating and seemingly insoluble difficulties of the nation-state" in India, they reexamined the colonial past and the language of nationalism in an effort to make sense of the present.[8]

In Africa, the union of imperial and colonial history led to a new and more subtle appreciation of the colonial relationship that combined attention to the "politics of collaboration" and the mechanics of imperialism on the one hand, with the study of African resistance on the other.[9] Historians began to register this change in the early 1980s by noting that the acquiescence of Africans in colonialism had been as significant as their protest against it.[10] This observation contributed to new work on the invention of tradition, which showed first, how the construction of imperial rituals, centered around the cult of the British monarchy, provided "models of subservience into which it was sometimes possible to draw Africans," and second, how the promulgation or codification of new traditions transformed "flexible custom into hard prescription."[11] This dialogue contributed to an ongoing debate about the meaning of modernity and the clash between old and new in a century of profound changes.

At the same time, Middle Eastern historians, working on the history of Egypt, the Fertile Crescent, and Turkey, began to confront the region's double imperial encounter in the twentieth century, with the Ottoman Empire before World War I and with the "mandatory powers" of France and Britain after World War I. In the more complicated case of Palestine, the colonial encounter worked in triplicate; besides the Ottomans and the British, there were the Zionists, who made the region into a Jewish settler colony which endured, as Israel, upon Britain's decolonization. Against this context, historians in the 1990s reassessed the region's major corporate nationalisms (such as Arab nationalism, or pan-Arabism) and country-based nationalisms, and began to explore the multilayered or polycentric qualities of social and national identities.[12]

In a similar vein but beyond the scope of the British Empire, East Asian historians began to debate many of the same questions about nationalism, imperialism, and modernity by considering the dual imprint of Japan and the West on twentieth-century China and Korea. For example, addressing multiple imperialisms like their peers in the Middle East, historians of Korea assessed the efforts of early-twentieth-century nationalists to assert cultural authenticity vis-à-vis China at a time when both Japanese power and Anglo-American influences were growing. Thus, they showed how early Korean nationalists, trying to find a balance between Korean and new Western ways (the one meant to embody local tradition, the other social progress), promoted King Sejong's fifteenth-century alphabet as a national writing system in the place of Chinese characters, but at the same time cut off their topknots to suggest that they were modern.[13]

As the twentieth century ended, the historical literature in India, the Middle East, and Africa had begun to shatter the national monolith into fragments, broken along lines of religion, ethnicity, social status, and even gender.[14] No longer approaching nationalism through the "Great Men" who first propelled it,[15] historians scrutinized the components and complexities of national identities; attended to groups, such as ethnic and religious minorities, that were outside the national mainstream; or became attuned to the local interaction of multiple imperialisms.[16] Even disciplinary moorings shifted, as some historians took a literary or linguistic turn, for example, by studying the language of Orientalism,[17] or took anthropological approaches toward popular culture.[18]

The early nationalists have now been demoted in studies of the colonial encounter, but they deserve renewed attention. They are, after all, the human bridge that joins the histories of colonialism and nationalism, since they were active participants in the cultures and processes of both. Moreover, in light of the interpretive developments of the past century, it is now possible to ask why leading nationalists actively maintained the colonial systems that they dreamed of displacing.[19]

In 1997, Ranajit Guha reflected on twenty-five years of subaltern studies in India and on the state of postcolonial studies in general. Reappraising the Indian colonial relationship, he wrote in terms that apply equally to African and Middle Eastern experiences. "Far from being blessed with the agreement and cooperation of those on whom it had imposed itself by conquest," he declared, "the incubus known as the Raj was a *dominance without hegemony,* that is, a dominance in which the movement of persuasion outweighed that of coercion without, however, eliminating it altogether."[20] The Sudanese example makes it clear that the "movement of persuasion," which enabled colonial rule, occurred above all in the bureaucracy, among the educated men who championed nationalism in its earliest, self-conscious forms.

TENSIONS OF SERVICE:
THE BRITISH—'EFFENDI' RELATIONSHIP

Colonial government employment offered the educated Northern Sudanese a livelihood. The pay was steady and the jobs held prospects for low-scale promotions and salary increases. A typical Gordon College graduate, at work for the regime, could hope to build a house (ideally in greater Khartoum) and support a family in reasonable comfort. "Life was easy," or so it seemed to one graduate in 1995 as he mulled over his youthful career as a customs assessor from the distance of more than fifty years.[21]

Government jobs satisfied basic needs, and yet many of the educated Northern Sudanese had wide grounds for frustration. They were sensitive to their low rank, exclusion from policy-making decisions, and subordination to British officials, some of whom were younger and less experienced than they were. Their jobs offered promotions, but mobility was limited; for filing clerks and typists especially, the work was dull. On top of it all, many felt patronized and, often, they were.[22] British sources, for example, sometimes confirm their junior status by labeling Northern Sudanese employees of 23 as "boys," while referring to British males straight from university as "men."[23]

On the surface, the British treated the educated Northern Sudanese with respect and addressed them with the polite Ottoman-Arabic title *effendi* (collective *effendiyya*). Akin to "mister," this title acknowledged their educational and professional attainments as modern men in government employ. (Exceptions were those individuals, *qadis* among them, who had had an Islamic education; such individuals were known as *shaykhs*, and wore robes and turbans, rather than suits and ties, as the outward manifestation of their status.)

Below the surface, however, the term *effendi*, to a Briton, signaled something worse: an overambitious, ever-complaining, potential political hothead. Contempt for *effendis* percolated down the British social scale. Even British missionaries felt it, warning newly arrived colleagues, as they learned their Arabic, above all to "avoid that strange office Arabic used unfortunately by so many of the effendiyya" and to cultivate "the rich and expressive living language" of the ordinary people instead.[24] Considering the odious connotations that the term *effendi* accreted, along with its humiliating associations of petty employ, it is no surprise that Arabic speakers abandoned the title upon decolonization in favor of the more neutral *sayyid*.

British contempt for the *effendiyya* had its roots in their own unease. As smoke-and-mirror rulers, dependent more on the spectacle of power than on its performance, the British were not entirely secure in their positions. *Effendis* (in their Egyptian or Northern Sudanese varieties), like *babus* in India, unnerved them on several counts. For a start, they were always pressing for more responsible jobs, and ultimately, for British jobs. They also dressed like Europeans (fez or tarbush aside), thereby undermining British exceptionalism in looks. Worse still, they could speak the language of British liberalism; their modern educations had taught them European political concepts such as "patriotism" (translated into Arabic as *wataniyya* or *qawmiyya*) and "independence" (rendered *istiqlal*), which they could deploy to contest the colonial presence. The British knew of these dangers from Egypt, where, since the Occupation of 1882, the *effendiyya* had been refining arguments for nationalism and freedom. As one British intelligence official suggested in 1910, it was only a matter of time before "the young generation" of Northern Sudanese would "imbibe obnoxious ideas at school" by coming under the influence of Egyptian teachers who were themselves "tainted with Nationalism."[25]

Disdain was reciprocal. While the British mistrusted or scorned *effendis* for their Western pretensions and social ambitions, *effendis* equally resented the British for thwarting their hopes and begrudging their efforts to be modern. Again, professional concerns were paramount. A recurring complaint of the educated Northern Sudanese was that their education had prepared them for petty jobs alone (and had not sought to cultivate knowledge for its own sake), that their jobs lacked sufficient mobility, and that their hopes to specialize or to extend skills were stifled. The British gave them limited educations and kept them down. "Employment was the end of the journey," lamented one.[26]

A lack of informal social contact between British officials and Northern Sudanese employees widened the gap of mistrust. In Khartoum and other large towns, British officials filled leisure hours with club visits, tea parties, sports matches, and dinners among Britons of commensurate social status.[27] In the first half of the colonial period, in a place like Port Sudan, contact between a British district commissioner and a district accountant or clerk was limited to the office. In the latter part of the colonial period, when some British wives were present, town-based officials occasionally invited Northern Sudanese colleagues to their homes. Yet these efforts to narrow the culture gap were often stilted affairs—little better, perhaps, than the "bridge parties" staged in the India of the Turtons and Burtons, about which E. M. Forster wrote.[28] As Jamal Muhammad Ahmad recalled:

Meals were rather rare, because meals meant handling forks and knives, and for some [Sudanese], forks and knives were not such a great amusement. Tea was all right because you just drank tea and had a bit of cake. It was stuffy because there was this tremendous effort on the side of the hostess to keep you happy. . . . I can't remember at all calling anyone by his first name. It was always 'Sayyid so-and-so' and 'Mister so-and-so.' . . .

There was one Briton who always told his Northern Sudanese guests to come in shorts. Jamal realized later that the man had been trying to put them at ease. "At the time we thought it was just a way to order us about. . . . We resented it. . . . At one stage, one or two people used to go in pairs of trousers, just to establish their personalities!"[29]

In remote outposts, however, where officials—British or Sudanese—were relatively few and far between, there were more opportunities for social contact: sharing cups of tea at the end of the day, meeting to discuss astronomy or English literature or the latest Reuters news, playing polo or tennis, and so on. Activities like these helped officials to overcome loneliness and boredom, though social ranks were maintained.[30] Often, such interactions led to the development of mutual respect, and occasionally, to lifelong acquaintances or friendships. When British writers in later years recalled Sudanese officials who had worked with them in remote outposts, praise and fondness for these individuals—and not contempt for the stereotyped collective—is invariably the keynote of their remarks. Part of the praise came from gratitude, for many Britons acknowledged that as neophyte A.D.C.'s, they had been taught their jobs or saved from administrative blunders by Northern Sudanese mamurs and others.[31] The educated Northern Sudanese felt much the same. Years later, many reminisced about specific Britons who had earned their grudging or wholesale admiration, or who had earned their gratitude by helping them progress in their educations or careers.[32]

This combination of mutual contempt on the collective level and mutual admiration on the individual level was a defining feature of the British–Sudanese relationship in particular, and the colonial relationship in general.[33] Hence, the complicated terms on which the educated Northern Sudanese worked for the regime: serving the Sudan with dedication, but only cooperating with the British at arm's length.

PROFESSIONAL GRIEVANCES AND REVOLT

For the most part, the educated Northern Sudanese coped with the frustrations of their government service or railed against its iniquities in minor ways. Cautious co-existence, not active hostility or resistance, distinguished their approach. Hence, some dragged their feet at work, while others simply asserted individualism through their clothes or manner of speech.[34] Many used literature to vent their feelings, by encoding anti-British or pro-Egyptian sentiment in Arabic poems that were intended for recitation among friends. In their fantasies, many would have liked to rupture the system, but reason kept them in check. The educated Northern Sudanese depended on government jobs for their livelihoods, for supporting their children and extended families. Moreover, many took pride in their jobs and had no desire to sabotage careers that were built on accomplishment. These internal tensions explain the absence of sustained, large-scale subversion throughout the Anglo-Egyptian period.

The uprisings of 1924 were an exception to this pattern.[35] Among the diverse participants of its urban demonstrations and seditious activities were many graduates of Gordon College and its feeder schools who had employment in government jobs. An abstract opposition to British colonialism and an attachment to Egypt may have figured strongly in the uprisings, but so, too, did discontent on the job, which underlines the importance of professional grievances to the growth of early nationalism.

Indeed, British intelligence reports support the view that many participants in the 1924 events were from among the professionally disgruntled. These reports profiled men like Ali Ahmad Salih, an out-of-work municipal tax collector and commercial press typesetter with a record of petty corruption, and a man with a large family to support, who joined the White Flag League and then turned government informant, presumably lured by an offer of money. The same Ali Ahmad Salih had been a soldier in the Camel Corps some years before, but was released after suffering injuries in a Nuba Mountains patrol which left him unable to hold his rifle.[36] There were dismissed sub-mamurs like Nur al-Din Faraj, who had earlier been released from military duty on medical grounds, for having come down with "religious melancholy" after joining a Sufi order.[37] And there were former postal employees like Kamil Hasan Yusuf, an unemployed half-Egyptian *muwallad* who had attempted to change his job and become a sub-mamur but who had failed out of the Sub-Mamurs Training Program.[38] Arabic biographical dictionaries tell a similar story. One biographer draws a straight line between disappointment and White Flag League membership for Ibrahim Abd al-Raziq (1896–1975), who came from a prominent family, but who had been turned down twice for opportunities he sorely wanted. First, he had been rejected for admission to Gordon College, where he dreamt of going to become a *qadi*. Later, while working as a *kuttab* teacher, he was turned down in an application to join the administration.[39] Like many ardent supporters of the 1924 uprisings, men like these nursed wounds of professional embitterment.

Personnel files, full of obsequious pleas for promotion, offer other windows into the professional frustrations that ate away at the educated Northern Sudanese and prompted them to develop anticolonial ideologies. The case of Arafat Muhammad Abd Allah (1898–1936), later distinguished as the founder and editor of the literary magazine *al-Fajr* (produced 1934–37), stands out.

Although Arafat Muhammad Abd Allah was one of the most brilliant students ever to pass through Gordon College, having been educated at government expense because of his rare ability, he failed the medical examinations that were necessary to secure a permanent government job.[40] (These health screenings began after 1910, when a doctor's examination revealed that at least 13 percent of the college's students were infected with bilharzia, and that 20 percent had seriously defective vision as a result of trachoma.[41]) Physical disability, therefore, became a barrier to his mobility, and not even steady intervention on the part of British officials enabled him to secure a government post that was equal to his talents. Ultimately, he got only a lowly job as a clerk in the Post and Telegraphs Department, with no prospects of mobility. (In this case, the job was lowly because it was "unclassified," meaning impermanent and unpensionable. By contrast, entry-level, English-speaking clerks in classified posts had relatively good prospects.) As one British official noted, it was particularly frustrating for Arafat that this job did not draw upon his exceptional English skills, and that it required so little initiative and intelligence.[42]

In letter after letter, penned in flawless, flowery English, Arafat begged for a better job. Yet the Financial Secretary (the ultimate judge in issues of hiring, salary raises, the granting of travel passes, etc.), rejected Arafat's pleas for promotion or transfer on the grounds of physical disability. Finally, in 1924, as Northern Sudanese discontent boiled over in a series of urban uprisings, Arafat fled to Egypt, where he took up his pen to assault British colonialism through the Egyptian nationalist press.[43] British officials registered his disappearance when he failed to show up for work.[44]

What moved Arafat to act as he did in 1924? The mounting frustration evident in his personnel file—as this "Obedient Humble Servant" "most respectfully" begged for promotion—appears to have contributed to his political decisions. How many of the Northern Sudanese *effendiyya*, like Arafat, were driven to action through bitter disappointment at work? As Arafat wrote in 1922, "It goes without saying that 'hope' is the one great stimulus for a man to 'hold on,' and if it is dashed to the ground, I would wonder what would become of him *as a worker.*"[45]

Job frustration played a role in the 1924 uprisings, though generational conflict had a part as well. Men of the young educated classes had strained relations not only with the British, but with their fathers, as their changing worldviews and expectations clashed with both colonial and parental authority. How else to explain the intelligence report which noted that after a group of boys had been sentenced and whipped for participating in some minor riots in Omdurman, some of their fathers approached the authorities and asked to whip them more?[46] Participation in the 1924 events cut across families, dividing not only father from son, but brother from brother. For example, one son of the Khalifa Abdullahi (d. 1899; ruler of the Mahdist state from 1885 to 1898), went to prison in 1924 after making a flamboyant attempt to convey a White Flag League petition of allegiance to Egypt,[47] while his sibling kept quiet and retained the goodwill of British officials. It is significant that the revolutionary brother, Muhammad al-Mahdi al-Khalifa Abdullahi, was a government employee (an English-to-Arabic translator) at the time, whereas his politically quiescent brother, Muhammad al-Sayyid al-Khalifa Abdullahi, was an independent farmer who proved filial piety by tending his father's grave at Umm Dibeikerat.[48] The difference in their attitudes followed the line separating *effendi* from *shaykh.*

LITERATURE AND SUBVERSION

Looking back on the 1924 uprisings, Gordon College graduates argued that they were the culmination of activities that had been stirring in literary circles for some time. To appreciate this view, it is important to understand the close relationship between Arabic literature and political expression in the Anglo-Egyptian Sudan.

The White Flag League was the group credited with organizing many of the 1924 events, but its literary forerunner was the League of Sudan Union (*Jami'at al-Ittihad al-Sudani*). Whereas the former included men like Ali Abd al-Latif, an officer of slave descent, the latter included mostly Gordon College graduates. Since winners and intellectuals write history, it is perhaps not surprising that the Gordon College set chronicled the League of Sudan Union so well.[49]

As a clandestine society, the League of Sudan Union formed around an Omdurman literary salon tended by a female singer and possible prostitute who went by the working name "Fawz."[50] Several Gordon College graduates gathered after work in Fawz's salon, along with the popular musician and oud player, Khalil Farah (c. 1892–1932)—a graduate of the Gordon College Technical Workshops. By day, Khalil Farah was a mechanic in the Post and Telegraphs Department, where he was frequently fined for arriving late. At night, he blossomed as a composer of songs that praised the Sudan's connections with Egypt and its spirit of Nile Valley unity.[51] Khalil Farah achieved fame on the basis of songs which blended literary and colloquial Arabic, and were thereby accessible to popular audiences.[52] For these songs, he is still hailed today.[53]

The regulars at Fawz's salon, who constituted the League of Sudan Union, not only sang and drank together, but also engaged in serious political discussion.[54] At some of their meetings they composed seditious proclamations, which they affixed onto pillars and walls at dusk. In 1922, assessing such posters, British intelligence concluded, "As far as can be ascertained, the later [post-1919] circulars and probably all the printed ones had their origin in Egypt and were brought for distribution to the Sudan."[55] This appears not to have been the case with the seditious documents from the League of Sudan Union. One of its former members recalled, years later, that the group had printed its circulars locally, using a type of rudimentary hand-press (*baluza*) that government employees readily found in their offices in Khartoum. The engineer and military officer Abd Allah Khalil (1892–1971), a Gordon College graduate and later a Prime Minister of the independent Sudan, was in charge of printing the anticolonial texts and distributing them to cells of other secret societies for hanging up around town or sending by mail.[56]

In other words, members of the League of Sudan Union, and by extension, the White Flag League, found the equipment necessary to print seditious circulars right in the workplace. The same was true for many other officials, who used workplace technologies to subvert the regime, especially in the lead-up to the 1924 events. The overlap between professional and political careers was thereby considerable.

Of all government employees, those attached to the Post and Telegraphs Department had greatest access to transportation and communications technologies, which they used to good effect. In 1924 the intelligence department reported that all Post and Telegraphs officials were in collusion with the White Flag League, sending free telegrams among members, bribing messengers to carry or bring information, and using the mails between Egypt and the Sudan to maintain contact with Egyptian sympathizers abroad. Telephone operators employed by the same department listened in on conversations among British officials and conveyed details to leaders of the League.[57] In an investigation of the 1924 uprisings, another intelligence report pointed to the role of traveling postmasters on trains, railway ticket inspectors and guards, and river (i.e., Steamers Department) workers in distributing subversive letters or Egyptian propaganda among White Flag League members, and in smuggling seditious documents by parcel post—the latter to evade the censors who watched the regular mails.[58]

A number of figures in the League of Sudan Union, and later the White Flag League, were postal employees. For example, Ubayd Hajj al-Amin (1898–1933) was an important organizer of White Flag League activities. A graduate of Gordon College, he served as a translator in the Post and Telegraphs Department. On the basis of his leading role in the uprisings, he was sentenced to a prison term in Torit, in the Southern Sudan, where he later died of blackwater fever.[59] Arafat Muhammad Abd Allah (1898–1936) reportedly used his Post and Telegraphs connections to pass messages to the postmaster in charge of the express Khartoum-to-Halfa trains, who in turn handed them over for smuggling into Egypt.[60] When news reached Arafat that he was under government suspicion, he fled to Egypt with the help of his friends.[61] Along with his colleague Ali Malasi, Salih Abd al-Qadir (1895–1968) helped to organize uprisings in Port Sudan, where he worked as a postal clerk. Salih, who was an accomplished poet, fit the profile of the disgruntled employee. As a student at Gordon College, he had rebelled against college injunctions that required students to revert to wearing the traditional robe and turban (as opposed to the modern suit and tie of the *effendi*) and had dropped out before finishing his studies in the teacher training program.[62]

Regardless of one's job, the political atmosphere was such in 1923 and 1924 that nearly every leisure-time activity took on political significance among the educated Northern Sudanese in the main towns. The *effendiyya* were contesting the British colonial presence even at the annual celebrations for *mawlid al-nabi* (the Prophet Muhammad's birthday), where poets gathered in government pavilions (set up temporarily for the occasion) to recite their works. At the Omdurman *mawlid* of Rabi' al-Awwal A.H.1342 (October 23, 1923), for example, young students and graduates of Gordon College delivered incendiary odes even while British officials were seated in front of them. (These Britons lacked the Arabic skills to perceive the challenge.) On the surface, these poems, with their emphasis on the glory of the Arab Muslim past, did not seem controversial. But through the manner and enthusiasm of delivery, they took on anticolonial significance. Hasan Najila later described the impassioned verses, championing nationalism and condemning imperialism in veiled words, that these poets recited on religious occasions.[63] Theatrical performances also took on political significance, as in 1923, when members of the Omdurman Graduates Club staged a fundraising production on the life of the Kurdish general Saladin (Salah al-Din al-Ayyubi), who defended the Levant and Egypt during the Crusades. An observer recalled that the man who played Saladin "acted so well that we believed that the glory of the Arabs had returned that night, and that we would triumph over our enemies, the imperialist intruders; many in the audience sobbed."[64]

CENSORSHIP, SURVEILLANCE, AND RESISTANCE

In the aftermath of the 1924 uprisings, the regime imposed heavy surveillance, placing the educated Northern Sudanese on their best behavior. Most of those who had participated in the League of Sudan Union or White Flag League continued in government jobs, performing them with the same dedication as before. While crackdowns pushed politics outside the public arena, political discussion did not disappear completely, but turned to literature instead. Contrary to expectations, therefore, the period from 1924 (the year of the uprisings) to 1938 (when the Graduates Congress emerged as a forum for open political debate) was a time of great intellectual vitality. Literary activity became the political ground par excellence, as the educated Northern Sudanese gathered after work in homes, employees clubs, and literary salons. Generally regarded as innocuous by the authorities, these activities stimulated debates on the cultural foundations of "Sudanese" society and discussions about a future without British rule.

The chill that followed 1924 began to thaw in 1930 when the regime promulgated its first formal press law. (Although the Sudan government had had no formal press law until that time, it had, from the early years of the regime, subjected Sudanese newspapers to censorship, defining it as a legal prerogative of the governor-general that derived from the martial law declared at the time of the conquest.[65]) This new law regulated the import, sale, and distribution of printed materials. As far as newspaper publishing was concerned, each prospective publisher had to apply for a permit; gain approval for the owner, printer, and editor(s); submit each issue for Intelligence Department review; pay a security fee; and, if requested, supply information on his writers.[66] In other words, the 1930 press law codified publishing practices but did not substantially differ from the regime's earlier informal policies. Although its provisions were strict, merely by signaling that the regime was prepared to consider new journalistic ventures, the promulgation of the 1930 press law marked an easing of the regime's post-1924 crackdowns.

Two literary journals emerged in the 1930s after the promulgation of the press law. The first, *al-Nahda al-Sudaniyya*, better known simply as *al-Nahda* ("The Awakening") came out only from 1931 to 1932, while *al-Fajr* ("The Dawn") ran irregularly from 1934 to 1937. Both had remarkably short runs, troubled by financial difficulties and by the illnesses and deaths of their editors.[67] Nevertheless, they were arguably the two most important Northern Sudanese journals of the twentieth century because they provided a forum for the exploration of Sudanese nationalism and national identity.

Some say that the founder and editor of *al-Nahda*, Muhammad Abbas Abu'l-Rish (1908–35), had been preparing the journal secretly, in handwritten form, when the authorities found out about it. Approaching Abu'l-Rish, they asked him to come into the open with his journal, on the understanding that government approval for publication would be forthcoming. The same was not true for another handwritten paper, called *al-Asil* ("The Steadfast"), published by a student named Muhammad Abd al-Wahhab al-Qadi, from the Ma'had al-Ilmi (where the Islamic sciences were taught), and containing praise poems as well as articles on Islamic reform and moral values. After watching the paper closely, the authorities asked the head *shaykh* of the Ma'had to put a stop to the journal and he complied.[68] These two cases suggest that some of the educated Northern Sudanese continued to engage in clandestine or semi-clandestine activity—however innocuous—by publishing secret papers in the aftermath of the 1924 events.

The *effendiyya* were the most active contributors to Northern Sudanese Arabic journals, including the government-approved newspaper *Hadarat al-Sudan* (founded 1919) and later *al-Nahda* and *al-Fajr*. Yet most published their essays and poems under pseudonyms, to evade laws which forbade government employees from publishing anything without first securing permission from the Civil Secretary's office. Obviously, the regime knew to whom the pseudonyms referred—the 1930 press law gave them access to information on writers' identities and through coercion they had obtained such information even before then. But if employees maintained the fiction by writing under pen names or initials, the government was usually content to leave them alone. For example, Khidir Hamad (1908–70), a typist in the Financial Secretary's office and a prominent nationalist politician of the early independence era, published in periodicals under the name "al-Tubji," whereas Ibrahim Hasan Mahalawi (1898–1977), a Railways employee at Atbara and in later years a trade-union organizer, used his initials "I.H.M." Little secrecy surrounded these noms de plume. An Arabic poetry anthology published around 1923, for example, announced that one young student at Gordon College (who later became a government accountant), Shafiq Fahmi Mina (1903–70), always contributed to the newspaper *Hadarat al-Sudan* under the name "Zuhayr."[69]

Occasionally, however, employees got into trouble by publishing in their own names, without permission, on delicate subjects. Yahya al-Fadli (1911–74), an accountant in the Finance Department and later a nationalist politician, was twice ordered before boards of discipline for this reason. On the first occasion, in 1936, when he published an unapproved article in the newspaper *al-Nil*, he was officially reprimanded. On the second occasion, in 1937, he was fined seven days' pay, apparently for publishing an essay on the problem of political sectarianism in the journal *al-Fajr*.[70]

In a similar vein, the poet, literary critic, and sub-mamur Hamza al-Malik Tanbal (1897–1951) was brought before a board of discipline after he published an unauthorized poetry anthology in 1931. Called *Diwan al-Tabi'a* ("Nature Anthology"), his volume would never have come to government attention except that a few of Hamza's former Northern Sudanese colleagues in El Dueim lodged a complaint that one of the poems contained insults to them.[71] The poet, historian, and accountant Muhammad Abd al-Rahim (1878–1966) was more cautious: not only had he secured government permission before publishing a literary study titled *Nafathat al-yara'* ("Effusions of the Pen") in 1936, he even reproduced his letter of permission from the Civil Secretary's office in the foreword of the book, along with several encomia written by friends.[72]

The delivery of incendiary nationalist poetry at public events was a prominent feature of the years between 1919 and 1924. But in later years, too, some poets continued to defy the government in poetry. According to one writer, the regime ordered the transfer of the Survey Department engineer Ali Nur (1903–72) from Wad Medani to El Damer in 1938 in order to prevent him from delivering nationalist poetry at the Wad Medani cultural festival. He had already been brought before a board of discipline for his earlier poetic exploits. Undeterred, Ali Nur sent a two-line telegram, in rhymed verse, to the festival organizers in order to explain his absence. It said, "*Aq'adatni majalis al-ta'dib, an qiyami bi-wajibi ka-adib*" (The Board of Discipline has prevented me from undertaking my duty as a *littérateur*).[73] Sending telegrams in verse was fairly common among Northern Sudanese poets, who went far afield on transfers in the course of their government jobs.[74]

The regime imposed restrictions and kept careful watch over the literary—and by extension, political—activities of the educated Northern Sudanese. It brought many errant officials before boards of discipline and penalized them not only with fines but with the threat of a stall on promotions. Nevertheless, officials did find ways to subvert the system, even with government surveillance in place. The story of Tawfiq Salih Jibril is instructive here.

Tawfiq Salih Jibril (1897–1966) was a member of the League of Sudan Union and of the White Flag League at the time of the 1924 uprisings. Tawfiq fit the profile of the embittered government employee. He served the regime as a sub-mamur from 1923 to his retirement in 1952, and unusually, throughout that whole time, never received promotion to mamur rank. One might argue that Tawfiq was never promoted because he did not curry favor with superiors—that he was a dedicated anticolonial. The truth may be that he was unsuited in temperament to his job. Over the years, various British superiors made the following comments in his evaluations: "He is not clever and is not quick to take responsibility" (1925); "He has been very careless" (1926); "He is NOT suitable to be in charge of a Merkaz . . . he is careless and his criminal work leaves a lot to be desired; lack of character and GUTS!" (1927); "I realize that his failings are constitutional and are not due to any deliberate laziness or vice, but . . ." (1928); "He is colorless and without personality and lacks initiative" (1933); and so on.[75] Over the years, too, other British officials praised Tawfiq for his strengths, notably his tact, trustworthiness, and gentlemanly manners, and a few even endorsed him for a promotion to mamur that never came. Yet it may have been, as one official wrote in 1948, that his "poetic and contemplative bent of mind" made him a kind man but an inefficient sub-mamur. Shortly before his retirement in 1950, another official reported, "It is a mystery how Tawfik Eff. became a Sub Mamur and how he has remained one. Apart from the fact that he is apparently a nice man I cannot think of a more unsuitable person for such a post. He should have been a curator at a museum or a post-master in a quiet little office."[76]

In literary circles, Tawfiq Salih Jibril was an accomplished and highly respected poet.[77] But somehow he appeared lackluster to superiors. Perhaps it was the case, as one British official surmised in 1938, that his "unassuming manner and a gentlemanly reluctance to thrust himself forward have tended in the past to make [officials] underrate his intelligence and his ability."[78] In any case, Tawfiq responded to his professional unhappiness in various ways, but especially through poetry that condemned colonialism. He kept this poetry private, and much of it was published posthumously. His experiences are reflected in the titles of poems such as *"Min dhikrayat al-isti'mar al-baghid"* (Some Memories of Loathsome Imperialism). In a comment that he penned in the margin of this poem, he painfully recalled that "when the British District Commissioner, Mr. Arthur, expelled me from the service [in 1953] . . . no one bade me off on the day of my departure except for my loyal friends."[79]

Tawfiq and his friends took comfort in knowing that they had shaken the regime in 1924 and that they had worked to subvert it in other ways. His trusted friend Hasan Najila recorded a story about Tawfiq when he was working as a sub-mamur at Umm Ruwaba in Kordofan.[80] The occasion was King's Day, the annual festivity of relay races, contests, and sports matches held throughout the Northern Sudan to commemorate the visit that King George V had made to the country in 1912. The year was 1929. As the district sub-mamur, Tawfiq was in charge of decorating the town square with banners and flags. On the eve of the festival and under cover of night, he crept into the square with his friend, Abidin Abd al-Ra'uf al-Khanji, the district *bashkatib* (head clerk), and ripped the British flags into shreds, throwing the pieces to the wind. At sunrise the British D.C. discovered the deed, turned red in the face, and raged. Tawfiq, who reached the scene before the D.C., sent a troop of police to look for the perpetrators, who were never found. On the margin of a poem that alluded to the incident Tawfiq later wrote, "The 'ruler' at that time was that brute of a District Commissioner, Armstrong. How often I experienced distress and tyranny from him!"[81]

A similar case of internal subversion occurred at Wad Medani sometime in the late 1930s or early 1940s. British intelligence had tried and failed to ferret out the source of some publications distributed in the name of the Graduates Congress without permission. Mahmud Abu'l-Azayim, then a young agricultural research intern in the town, recalled that the source of the illicit documents was none other than Mustafa Sa'id, the mamur of the local prison and one of the biggest, toughest men in town. A few young Northern Sudanese drafted the documents and went on a visit to Mustafa Sa'id, whose house was attached to the prison. The burly mamur passed the documents to a prisoner (a former government employee who had been convicted for embezzlement) who could type, and then mimeographed thousands with the help of the prison's office equipment.

Abu'l-Azayim commented, "The idea of printing the publications in the prison was the idea of the prison mamur himself. That's because it was the one place that it would never occur to the security men to suspect. And Mustafa Sa'id himself would be the last to be suspected of participating in this type of activity."[82] The case of the mamur Mustafa Sa'id represents a type of on-the-job resistance that was probably more common than British officials knew.

ON THE RECEIVING END OF RESISTANCE

Their government employment notwithstanding, self-proclaimed Northern Sudanese nationalists fancied themselves stalwart foes of the regime and looked to 1924 as their great heroic moment. However, their roles as resisters did not change the fact that their jobs placed them in positions of power over Sudanese populations. In remote parts of the territory, officials had latitude and power within their petty spheres.

Among Northern Sudanese officials, the mamur had the most tangible local authority. With a title that literally meant "commissioned" or "ordered" in Arabic, the mamur had a deputy in the sub-mamur, who was in charge of police and prisons. Analogous to the British district commissioner and assistant district commissioner, respectively, the mamur and sub-mamur had wide-ranging duties and were responsible in general for the maintenance of law and order. They collected taxes (and liaised with local notables to do so), supervised police business, maintained public security, surveyed and registered lands, directed upkeep of government buildings, and helped semiliterate or illiterate "sanitary barbers" (the *hakims*, or medical assistants) to register births, deaths, and smallpox vaccinations.[83] They supervised public health measures, such as anti-malarial mosquito control. They apprehended criminals, conducted murder investigations, and either tried cases or passed them on to a higher authority.[84] Mamurs and sub-mamurs, in short, acted as the long arm of the colonial state, reaching from Khartoum into the peripheries. Mamurs like Yusuf Saʻd—known half-jokingly by the Baqqara among whom he collected taxes as "Awz Feloos Bas Effendi" (Mr. Just Gimme the Money)—took a stern and thorough approach to their tasks. According to a Briton who fondly remembered him, the Baqqara "respected [Yusuf Saʻd] as a man you couldn't bamboozle."[85]

Because jobs obliged many educated Northern Sudanese to impose colonial authority over subject peoples, they sometimes found themselves on the receiving end of other people's resistance, particularly in rural areas. Hence, the assault or even assassination of tax-collecting sub-mamurs and mamurs was not unknown, particularly in the South and in the Nuba Mountains.[86] There, tax-collecting, from the perspective of the locals, looked like wanton seizure of cattle and other wealth and was a major cause of discontent. The resistance of Southerners and Nubas to tax-paying, in particular, often led to government reprisals, during which Northern Sudanese officials, policemen, and soldiers killed and were killed while attempting to impose colonial authority.[87] Sometimes mamurs were part of the problem, through corruption or personal tyranny. In 1919, for example, the Aliab

Dinka tried to convey the locals' grievances to British authorities but had to rely on the mamur, whom they were implicating, for the transmission; the mamur distorted their story to protect himself.[88]

Mamurs and sub-mamurs of the provinces were not the only officials charged with power. Even relatively minor employees wielded forms of authority. In his memoirs of growing up in Wad Medani, the writer Mahmud Abu'l-Azayim recites cases of anticolonial subversion with relish—such as the time, for example, when some local youths blocked irrigation canals so as to flood the field where the annual King's Day celebration was about to be held.[89] But, in one case, Mahmud acknowledged his own role in imposing, rather than resisting, an unpleasant policy. As a young intern in the entomology section of the Agriculture Department, he set out on a month-long inspection tour of Blue Nile villages between Hantub and Katranj, an area that was part of the commercial cotton-growing Gezira Scheme. There, the Agriculture Department had forbidden the planting of okra, a food crop, until after the cotton harvest. It was Mahmud's job not only to identify farms which contravened this rule, but to uproot okra plants and to report okra planters to the court at Rufa'a, which was headed by the "oppressive D.C.," Mr. Hawkesworth.[90] Along with a police sergeant named Bashir, Mahmud rode from village to village on camel (his first time riding one) and was generously fed and housed by villagers. How it pained him, he recalled, to give orders for uprooting okra, when it was that very food that the villagers had cooked to nourish him, and when the people could not understand the reason for the law.[91]

Mahmud Abu'l-Azayim felt twinges of guilt for his role vis-à-vis the cotton-cultivating villagers because they were, in important ways, his cultural compatriots. Like himself, they were Arabic-speaking, Muslim, Blue Nile dwellers. Bonds of allegiance were not strong, however, when officials found themselves serving in culturally alien zones—in places where Arabic was not spoken and where Islam was absent, or where it was practiced differently. Making the transition from colonial resister to colonial law enforcer was probably easier for the educated Northern Sudanese in such culturally distant places. Confronted with alien customs, the educated Northern Sudanese were as likely to find themselves perplexed as their British superiors—especially when these practices collided with the law, as in the case of witchcraft- or superstition-related homicides and other crimes.[92]

Some Northern Sudanese officials were shocked to encounter Muslim communities that engaged in "un-Islamic" practices. Khidir Hamad recounted his surprise, for example, when on a trip to El Fasher (capital of

Darfur Province), he encountered people calling themselves Muslim who allowed their daughters to marry Christian men right before the eyes of their chiefs. Similarly, Babikr Badri expressed shock over a visit he made to Darfur around 1927 as an education inspector, where he met Zaghawa men who claimed to be Muslims and yet had ten or twenty wives.[93]

Cultural contrasts were even more dramatic for Northern Sudanese officials posted to non-Muslim regions. Some responded by using their jobs as an opportunity to proselytize. For example, when posted to the Nuba Mountains in the 1940s, the *qadi* Muhammad al-Amin al-Qurashi (1886–1976) "rolled up his sleeves to . . . propagate the Islamic religion."[94] Others interpreted their work as a modernization crusade. Khalaf Allah Babikr (b. 1910), a Gordon College graduate who worked as a public health officer for many years, was reportedly happy with the self-sacrifice of serving in far-flung areas of the Sudan, "even when he rushed into battle unsheathing the weapons of modern science amid surroundings . . . like something from the Stone Age."[95] Other officials expressed disapproval over Nuba or Southern nudity[96]; some pressured British officials to ban it. As one Briton later reflected, "It is true that some of the educated Sudanese criticised us for allowing the Nuba to go about naked; they felt it was shameful in that it made their country appear backward and uncivilised. One can understand this, but how could we have imposed an order on the Nuba obliging them to dress?"[97]

A photograph album, compiled by a young British A.D.C. in 1935 to commemorate his Kordofan service, illustrates the foreignness of the educated Northern Sudanese in the Nuba Mountains. There, amid pictures of naked Nuba wrestlers, decked in feathers and ash, and of young women with abdomens intricately scarred, are photographs of a tea party for the members of the Rashad government employees' club. This small, all-male crowd looks solemnly into the camera as they sit attired in the suit and tie of the *effendis,* and the *jallabiyya* and *imma* of the *shaykhs,* with their china cups beside them.[98]

THE TERMS OF SERVICE, IN SICKNESS AND IN HEALTH

Ultimately, the educated Northern Sudanese worked for the regime because they wanted the jobs and needed the income. For all their connections to government, their working conditions were hardly glamorous, particularly outside the big towns. Doing their jobs, supporting their families, coping with discomforts, and passing the time—these were their major concerns. In this they shared experiences with Britons, Egyptians, and Lebanese, particularly in the early years when district officials of all ranks were likely to live in hovels. In his memoir, H. C. Jackson recalled his service in Sennar in 1909: "There was a red-brick office, and some of the clerks were accommodated in mean, single-roomed dwellings also of brick. In them the clerks sweated in summer and shivered in winter, while they counted their piastres to see if they could afford to go on leave when the time came." Jackson's own brick house was not much better, except that it had two rooms instead of one. "Nor was it very cheering," he recalled, "as I looked up at the ceiling [of my house] through which the water was dripping, to note a mark made by the revolver bullet of a predecessor who had shot himself in the madness of malaria."[99]

Sickness was indeed one of the hardest parts of service, for all officials. Malaria, in particular, went with the job, and sometimes (in the early years) took a turn for the worse, developing into deadly cases of blackwater fever. Malaria was "inescapable," said one British official, who remembered the quinine he took through painful injections.[100] The incidence of death among Northern Sudanese officials as a result of this disease and others is unknown, but references to sickness abound in memoirs, personnel files, and medical reports.[101]

Officials had to cope not only with sickness but with insects, heat, and dust. Recalling his service in the mid-1940s, a British agricultural inspector described sharing a mud-brick cottage with termites who ate his books and photographs. He considered himself lucky, however, to have avoided the Tokar delta cotton-growing area, where the dust was sometimes so thick that "people ate their meals from table drawers which were shut between mouthfuls."[102]

Service in remote areas placed extra strains on officials, physically and emotionally. In a chapter of his memoir entitled "Round the Bend," Alexander Cruickshank, a Scottish doctor, described the erratic behavior of a British official and a Lebanese doctor who "cracked" under the pressures of isolation and illness in the South. He called their malaise "Sudanitis" and described its symptoms as bad temper, use of bad language, "making mountains out of molehills," and loss of appetite. A Sudanese policeman reported one case of a British official to Cruickshank who trekked a distance to the official's house to investigate.

> Getting no answer to my shout [I] walked in. I found him naked in the bathroom making frightful grimaces into his mirror and shouting abuse at himself. He had been all alone for six months, was continually getting attacks of malaria and had been steadily overworking.

Cruickshank sent a runner to the nearest telegraph station and wired Khartoum to call for this man's immediate evacuation. After four months of leave, this Briton returned to work restored. The Lebanese doctor was not so fortunate. After weeks of exhausting treks to remote villages to inspect for sleeping sickness, he developed a severe case of paranoia (fearing that he was about to be attacked by a wild animal and isolating himself with a rifle), then had a nervous breakdown, and finally had to resign permanently.[103]

Northern Sudanese officials were susceptible to "Sudanitis," too. One Northern Sudanese official had to be retired, or "invalided," when he was hospitalized for a month with "neurasthenia." According to the senior surgeon, this man's illness took the form of a "dread of Tuberculosis and a conviction that he has this disease."[104] Preserved among the papers of Sir Harold MacMichael is a spoof by an anonymous British official for the entertainment of British colleagues. "Proceedings of a Medical Board on XXX Effendi, a Clerk" mocks the hypochondriac *effendi* who is physically but not mentally fit for service and who is seeking retirement on the grounds of disability. The sight of work causes the clerk great pain, his house is small and makes him short of breath, the office is too small and gives him headaches, his frequent transfers badly affect his health, and so on.[105]

Like Cruickshank's descriptions of officials gone "Round the Bend," the joke of MacMichael's "Proceedings of a Medical Board" tells a tale of the discomfort of the provinces. Service in the South, especially, was a serious matter. In 1911, the director of the Post and Telegraphs Department explained that clerks in the South (who would at this time have been Egyptians and Northern Sudanese) could serve for eight months a year at most, and stressed that it was essential for them to be relieved punctually (implying that they could not cope with more).[106] Recognizing the hardships of Southern service, the regime granted officials serving south of 12° latitude a "climate allowance" on top of their regular salaries, until the austerity measures of the Depression led to its rescinding by 1931.[107] A special breed of Northern Sudanese employee—men like the Gordon College graduate and mamur Ibrahim Badri—dedicated entire careers to service in the most remote parts of the South.[108] Yet many other officials who served in such areas pined for the comforts and company of urban life and looked forward to the day when a transfer would send them northward along the Nile.

From reading the memoirs of British officials, one gets the sense that colonial service in the Sudan—no matter how physically uncomfortable or isolating—was a high point in their lives. To friends, family, and colleagues at home in the metropole, colonial service had glory, romance, cachet. Empire was an adventure.

For the Northern Sudanese employees of the colonial regime, colonial service had much less romance and glory. It offered a livelihood—a way of eking out an existence, sending sons to school, and feeding and clothing dependents of the extended Northern Sudanese family. Their personnel files reflect prosaic but very serious concerns. In correspondence they make arrangements for the all-important pension plan which would provide for them after retirement, plead for pay raises, or for a free railway pass for a grandmother in their charge, negotiate transfers or express interest in new job openings, and so on. At the end of the day, stark realities more than abstract ideals shaped their commitment to service.

CONCLUSION: LIFE, THE REGIME, AND THE NATURE OF SERVICE

The sub-mamur and poet Tawfiq Salih Jibril envisioned the Northern Sudanese government employee as having two heads: one for work, the other for private life. When the employee went to the office in the morning, he donned his work head, which was stuffed with the regulations, instructions, and files of government service. After hours he removed the office head, washed it out, and put on his private head, to spend the rest of the day as a human being, gathering with friends and doing as he pleased. Tawfiq undoubtedly liked to envision his own life that way, disappointed as he was with his stunted career and pouring his heart into the poems that he composed and shared with friends at the end of the day.[109]

But in certain ways, the line that Tawfiq imagined between work and leisure did not exist. Even the most cursory look at Tawfiq's poetry shows that professional experiences weighed heavily on his private life. His colonial job left a lasting mark on his poems, whether they represented fiery nationalist odes, calm reminiscences, or elegies for friends deceased. He wrote some poems in the field, for example, in Bara (1931), Managil (1937), and Rashad (1946), and later composed poems in honor of remote stations where he had served, such as one entitled "Delami" (in the Nuba Mountains). He wrote some in honor of lifelong friends, like Ibrahim Badri, who had studied in the Sub-Mamurs Training Program with him, and he composed one poem about the sub-mamurs' school itself. He even prepared poems as telegrams, which he sent to colleagues posted around the country. As much as he loathed British colonialism in the abstract, Tawfiq even composed a *qasida* of farewell to Sir James Robertson, the Civil Secretary, as he was preparing to leave the country in 1953. By doing so, Tawfiq showed courtesy, since the preparation of praise poems for officials (Northern Sudanese, Egyptian, British, or otherwise) upon their transfer or retirement was a way to convey respect and good wishes.[110]

Tawfiq Salih Jibril was not unusual in revisiting his job through his poetry. Colonial employment and professional disappointment left their mark on the literary output of many educated Northern Sudanese. For example, the poet Hasib Ali Hasib (b. 1899) left Gordon College before completing his studies. Much to his disappointment, he was only able to secure a job as a Shari'a court clerk, making a paltry £E4 a month when he began in 1920. In 1923, while serving in Rashad in the Nuba Mountains, he composed a poem that deplored his low rank in the colonial service, mentioning that of the eight government salary grades, his grade was the eighth, or lowest. Perhaps still disheartened with his lot, Hasib dropped out of government service in 1929 after fewer than ten years in the administration.[111] Similarly, the government job and its disappointments cast echoes into the plots and characters that featured in the early prose experiments of Northern Sudanese writers who worked with the short story and play. For example, one short story published in *al-Fajr*, entitled "Prisoner Number 108," plotted the fate of a government employee whose small salary was insufficient to support his wife and growing family. Faced with mounting debts, and driven to desperation, he filched money from his office treasury, only to be sentenced to three years in prison.[112] The poet and sub-mamur Hamza al-Malik Tanbal, meanwhile, used poetry to vent his resentment against his former Northern Sudanese co-workers at El Dueim. Hamza, who had served there in 1924, likened the mood of the workplace to "a volcano, with malice boiling up within it."[113]

Colonial employment also left its mark on literature by exposing authors to far-flung places and cultures in the course of their jobs, as a consequence of the frequent transfers that many experienced. Several writers wrote accounts of these experiences. Muhammad Abd al-Rahim (1878–1966), for example, a government accountant who wrote histories in his spare time, acknowledged the impact of his job on his first book, *Al-Hadiyya an khitat al-sudaniyya*, written in 1920.[114] He explained, "What helped me to collect the information was my long service within the borders of the Sudan, in Mongalla, Wau, Raja, Kafia Kingi and Kuttum, and my mixing with its different peoples. I was in touch with the intelligent among them and asked them about their tribes. They would recount the history of their tribes, their beliefs, and superstitions, and I would copy them down."[115] His transfer to Darfur in 1930 prompted him to write his second book, *Nafathat al-yara'* (published in 1936), which discussed not only Darfur, but also Waday and Nigeria. A couple of officials even contributed English essays to the government-sponsored journal, *Sudan Notes and Records*, drawing upon their professional insights and regional expertise.[116]

The jobs of the educated Northern Sudanese were often so important to their lives that they became enshrined in their identities. Visiting the historic Ottoman Red Sea town of Suakin around 1950, one travel writer met a gentleman named Muhammad Ahmad Abu'l-Dhahab, whose calling card evinced an essentially colonial identity. Below the man's name, the card read "Mamur on Pension."[117] Similarly, on the title page of his poetry anthology, published in Cairo in 1931, Hamza al-Malik Tanbal chose to print his job title and post in large script immediately below his name, to read "Sub-Mamur, Bara District" (*wakil ma'mur, markaz Bara*).[118] In some cases, it appears that one's job title became part of one's name, as a kind of formal nickname. The biographer Mirghani Hasan Ali refers to the fiery nationalist poet Ali Nur not as "the nationalist Ali Nur" or "the poet Ali Nur," but rather as *al-Muhandis* ("the Engineer") Ali Nur.[119] Similarly, the nationalist Ahmad Khayr (d. circa 1995), a founding member of the Graduates Congress, published his political memoir, *Kifah jil* (*The Struggle of a Generation*) in 1948, not under the name Ahmad Khayr, but under Ahmad Khayr al-Muhami ("Ahmad Khayr the Attorney"), referring to his career in law. Successive editions of *Kifah jil* continue to have his name thus emblazoned on the book's cover.[120]

In sum, two points stand out regarding the relationship of the educated Northern Sudanese to the colonial system. First, no matter how ill at ease Northern Sudanese officials felt with colonialism, and no matter how they felt it wronged them professionally, these individuals shaped and were shaped by its system. Colonialism "got under their skin" in more ways than one. It irked them, even while it became part of them. Sometimes they challenged it or railed privately against it, but most of the time they lived with it. Second, by playing manifold administrative roles, Northern Sudanese employees made colonial rule possible. They typed, filed, and delivered the regime's letters; they collected its taxes; they even imprisoned its challengers. Serious and sustained internal subversion was rare. It was far more common for officials to confirm their stake in the colonial system by seeking promotion within it, and by taking pride in the jobs which they were appointed to fill. Colonial service was a way of life for most Northern Sudanese officials, even though nationalist agitation came from their ranks. They were as much a part of the colonial system as the Britons who ruled it.

6 The Nation after the Colony

In the mid–twentieth century, as decolonization swept through Africa and Asia, each moment of independence transformed a colonial state into a nation-state in the eyes of the world community. Euphoric, nationalist politicians hailed independence as a fundamental break with the past: the start of an age when free governments would depart from and excel over their colonial predecessors in aspirations, achievements, and methods.

In theory, colonial-states and nation-states *were* things apart. As pieces of empires, colonial states had been maintained, by force, for the sake of a distant metropole. By contrast, nation-states were meant to be autonomous, dependent on and responsible to the collectives of people within them.

In practice, however, colonial states passed many features to their successors. As a result, postcolonial nation-states often combined powerful features of colonies—above all, fixed borders and centralized governments that tended to be more autocratic than popular—with the high cultural ambitions of nationalism, based on a desire to forge a community in light of social ideals. Many postcolonial nation-states therefore found themselves struggling with a mismatch between the tools and goals of ruling, as their leaders resorted to autocratic methods and top-down directives in their quest for national consensus.

The following pages examine efforts to define the nation, in theory and practice, during and after colonialism. By tracing the career and plight of Sudanese nationalism over the course of the twentieth century, as its ideas first originated in literary debates, later gained application in government policies, and finally became ensnared in civil war, one can better appreciate how the colonial state evolved into the nation-state, with far-reaching social consequences.

THE NATION ENGINEERED

Years before concepts of nationalism commanded mass appeal, educated male elites in Africa and Asia first perceived nations in colonies. Many of these men were petty government employees, hired to bolster skeletal colonial staffs. Highly literate, increasingly conversant with European political ideals (for example, about liberty and patriotism), and drawn together through common educations, lifestyles, and careers, these men came to feel a special sense of community within the expanse of the colonial territory. They called this sentiment nationalism, and in the years before independence, debated what it meant. Through poems, essays, and other literary forms, which they exchanged above all in print, they discussed the languages and customs, religious beliefs and histories, that gave their communities meaning.

At decolonization, these bureaucrat-nationalists gained the authority to translate their ideas into policies and to impose them from above. Surveying social landscapes where diversity prevailed, they typically reached two conclusions. First, where nationalist sentiment did not exist, it would have to be engineered. Second, to forge a sense of community and make administration logistically easier, authorities should promote a single national language or set of languages. Taking action on both points, many focused efforts on schools, where educators could promote a public culture and esprit de corps by determining the languages that children learned as well as the histories that they studied. In this way, the postcolonial expansion of government education helped nationalism to gain a more popular following, by convincing some members of an up-and-coming generation that the nation was self-evident.

However, problems surfaced with time, showing that attitudes which had seemed so natural to early nationalists, toward cultural values such as language, religion, and ethnicity, often lacked widespread support. And so, instead of complying with government efforts to promote a national monoculture, some groups began to resist.

Controlling powers have often sought to homogenize culture within territories of inherent diversity. In nineteenth-century France, for example, policy-setters in the Paris metropole promoted a national monoculture based above all on a standardized French, and took special efforts to acculturate and assimilate speakers of non-French regional languages. In the twentieth century, authorities in Mexico and Turkey did much the same, respectively promoting Spanish among Amerindians and Turkish among Kurds.[1] These lessons of history suggest that the success and totality of assimilation has varied according to the resources that governments marshal, in building schools, training teachers, and developing infrastructures to make the even application of policies possible.

Hobbled by meager resources, leaders of postcolonial African and Asian countries faced particular difficulty in imposing their nationalist visions. At decolonization, they inherited control of territories that were products of rule on the cheap, where imperialists had developed minimal infrastructures to guarantee the flow of commodities and armies as necessary. (In parts of Africa, for example, Europeans had first laid rail lines to carry the weapons and soldiers of conquest; railway maps still bear the evidence of the few later extensions that insured the transport of raw materials such as cotton, groundnuts, and gold ore from their sites of production to the coasts.[2]) The early nationalists, as colonial bureaucrats and urban-dwellers, had prime access to new communication routes. However, many people did not. Lacking access to roads, railways, or river steamers that could connect them to urban networks, the populations in remote regions were atomized rather than integrated within colonial territories. Thus, when the transfer of power occurred, many groups did not apprehend their nationhood and felt little or no allegiance to a central government and to the unknown peoples in its realm. Resistance was bound to occur as postcolonial central governments tried to subject people to state control on a scale they had never known, and then to impose their vision of a nation that many people had still not perceived.

Although this view of nationalism as a consciousness not only invented, but engineered, has gained ground in recent years, it runs counter to ideas of nations as manifestations of extant, deep-seated popular sentiment and as products of rational political forces. For example, the latter view prevailed in the years after decolonization among historians of Africa, who hailed emergent nation-states and lent support to their cause. Seeking proof of social solidarity and broad-based participation in grassroots, anticolonial protest, many historians suggested that independence in Africa marked the culmination of widespread, nascently nationalist agitation. They implicitly argued that a tradition of "primary resistance," which had involved men and women in tax revolts, rural insurrections, and urban strikes, gave the people of the new nation-states a common past and future.[3]

In the aftermath of imperial encounters, most recently within the Soviet Union, this romantic ideal has faded. Against a background of chronic communal discord or political repression, the lack of consensus in early nation-building, as well as the processes that empowered nationalist elites, have come into sharper focus. So, too, have the efforts of politicians to manufacture or manipulate the idea of the nation with their special group interests in mind. For example, nationalist elites in China, Korea, and South India, "with their control of the means of knowledge production and, in some cases, with their positions in state bureaucracies . . . could make sweeping claims for the nation, often conflating their own group needs with particular definitions of the nation and leaving little room in public forums for alternative voices."[4]

These words about early Asian nationalists apply equally to the Sudan. There, at decolonization, the British transferred power to a monocultural elite: Arabic-speaking Muslim males from the riverain North, who had been the primary beneficiaries of colonial educational and hiring policies. Drawing upon ideas that they had discussed in literature at a time when they still lacked power, these nationalists prepared to press a vision inspired by Arabic and Islam.

But dissent surfaced almost immediately. In their plans for the transfer of power, neither the British nor the educated Northern Sudanese had accounted for the opinions of a budding Southern intelligentsia, of Anglophone, Christian mission-school graduates, who watched the exclusive ascendance of Northerners with growing, astonished dismay.[5] Spreading beyond the small circles of the educated just months before independence, tensions erupted in the South in the form of an army mutiny and demonstrations, as well as attacks on Northern officials. As the years went on and patterns of violence persisted, many historians came to see this mutiny as the start of civil war—the battle over economic resources, political power, and cultural clout which has ravaged the country throughout most of its independent existence.

The idea of the Sudanese nation was nebulous when colonial bureaucrats first discussed it. After years of civil war, and in the absence of widespread communal consensus, its definition is nebulous still. The Sudan's history of strife raises a question relevant worldwide but difficult to answer—namely, what conditions are necessary to make a stable nation-state?

COLONY, NATION, AND STATE

"Qu'est-ce qu'une nation?" What is a nation? Even at its most theoretical level, the question is as elusive now as it was in 1882, when the French philosopher Ernst Renan posed it before an audience at the Sorbonne. At the time, Renan proposed defining the nation as "a soul, a spiritual principle . . . a moral conscience"[6]; nearly seventy-five years later, Hans Kohn defined it with equal abstraction as "a state of mind . . . a living and active corporate will."[7] In 1996, Benedict Anderson, whose description of the

nation as an "imagined community" transformed the study of nationalism in the late twentieth century, admitted that "it is hard to think of any political phenomenon which remains so puzzling and about which there is less political consensus. No widely accepted definition exists."[8]

While the modern nation withstands easy definition, it has certain distinguishing features nonetheless. As an idea among people who share a common cause, the nation gains specificity through its relation to a territory (its claim to a particular land),[9] a polity (its claim to an autonomous state),[10] and a history (its claim to a common past, based on a cult of heroic ancestors,[11] which "legitimates the present and offers signposts for the future"[12]). More ambiguously, the nation gains focus through some kind of "common public culture," which may involve ethnic, linguistic, and religious practices as well as attitudes toward mutual self-conduct.[13]

The debut of a full-fledged nation is hard to pinpoint, so that the question, "When is a nation?" also eludes easy answers. Must nationalism have a mass following before a nation can be said to exist, or are the words and deeds of elites sufficient to mark its beginning?[14] Since communal perceptions are neither fixed nor uniform but subject to steady mutation, gauges for its timing can only calibrate degrees, not absolutes, of nationhood.

If nations are souls, then states are bodies, giving form and function to corporate organizations. States are, in short, the structures of government. Yet, although a nation is not the same as a state, the two are connected and often conflated as a "nation-state." This term implies that a national community and the administrative "roof" above it are, or should be, congruent and mutually reinforcing.[15] Stable countries that are fortified by a high degree of popular participation in government and public life often fulfill the nation-state ideal because they enjoy the sense of citizenship—of common rights, responsibilities, and concerns—which promotes social cohesion. By contrast, countries that have low levels of popular involvement in the public sphere and little integration across layers of ethnicity, religion, and class often fall short of the nation-state ideal. In a weak nation-state the ruling structure may be strong even while the population lacks cohesion and group morale. The result, in such a case, is a disjuncture between people and polity which places the nation-state in crisis, leaving it vulnerable to chronic ethnic, religious, or civil strife, and dictatorial, corrupt, or unresponsive government.

The former European colonies of Africa and Asia have been so susceptible to crises of this kind, that observers have coined a term to describe their situation. They call it the postcolonial predicament,[16] implying that the colonial legacy bears some relationship to, and responsibility for, the nation-state in crisis. Indeed, colonial states often passed four congenital weaknesses to their independent heirs.

First, and most obviously, colonial states imposed borders, which were as arbitrary for the Sudan as they were for countries like Gambia, Iraq, and even India (where no empire-builders before the British had subjugated the entire subcontinent, including the Dravidian south).[17] Hence, nationalists in colonial territories had to invent nations to match borders, a process that barely had time to start in many regions before the "colonial moment" ended.[18] Whereas by the mid–twentieth century, a country like France had spent centuries elaborating its nation and state,[19] a country like the Sudan, by contrast, had less than sixty years to cohere within its borders before gaining independence. Modern borders have also been restrictive, relative to borders centuries ago, because they have been so inflexible, recognized by international communities like the United Nations and fixed on paper maps.

Second, colonial states encouraged cultural plurality, rather than homogeneity, as an instrument of control. The more mixed a population was, the easier divide-and-rule became.[20] This very diversity, which worked to the advantage of colonial rulers, posed grave challenges to the independent "national" state as it sought to integrate constituent groups. As one political theorist points out, "It is incompatible with nationality to think of the members of the nation as people who merely happen to have been thrown together in one place and forced to share a common fate, in the way that the occupants of a lifeboat, say, have been accidentally thrown together."[21] But in fact, in many colonies, various groups did feel tossed together and feared the prospects of living communally. In British India, for example, many Muslims, as a minority vis-à-vis Hindus, feared being outnumbered in a secular system based on individual votes. Hence, Muslim leaders chose partition in 1947, creating an eastern and western Pakistan. In the Sudan, Southern peoples, coming from underdeveloped regions far from the Khartoum core, objected to the imbalance of power—economic, political, and cultural—that would allow Muslim Northerners to rule and set policy alone. These objections sparked an army mutiny in 1955, months before Britain's final withdrawal, signaling the start of the first civil war between North and South. In Nigeria, meanwhile, the turn to civil war in 1967 (when the southeast tried to secede as Biafra), was simply a delayed reaction to the decolonization process, arising, as in the Sudanese case, from the regional and ethnic inequalities that were affecting representation quotas in the civil service and military especially.[22]

Third, colonial states were highly autocratic—benign despotisms at best. Lacking local parliaments to keep them in check, they developed all-embracing powers. "The result," noted one analyst, with Africa in mind, "[was] not only a stronger bureaucracy in relation to society as a whole, but also in relation to the rights and liberties of its individual members. The state [was] on the way to becoming stronger than society in a colonial territory."[23] Given such strong-arm states, the postcolonial shift in many countries to one-party or military rule was not surprising; nationalists who inherited the reins of control at independence—like, for example, Kwame Nkrumah of Ghana—found autocracy more amenable than government by consensus in managing their young regimes.[24] In the Sudan, too, General Abboud stepped into power in 1958 (just two years after formal independence) with a mission to rescue the government from factional paralysis—the result of too many opinions, and too little consensus, in the fledgling Parliament.[25] Autocratic military rule emerged in several other Arabic-speaking countries. In Libya (independent 1951, army coup 1969) and Iraq (nominally independent 1932, army coup 1958), military dictators emerged in the aftermath of European, post-Ottoman colonialism, in contexts where British-enthroned monarchs stood on shaky ground.

Fourth and finally, for educational and professional advancement, colonial states tended to favor specific groups whose members later became early nationalists. Their selection policies guaranteed in the long run that the power to define national values and later, at independence, to preside over national politics, would fall to a particular cadre. There were two variations on this theme. In regions that had established traditions of literacy, like Sierra Leone (among Freetown Creoles)[26] and India (among Brahmins, Parsis, and Muslim elites),[27] colonial states concentrated educational funds on young men from clerical families to ensure continuity and stability in bureaucratic practice, diffuse potential opposition from local intelligentsias, and save money in training (by extending rather than initiating literacy). By contrast, in territories that had no traditions of literacy, such as southeastern Nigeria and inland Kenya, the need for clerical workers produced opportunities for rapid social mobility, notably among Christian missionary-school converts. The result, in either case, was the rise of modern educated classes who were often drawn from uniform ethnic and social backgrounds.

In the Anglo-Egyptian Sudan, which had some traditions of Arabic–Islamic scholarship, this policy meant that the beneficiaries of advanced education and bureaucratic hiring were high-status Muslim, Arabic-speaking males from the central riverain North. Most were graduates of one government school, Khartoum's Gordon College. Relative to a population that included speakers of scores or even hundreds of languages, the educated

Northern Sudanese were strikingly homogeneous.[28] (In this regard they were unlike the Brahmins in India, who were diversified by ethnicity, effectively defined by language.) It was therefore unsurprising that as Arabic-speaking Muslims and as early nationalists, these men regarded Arabic and Islam as their nation's cultural bulwarks. After independence, they used the powers of the central government to promote their cultural vision.

DEFINING THE SUDANESE NATION

Literature was a laboratory of early nationalism throughout the colonized world. Whether writing in Bengali, Swahili, Arabic, or French, poets and essayists used literature to test their budding ideas about culture and society.[29] Thus cultivated among the literati, nationalism flourished. Its ideas often fared less well, however, when nationalists at decolonization translated them into policies and introduced them countrywide. Early Sudanese nationalism followed this course, as a study of its literary origins, intellectual development, and later translation into practice suggests.

In general, Arab and Arabic culture figured more prominently than Islam in early Sudanese nationalist thought. This was not because educated elites were inherently secularists, as some have argued,[30] but because their early nationalism was so steeped in the Arabic language and its literature. Arabic was the vehicle through which they debated the features of national identity and the goals of national progress, and extolled the nation's virtues. Arabic literature was the art form through which they portrayed the nation in words, making its territory seem more tangible, and its collective people less anonymous. Arabic literature also offered early nationalists a safe haven at a time when the colonial state stifled public criticism and agitation, particularly before the founding of the Graduates Congress in 1938. The metaphorical and allusory possibilities of literature enabled early nationalists to evade colonial censors while conveying potentially subversive meanings to peers. Harnessed to social reform, and disseminated in print, poetry and new prose forms, such as the critical essay, endorsed educational and technological developments and modernity in general.

Among the educated Northern Sudanese, the first conscious step in the process of defining a specifically Sudanese identity occurred in 1927, when the newspaper *Hadarat al-Sudan* published a series of essays by an obscure poet and sub-mamur named Hamza al-Malik Tanbal (1897–1951).[31] Writing from his post in Managil, Blue Nile Province, Tanbal argued that there could and should be a distinct Sudanese Arabic literature. Literature, he insisted, "was a weighty, momentous subject. Every writer and thinker ought to concern himself with it, because the value of the nation (*al-umma*) or its character comes out most clearly in its literature."[32]

Tanbal's ideas were radical. For the first time, a writer was adding the term "Sudanese"—still laden with its connotations of slavery and low status—to the noble Arabic language, and nevertheless was suggesting something positive.[33] Tanbal's usage signaled that the meaning of "Sudanese" was changing, taking on associations of a territorial, rather than a status-based, identity. Readers responded immediately, flooding the newspaper with letters, expressing hostility, curiosity, or doubt. In the debate that followed, literati from the riverain North argued about whether a Sudanese literature, and by extension, a Sudanese identity, was conceivable.[34]

This debate over a Sudanese literature—did it, could it, or should it exist?—touched a political nerve, helping to enflame a local controversy about the Sudan's political and cultural relationship to Egypt. Whereas some educated Northerners sympathized with the cause of Nile Valley unity, implying solidarity with Egypt in the face of British colonialism, others took a staunch separatist line under the motto of "Sudan for the Sudanese." This dispute, which whetted the factional rivalries of the colonial and independence eras, divided the two large Muslim sectarian groups of the Northern Sudan, namely, affiliates of the Khatmiyya Sufi order, who leaned toward Egypt, and of the neo-Mahdists, who stressed autonomy from Egypt.[35] This Nile Valley debate notwithstanding,[36] the idea of a special Sudanese national literature, like the idea of a distinct Sudanese nation, gained such wide appeal that even those who were "unionists" took pride in it. In other words, some maintained an abstract attachment to the cause of Nile Valley solidarity while asserting Sudanese distinction all the same.[37]

To many, the idea of a Sudanese literature sounded fine; the challenge was how to produce it. Readers wrote to ask, "What would a Sudanese literature look like?" Tanbal suggested that such a literature would convey settings, customs, and concerns that were rooted in the territorial Sudan, implying the region defined after the 1898 conquest. He applied this literary agenda to his *Diwan al-Tabi'a* (*Nature Anthology*) (1931), which contained poems that evoked different Sudanese landscapes, from sunsets in Nubia to mountains in Kordofan, and thereby staked a nationalist claim to the terrain.[38]

Over the course of the 1930s, other young writers extended Tanbal's agenda. They experimented above all on the pages of *al-Nahda* and *al-Fajr*, two literary journals which used "Sudanese literature" (*al-adab al-sudani*) to address explicitly the cause of "Sudanese nationalism" (*al-qawmiyya al-sudaniyya*). For example, they wrote stories and plays that portrayed the daily lives and worries of ordinary *effendis*, including government mamurs or clerks, and composed poems that referred to the folkloric traditions of local Muslim communities. As one writer explained, their goal through such exercises was to produce works that were genuine Sudanese, as if possessing a deep-rooted pedigree (*sudaniyya ariqat al-nasab*).[39] In retrospect, the imagery and situations of this emerging national literature drew upon the Northern, but not Southern, Sudan, illustrating the cultural specificity of the nationalist model.[40]

Muhammad Ahmad Mahjub (1905–76), a Gordon College–educated engineer, *littérateur*, and future Prime Minister, took a leading role in the literary-nationalist movement. In a series of essays printed in *al-Nahda* and *al-Fajr* and later published collectively in a volume entitled *Nahwa al-ghad* (*Toward Tomorrow*), Mahjub urged his peers to cultivate a solidarity (*asabiyya*) that would be national, rather than tribal, and stressed the Arabic language as the medium for its growth. He pressed his colleagues to develop a "national poetry" (*shi'r qawmi*) to bolster national sentiment, and encouraged them, as the country's literati, to recognize their duty toward their nation and their art.[41] In other words, Mahjub recognized that Sudanese nationalism would require active construction.

Others used *al-Nahda* and *al-Fajr* to call for the writing of a Sudanese national history, to replace the unsympathetic accounts of British, Egyptian, and Lebanese writers. One contributor lamented, for example, that the educated classes knew no more about their own country than they knew about Siberia or the Himalayas. He explained grandiloquently that the lack of historical knowledge would impede national development, because "the past is the magnifying glass through which we see the route of the future . . . [I]t is the wise guide which stands at the pulpit of the years, delivering the sermon of the ages and the warning of the epochs, clarifying in solemn silence how to surmount difficulties and pave paths, how to elevate truth and annihilate falsehood."[42] Years later, a Gordon College graduate and former *al-Fajr* essayist named Makki Shibayka became a professional historian and fulfilled this bid for national history writing; the very title of one of his books, *Al-Sudan abra al-qurun* (*The Sudan across the Centuries*) gave the nation a historical lineage that far predated the Anglo-Egyptian conquest.[43]

The educated Northern Sudanese wanted their nation's history to be old, and therefore venerable, pedigreed, and eminently justifiable. At the same time, they wanted their nation's society to seem new, and they argued that it was progressive, changing for the better, and modern.

Calls for the reform of the Northern Sudanese Muslim woman reflected this urge to be modern. On the pages of *al-Nahda* and *al-Fajr*, nationalists argued that women's un-Islamic practices and superstitions were leading to social stagnation (*jumud*) and ignorance (*jahiliyya*) and were impeding national progress. In 1931 a pseudonymous writer called "Ibn Sudan" (Son of Sudan) criticized the tattooing of women's gums and lips (*al-washm*) to signify married status, the practicing of radical "Pharaonic" female circumcision (*al-khitan al-fir'awni*), and the scarring of cheeks (*al-shillukh*) in specific patterns as a marker of Arab ethnicity.[44] More than a decade later, Sayyid Abd al-Rahman al-Mahdi, leader of the neo-Mahdists, condemned the same practices, declaring, for example, that women's tattooing of lips, like cheek scarring, was "a survival from barbarous times, and a characteristic of backward nations."[45] Ethnic scarring, in particular, came under attack as nationalists felt a growing need to abandon primordial loyalties based on "tribalism" (*qabaliyya*) in favor of a broader "Sudanese" (*sudani*) identity. Curiously, although nationalists associated scarring primarily with women, it was common among men and women alike, which points to the symbolic position that women held in the nationalist mission as objects of social reform.

In part, the nationalist mission was responding to the widening cultural gap between the sexes. Very few Muslim Northern women in the Anglo-Egyptian period gained formal educations that stressed literacy, so that females could not read about, much less contribute to, the nationalist literary debates. Coming from families of high social status, moreover, the female relatives of the early nationalists did not circulate in the public sphere. The worlds of the nationalists were changing—as a result of encounters in schools, offices, cinemas, and on the printed page—but women, in this period, shared few of their experiences.[46]

However, the reform of women had its limits; nationalists did not want them to change too much. Women may have been forces of backwardness, but they were also bearers of indigenous culture, so that their traditionalism had both negative and positive features. Indeed, precisely because of their local particularity, women's customs provided a rationale for Sudanese nationalism. For how else could one justify a separate Sudanese state within colonial borders if there were no specific cultural practices to distinguish it? More specifically, how could one rationalize a Sudan independent of Egypt, which maintained claims to unitary Nile Valley leadership throughout the Anglo-Egyptian period?

In short, the enterprise of journalism showed that the nationalist movement was concerned with Arabic as the language of literature, culture, and politics, and as a vehicle for social reform. But Arabism (*uruba*), meaning an ethnicity rooted in Arab ways, was equally important to their endeavor, as was the insertion of the Sudan in Arab history. Thus, nationalist literati took pains to connect Sudanese Arabic culture to the glorious history of Arab expansion and state-formation that had followed the rise of Islam in the seventh century. They also stressed connections to the noble Arab past in two other ways: first, by writing about Abbasid and Andalusian themes;[47] and second, by surveying Northern Sudanese social and literary conventions (for example, among Kordofanian bedouin) and attributing them to ancient Arabian practice.[48] *Kitab al-arabiyya fi al-Sudan* (*The Book of Arabic/Arabness in the Sudan*) was one such cultural survey affirming local Arab authenticity. Written by a Gordon College graduate and schoolteacher who was also known for having published an "Arabism anthology" (*Diwan al-Uruba*), *Kitab al-arabiyya* was one of the first Arabic monographs ever printed in Khartoum.[49] In the words of a skeptical British reviewer, "The author champions the thesis that the modern inhabitants of the Northern Sudan are of pure Arab descent, and one of the objects of the book is to refute the contrary view which would reduce the Arab influence to a comparatively slight infiltration acting on the aboriginal Nubian stock."[50] The educated Northern Sudanese held the book in such high esteem that it was reissued in 1967 with the backing of the Minister of Education, who praised it "as an index of the deep-rootedness and faith of the Sudan in its Arabism."[51]

In a 1932 article titled "Al-Shu'ur al-qawmi wa-hajatuna ilayhi" ("Nationalist Sentiment and Our Need for It"), Muhammad Ahmad Mahjub stated that the Sudan was held together by bonds of geography, ethnicity (*al-jins*), religion, and language. He asked, therefore, why nationalist sentiment was not stronger. Nationalism (*al-qawmiyya*), he argued, "rests, at its heart, on a unity of language and ethnic characteristics, and on agreement in religion and on the ideal which the group seeks to realize."[52] Although the colonial territory of the Sudan contained peoples who spoke scores of languages and professed local religions, Mahjub and his peers (regardless of the sectarian differences among them) felt that the Sudan derived, or should derive, a fundamental unity from Arabic and Islam. To develop a strong nation, Mahjub contested, "it is inevitable that we embrace the Arabic Islamic heritage."[53]

Mahjub's fellow nationalists shared these convictions and tried to act on them, during decolonization and after. In 1949, for example, they used newly acquired powers over educational policy to declare Arabic the official national language of school instruction. Northern educators went on in the

1950s and '60s to pursue this agenda with zeal, particularly in the South, where colonial government and missionary schools had promoted English and local vernaculars as languages of learning and print.[54] They decided, in other words, that if Arab or Arabic identity did not exist in certain regions, then their policies should help to create it. At the same time, politicians reversed the exclusive educational privileges that Christian missionaries had enjoyed in parts of the South and in the Nuba Mountains, and opened educational and charity-based opportunities to Islamic organizations.[55] Believing that Christian missionaries had inhibited national unity by propagating Christianity instead of Islam, Northern politicians went further in 1957, a year after independence, by nationalizing mission schools, and later, in 1964, by deporting foreign missionaries.[56]

As champions of social progress, early nationalists viewed themselves as standard-bearers for modernity. Thus, they developed a *mission civilisatrice* that paralleled the colonial confidence of the British, or emerged as a defensive reaction to it. While not writing explicitly of their "civilizing mission," they conveyed the idea through metaphors of cultural conquest and battle that posed Arabism and Islam against the forces of backwardness, ignorance, and superstition.

The writings of Ahmad Khayr (1905–94), a Gordon College–educated translator and later lawyer, helped to set this tone. In *Kifah jil (Struggle of a Generation)*, a 1948 treatise which he intended as "the biography of a generation," Ahmad Khayr argued that his cohorts had promoted progressive nationalism in place of the retrograde tribalism that the British had boosted in the heyday of indirect rule. He and his fellow nationalists "shook the dust off the years, triumphed over antiquated traditions, and shattered the chains of a people living amid fetters of the Middle Ages." They "triumphed in the battle against tribalism" and "liberated thought from the delusions of superstition." They won a war against ignorance and illiteracy, and founded a movement aiming for independent and democratic government.[57] Through these victories over backwardness, he argued, the Sudan was earning itself an important place in the nascent Arab East, which was "getting ready for a great jump forward, a total revolution, thereby ending . . . the ages of ignorance."[58]

None of the nationalists of the colonial period assigned importance to the Sudan's African heritage or drew pride from its non-Islamic and non-Arabic cultures.[59] Nor did they praise non-Muslim, non-Arabic-speaking peoples in the poems and other literary forms that were so important to their construction of the "Sudanese." Hence, in 1941, when Muhammad Ahmad Mahjub suggested that the peoples of the Sudan were the historical product of a "mixing" or "commingling" of immigrant "Arabs" with an original population of "Blacks" (*al-sud*, or *al-zunuj*), he attributed cultural superiority, acquired through reason, intelligence, and courage, to the "Arabs."[60] Many Northern Sudanese thinkers of the generation that followed continued to hold assumptions of the Sudan as a "fortress of Arabism and Islam" in Africa.[61] As late as 1985, al-Sadiq al-Mahdi, political heir of the Mahdi family, continued to aver that full-scale Arabization and Islamization were imperative for national unity, particularly in light of the "Southern problem."[62]

Writing in 1965, the historian Ja'far Muhammad Ali Bakhit (who had briefly served as a sub-mamur in the early 1950s) argued that the Sudanese nationalist movement was stronger than those of all other African colonies because of Islam, which had endowed the North with "a higher sense of community than most African dependencies and a talent for absorbing alien cultural and political imports." The alien was above all the African, with its divisive tribal dynamics. "Culturally and politically," he explained, "the Northern Sudan from the fourteenth century had been an Arab salient of Muslim Egypt and the Middle East into the negroid and pagan civilisations of tropical Africa."[63] In a history of modern Sudanese thought written in the mid-1960s, another writer made this cultural prioritizing of the Arab over the African even clearer. "Through this [cultural] cross-pollination," he wrote, "emerged a new creature: the modern Sudanese, who was not formed of pure Arab or of pure African (*zanji*) blood, but who certainly combined in his tissues the two kinds of bloods, and carried in his brain the product of the more powerful and more perfect culture: Arab culture."[64]

Southern intellectuals have rejected this view of Arab supremacy, in peacetime and in war. Individuals like the anthropologist and novelist, Francis Mading Deng, or the hydrologist turned military leader, John Garang (head of the Sudan People's Liberation Army), have maintained that Sudanese identity should be recognized as a hybrid identity, to which Arab and African cultures have equally contributed.[65] Some Muslim non-Arabs, representing communities like the Fur or the Beja, have also raised their voices to reject Arab supremacy, affirming instead the legitimacy of subnational cultures, as well as the continuing relevance of ethnic or tribal identities, within the modern system.[66]

This divergence of views over national identity underlines complex questions for dispute. How monocultural must a national identity be, and, by extension, can a theory of national oneness accommodate social diversity? Most nation-states struggle to answer these same questions; a few, like the Sudan, succumb to war.

UNCIVIL WAR

On January 1, 1956, the Sudan entered independence with fixed borders, an administrative apparatus inherited from the colonial state, and a nationalist agenda set by former colonial employees. Since then, the country has spent all but twelve years of its independent existence embroiled in civil war. Available statistics for the years from 1983 to 1998 (during the country's second and ongoing war) suggest that in this period alone 1.9 million died, 350,000 fled abroad as refugees, and 4 million fled inside national borders—giving the Sudan the largest internally displaced population in the world.[67] Sudanese death tolls and population displacements far exceeded those of the Arab–Israeli conflict, the Iran–Iraq War, and the Lebanese civil war—indeed, of all individual intra- and interstate conflicts that occurred in the Middle East and North Africa after the foundation of Israel in 1948.[68]

The civil war has been a fight to define the nation-state—its official legal, linguistic, and religious codes, and its division of powers. Centered in Khartoum and dominated by riverain Northerners, successive Sudanese governments—the democratically elected and the dictatorial alike—have maintained the ideals of the early Northern nationalists, who as a narrow elite, sought to construct a nation in their own cultural image. Their political heirs have therefore asserted that the Sudan is and must be defined by Arabic and Islam, and have believed that cultural homogeneity, not plurality, is required for national unity. For this reason, Northern politicians at the end of the twentieth century, like their nationalist predecessors a half century earlier, saw assimilation, through the spread of Arabic and Islam, as imperative.[69]

But Southerners and other non-Arabic-speaking peoples have resisted assimilative efforts. They have resented the unilateral nature of central government policies which have failed to account for and accommodate regional viewpoints, as well as the unequal distribution of power which has allowed riverain Northerners to dictate terms of government. A result has been the politicization of language policies, with Northerners insisting on Arabic as the country's sole official language, and Southerners pushing for the dual recognition of English and Arabic, as well as indigenous languages in some situations.[70] Most Southerners in the postcolonial period have not resisted Arabic education per se; they have only resisted its exclusivity and the idea of its supremacy. A sense of cultural assault, coupled with wider grievances over chronic economic underdevelopment and political under-representation outside the riverain North, have fueled the two rounds of civil war. Added to this has been resentment among Southerners over the central government's exploitation of Southern natural resources[71]: first water (a struggle manifest in the stalled Jonglei Canal Project in the Upper Nile swamplands, which would have benefited the North and Egypt), and later, oil, developed with the construction of a cross-country pipeline and first exported in 1999.

Along with Rwanda, Burundi, and the constituent parts of the former Yugoslavia, the Sudan in the 1990s illustrated the crises of nationalism and the nation-state and confirmed a mood of pessimism among scholars with regard to identity politics. In the words of one historian, nationalism had become a "matter of ethnic politics, the reason why people in the Third World killed each other—sometimes in wars between regular armies, sometimes, more distressingly, in cruel and often protracted civil wars, and increasingly, it seemed, by . . . virtually unstoppable acts of terrorism."[72] As if to acknowledge complicity in a problem, another remarked that "historians are to nationalism what poppy-growers in Pakistan are to heroin addicts: we supply the essential raw materials for the market."[73] Harsher still was a political theorist who denounced nationalism as "an upwardly mobile, power-hungry and potentially dominating form of language game which pretends to be universal," destroying cultural plurality and oppressing domestic critics. "Nationalism," he added, "is a scavenger . . . a pathological form of national identity."[74]

Observing the plight of nation-states in crisis, some political analysts began to call for the development of a stronger "civil society," in which the state would have to establish a new contract with the nation: a basic agreement on cohabitation entailing a commitment to mutual well-being and tolerance, not uniform culture, as the source of common cause.[75] A move in this direction occurred in the Sudan once before. By the Addis Ababa Agreement of 1972, Ja'far Numayri (military dictator from 1969 to 1985) addressed the grievances that had propelled the first civil war by agreeing to decentralize power, develop the South, and show tolerance for diversity. Within a decade, however, the Numayri regime had reneged on most of its promises. Moreover, following what observers described as a personal Islamic awakening, Numayri, toward the end of his reign, promoted assimilationist agendas again, notably by declaring the nationwide imposition of Shari'a law in 1983—a move that deepened Southern alienation. This failed experiment illustrates the basic obstacle to the creation of a civil society: it depends on the willingness of the strong to curb their own power.

In the 1990s, as the civil war raged and hopes of reconciliation dimmed, Sudanese living abroad increasingly alluded to the possibility of break-up— of legal divorce between North and South.[76] One historian and SPLA fighter even mentioned a possible name for a breakaway, independent South: Nilia, named after the Nile, as an "eternal commemoration of [Southerners'] prolonged suffering while defending it and the entire land."[77]

There are, however, few precedents for redrawing national lines. As arbitrary as they were, the colonial borders of Africa and Asia have stuck.[78] In Africa, in spite of protests by early nationalists over the continent's "Balkanization,"[79] the Organization of African Unity, or OAU (founded in 1963), pledged and backed up a commitment to respect political borders.[80] In the Middle East, years of pan-Arabist rhetoric condemning colonial borders and calling for their erasure had little effect, except perhaps in the two Yemens, which cautiously reunited in 1990.[81] According to one historian, the Gulf War finally dispelled the pan-Arab "myth" that condemned colonial borders, by showing that even Kuwait—a "despicable emirate" which was an "utterly artificial British creation"—was able to proclaim national distinction in order to resist absorption into neighboring Iraq.[82]

Borders have stayed firm in the "nation-state" system for two reasons: first, because individual states have resisted yielding or sharing access to power and local resources, such as oil, through mergers; and second, because changing borders might court mayhem by setting a precedent for others to follow. For the sake of preserving the status quo, the Arab League and the OAU have discouraged the redrawing of lines, as have other postcolonial countries, such as India and Indonesia, which have both been struggling to prevent regional secessions.

The colony and the early nationalists bequeathed two incompatible legacies to the Sudan and to other African and Asian nation-states: fixed borders and the premise of monocultural national identity. In the absence of sufficient power to erase local diversity, one or the other must give way.

Conclusion: The Colony and the Nation
Lessons from the Sudan

This book originated in a desire to understand how colonialism worked on the ground, affected local cultures, and influenced the genesis and substance of the nationalism that arose in its midst.

It began with a specific concern: to understand how a small number of Britons in one large piece of Africa, namely, the Anglo-Egyptian Sudan, had developed a reputation for such efficiency in running a vast and diverse territory. Time and time again, in history books, in memoirs, even in casual conversations with people who were born or had spent years in the place, words of awe resurfaced. "They ran the place like a Swiss watch," a Sudan-born expatriate declared.[1] A mentor once confided, "When they left, the Sudanese pound was stronger and worth slightly more than the British pound itself!"[2] "The Sudan was poor," a historian noted soberly, as if by way of explanation; its administration "did not allow extravagance." Its rulers, he suggested, had a genius for stretching pennies—not Britain's own pennies, just Egypt's and Sudan's.[3] When a former British official revisited the country in 1972, years after independence, the Sudanese president reportedly volunteered (much to the later chagrin of a compatriot) that "The Sudan is not as efficiently and competently run as when you British were here!"[4] Even their sex lives were impeccable. A chronicler of imperial sexuality noted that the Sudan's British administrators had a moral code so high and a regime "so free of scandal as to be in itself scandalous."[5]

How did they do it? How did they convince so many people of their mastery and rectitude, producing legends that outlived them?

Their apparent mastery was all the more puzzling because the Sudan after independence seemed to be unmanageable, a discordant assemblage of peoples locked for years in civil war. The image of colonial calm and stability therefore contrasted with the violence and crisis that followed; it seemed as if a break in the past had occurred. As if to lament a colonial influence that had been transitory and whisked away, historians of the colonial era and retired British officials wrote books whose very titles evoked winds passing, sands shifting, and shadows slipping, fading.[6]

Of course, in facing a postcolonial crisis, the Sudan was not alone. After World War II, the collapse of the British Empire in sub-Saharan Africa, the Middle East, and across the globe left a string of countries inhabiting borders that were impositions of colonial conquests. In many of these, populations and governments were still struggling to find stability and communal cohesion.

Thus, a question begged for an answer: What was the relationship of the nation-state to the colonial order that came before it, and how did the history of colonialism bear on communal identities? Investigating these questions, this book set out to examine colonialism, not as an abstraction of power, but as a feature of everyday life—the sum of manifold social encounters and small administrative deeds that affected how people lived and related to each other. It focused on the petty local employees of the colonial regime: men who, as administrative mediators and cultural conduits, lived intimately with colonialism yet yearned to live without it. In the process, the book reached several conclusions which have broad comparative relevance for understanding the connected histories of colonialism and nationalism in Africa and Asia during the twentieth century.

(1) The colonial system depended on a wide participatory base. To run each territory cheaply, the ruling class of Britons trained and hired vast numbers of local recruits and paid them local salaries. These individuals performed the myriad small tasks of government, from filing papers to counting taxes. The great British achievement was in managing these staffs and deploying limited financial, educational, and military resources to the maximum advantage of the colonial state.

(2) Petty employees were as much a part of the colonial system as the Britons who ruled it. Throughout their empire, and in order to maintain control, the British relied on what historians have variously called confidence tricks, bluffwork, smoke-and-mirrors maneuvers, and pageantry. But even in this, they did not act alone. Colonialism was a day-to-day performance of power, in which petty employees took part by presenting the face of government to the general populace in their capacity as inspectors, collectors, law enforcers, teachers, and clerks.

(3) The petty employees in colonial service were often highly educated and literate men, who left records that make their lives and careers recoverable. British sources alone do not tell the stories of these men; they more

often give an impression of their underlings as social ciphers, or as characters kind-hearted but befuddled (an impression which serves to emphasize British competence by contrast). In fact, many of these petty employees distinguished themselves in clubs and literary circles after work, pouring efforts into poems and essays that they sometimes published in periodicals or collective anthologies. Years later, the most accomplished among them even wrote memoirs. In short, these men were members of a thriving culture of print and increasingly, too, of images. Possessing the power of writing as well as access to film technologies, they left behind texts and photographs that have made them historically accessible.

(4) Petty colonial employees were early nationalists, who, in poetry and prose, called forth a nation in their own cultural image. In the course of their educations and careers, petty government employees came to see the colonial territory as congruent with a nation—their nation—consisting of a common people, occupying a land, and having an intrinsic right to self-rule. Relying on the periodical press to share and exchange their ideas, they explored in words the nation's values, landscapes, and heritage. Yet, their ethnic and social limitations—the product, in part, of educational selection policies—constrained their view of the nation, by convincing them that their own cultural traditions were its definitive features.

(5) The conditions of colonial employment were conducive to the creation and growth of nationalism. Privileged to attend British-style schools that groomed them for government service, the men who became petty colonial employees developed a firm grasp of literacy (often in both English and an indigenous written language), a familiarity with new print and film media, and a confidence based on their cultural savvy, professional knowhow, and connection to the ruling class. When they graduated and took jobs in the regime, authorities sent them on professional migrations that periodically transferred them from post to post within the territory's fixed borders. Their exceptional familiarity with the landscape made them the first to perceive the colonial territory as a national unit. Meanwhile, meeting colleagues in employees' clubs and at Old Boys school events, and engaging in discussions on the pages of journals, they described, discussed, debated this nation and gave it a clearer shape. At the same time, in private gatherings, they shared grievances about their professional subordination to Britons, and more abstractly, about their opposition to foreign control. Yet, for the most part, and despite their frustrations, they were not agitators or subversives; their livelihoods depended on government jobs, in which they also took pride. As their confidence grew in their collective abilities, so did their calls for greater administrative autonomy and, ultimately, for self-rule.

(6) When decolonization occurred, the bureaucrat-nationalists were obvious heirs to political power, but tensions soon grew, within their ranks and without. Decolonization, by producing dramatic and sudden opportunities for professional mobility, turned province tax-collectors into province governors, engineers into ambassadors, and teachers into prime ministers. Yet, ideological differences, ethnic biases, and professional or social rivalries soon surfaced among the nationalists once their common opponents, the British, were gone. In the long run, these internal rivalries and disagreements contributed to and compounded political instability in the postcolonial period. So, too, did resentments among those who questioned the allocation of power and resources within the new government and called for greater countrywide parity, in educational and professional opportunities, in levels of economic development, and in political representation.

(7) After independence, nationalist politicians worked to engineer nationalism by making their elite ideology more popular, but often lacked the resources to impose their vision successfully. Elected in parliaments or appointed to high posts in ministries and provinces, these new men in power set about implementing policies that reflected their nationalist ideals. In their quest for a national monoculture, they were far more ambitious than the colonial rulers had been before them. For, whereas the British had welcomed diversity as a tactic of divide-and-rule, nationalists saw the existence of too much diversity as a problem that would complicate the tasks of a central government and undermine the social unity on which the ideal of the nation was built—hence, the application of universal educational, linguistic, and legal policies. However, unevenness in infrastructural development and in the distribution of schools meant that nationalist politicians had trouble imposing their vision, particularly in peripheral and underdeveloped regions. Moreover, some groups outside the politicians' cultural mainstream resented attempts to impose cultural strictures upon them and grew increasingly alienated from official nationalism as the postcolonial period progressed.

(8) Some of the very features that benefited the colonial state hobbled the nation-state that followed. The colonial state had presumed no consent; as a piece of a larger empire, it was ultimately maintained by the coercion of its administrators, with the financial and strategic interests of the distant metropole in mind. The nation-state required something different: a degree of consent in the affairs of the state based on the perception that the state was acting in the popular interest. The nation that inherited the state of the colony lacked wide consent and therefore faced many problems.

(9) Colonialism had a transformative, not transitory, impact, and left enduring legacies, among them fixed borders, centralized states, and sharp

inequalities in social and regional power. The nation-states of Africa and Asia are still living with colonialism, their vitality often sapped by internecine conflicts, coercive central governments, and culturally exclusive conceptions of nationalism fashioned by the colonial employees of a bygone era. Nevertheless, their borders seem likely to endure, leading to calls for less rigid notions of corporate identity and a diffusion of power and resources.

As nationalism comes under scrutiny, historical understanding must figure into the process of consciously revising communal identity, because history is a central element in the engineering of a nation and because history can make sense of the present by offering guidance, warnings, and lessons. "To know about the past," wrote one historian, "is to know that things have not always been as they are now, and by implication that they need not remain the same in the future."[7] Ernst Renan, the late-nineteenth-century French philosopher, would have agreed. While discussing the meaning and nature of nations, he asserted, "Man is a slave neither of his race nor his language, nor of his religion, nor of the course of rivers nor of the direction taken by mountain chains."[8] People can make their nations and communities as they please, by interpreting the past for their present and future.

What makes nations and empires succeed or fail, flourish or collapse? This question has been fascinating historians perennially. The fourteenth-century historical philosopher, Ibn Khaldun, was one of the most distinguished to seek its answer. Setting out to explain "how changing conditions affected human affairs, how certain dynasties came to occupy an ever wider space in the world, and how they settled the earth until they heard the call and their time was up," he produced a grand synthesis of Islamic world history, a masterwork in comparative study for his time.[9] Reflecting on communal identities, Ibn Khaldun described the sense of solidarity, or *asabiyya*, that makes social groups cohere or fall apart in its absence. In contemporary Africa and Asia, achieving *asabiyya* will require, at the very least, reaching some consensus on what the nation should be and how it should live with its colonial past.

Glossary

The definitions below explain terms as they were or have been used in the Sudanese social context.

ahfad
: "grandchildren" or "descendants"; name given to the set of schools founded by the educator Babikr Badri and retained today by the Ahfad University for Women in Omdurman, Sudan.

ahliyya
: adjective meaning "people's" or "popular"; term used to describe the popular movement for founding non-government schools in the Northern Sudan after 1926, as well as the schools that resulted from the movement. The name is retained today by Omdurman Ahlia University.

babu
: title of address formerly used in British India to refer to a local gentleman educated in a "modern"-style school, proficient in English, and typically employed in a civil administrative or clerical job; the Indian analogue of *effendi* (q.v.).

bashkatib
: head clerk.

Bilad al-Sudan
: "Lands of the Blacks"; term used by early Muslim geographers to describe the lands stretching from the Red Sea in the east to the Atlantic Ocean in the west; the Sudan derives its name from this term.

effendi
: title of address for a non-European Muslim man educated in a "modern"-style school and accustomed in the early-twentieth-century Sudan to wear the Western suit with a Fez or tarbush (q.v.); the term is now defunct.

effendiyya the "modern" educated class; collective plural of *effendi*.

al-Fajr "The Dawn"; literary journal published in Khartoum from 1934 to 1937; like the journal *al-Nahda* (q.v.), it played a leading role in the development of nationalist ideologies.

Hadarat al-Sudan government-subsidized Arabic newspaper published in Khartoum from 1919 to 1938; its owners and editors took a nationalist "Sudan for the Sudanese" stance against Egyptian claims to a role in the Sudan.

hakim a medical assistant; or one of the "sanitary barbers" who vaccinated, set broken bones, registered births and deaths, and circumcised boys.

imma turban; in the Sudan, it is usually formed from loosely wound, white cotton.

jallabiyya long, loose robe worn by males, generally made from white cotton.

khalwa village school teaching rudimentary literacy, traditionally through Qur'an recitation.

kuttab village or district school teaching basic reading, writing, and arithmetic, in addition to Qur'an study.

Ma'had al-Ilmi religious institute organized in 1912 around the Omdurman mosque, offering certificates in the Islamic sciences and staffed by members of the *ulama* (q.v.); this institution was the predecessor to Omdurman Islamic University.

Malja' al-Qirsh "Piaster House"; an orphanage school organized in 1931 by Northern Sudanese graduates; its name referred to its mode of fundraising through the collection of piaster donations from the public.

mamur a petty district official responsible for collecting taxes, investigating crimes, etc.

markaz district office or administrative center.

muwallad term used particularly to refer to an individual born in the Sudan of mixed parentage, especially Egyptian-Sudanese parentage; plural *muwalladin*.

al-Nahda "The Awakening," or "The Revival"; literary journal published in Khartoum from 1931 to 1932; like the journal *al-Fajr* (q.v.), it played a leading role in the development of nationalist ideologies.

nazir	leader of an Arab tribe or of an Arab tribal section.
qadi	a judge in the Islamic law courts.
qasida	an ode or praise poem.
Shari'a	Islamic law.
shaykh	title of respect used for elderly gentlemen, religious scholars, and local dignitaries.
shillukh	a pattern of facial scars on the cheeks or temples, used to signify membership in a Sudanese Arab tribe or tribal section.
sub-mamur	a deputy mamur (q.v.), who served as an officer of police.
Sudan Political Service	during the Anglo-Egyptian period, the elite, exclusively male and British civil administration of assistant district commissioners, district commissioners, province governors, and policy makers; abbreviated S.P.S.
tarbush	a Fez hat.
ulama	those highly learned in Islamic law and scripture; singular *alim*.
umda	head of a village or town; mayor. It is sometimes rendered in English as "omda."

Abbreviations

A.D.C.	Assistant District Commissioner
CMS	Church Missionary Society archives, University of Birmingham
D.C.	District Commissioner
EUL	Manuscripts and Special Collections, University of Edinburgh
FO	Foreign Office Papers of the Public Record Office, London
GMCR	Gordon Memorial College at Khartoum, *Report and Accounts*
IJAHS	*International Journal of African Historical Studies*
IJMES	*International Journal of Middle East Studies*
JAH	*Journal of African History*
NRO	National Records Office, Sudan Government, Khartoum
PRO	Public Record Office, Kew Gardens, London
SAD	Sudan Archive, University of Durham
SGED	Sudan Government, *Annual Report of the Education Department*
SGR	Sudan Government, *Reports on the Finances, Administration, and Condition of the Sudan*
SNR	*Sudan Notes and Records*
SOAS	School of Oriental and African Studies Archives, University of London
S.P.S.	Sudan Political Service
WO	War Office Papers of the Public Record Office, London

Notes

1: LIVING WITH COLONIALISM

1. Macaulay, "Government of India," 8:122.
2. I have adapted the phrase "intimate enemies" from Nandy, *The Intimate Enemy*.
3. Billig, *Banal Nationalism*.
4. For a recent work on this theme in Middle Eastern studies, see Thompson, *Colonial Citizens*.
5. See Tosh, *The Pursuit of History*, ch. 1, "The Uses of History," 1–26, esp. p. 7.
6. Lenin, *Imperialism*.
7. Mamdani, *Citizen and Subject*, 16.
8. Osterhammel, *Colonialism*, 63.
9. Kirk-Greene, "The Thin White Line."
10. Anderson and Killingray, "Consent, Coercion, and Colonial Control." For comparisons with France's African empire, see Echenberg, *Colonial Conscripts*.
11. Guha, *Dominance without Hegemony*.
12. The phrase *Europeanized native* comes from Lugard, *The Dual Mandate in British Tropical Africa*.
13. I use the term *intellectuals* not only as a synonym for the highly educated but as a designation for articulators, interlocutors, and agitators. See Gramsci, *The Prison Notebooks*; Said, *Representations of the Intellectual*, 11.
14. Bayly, *Empire and Information*.
15. Boehmer, *Colonial and Postcolonial Literature*; MacKenzie, *Imperialism and Popular Culture*.
16. Anderson, *Imagined Communities*.
17. Goody, *The Power of the Written Tradition*.
18. Renan, "What Is a Nation?"
19. Brook and Schmid, *Nation Work*.
20. Mahjub, *Nahwa al-ghad*, 228.

21. Osterhammel, *Colonialism*, 4, 10.

22. Eagleton, *The Idea of Culture*, 34.

23. Said, *Culture and Imperialism*, 14.

24. Dirks, *Colonialism and Culture*.

25. Headrick, *The Tools of Empire*, 117–19; Zulfo, *Karari*, 98–107.

26. Holt and Daly, *A History of the Sudan*, 96.

27. Churchill, *The River War*, 2:164.

28. Kirk-Greene, *The Sudan Political Service*.

29. Letter from Sir Donald Hawley to the author, dated Little Cheverell House, Nr. Devizes, Wiltshire, August 4, 1997. Donald Hawley served in the Sudan from 1941 to 1955.

30. PRO, FO 371/13151: Foreign Office minute, "Participation of Sudan Government at Imperial Conferences," dated September 25, 1928.

31. Powell, "Colonized Colonizers."

32. Sharkey-Balasubramanian, "The Egyptian Colonial Presence in the Anglo-Egyptian Sudan, 1898–1932"; and al-Hardallu, *Al-Ribat al-thaqafi bayna Misr wa'l-Sudan*.

33. Barbour, *The Republic of the Sudan*, 15.

34. Estimates range from 33 languages on the low end in *The New Encyclopaedia Britannica* (Micropaedia, 1990 edition), 11:349–50, to 595 on the high end, cited in Harir, "Recycling the Past in the Sudan," 18. Metz, *Sudan*, suggested about 400; Nelson et al., *Area Handbook for the Democratic Republic of the Sudan* , vii, suggested that the Sudan had "roughly 115 languages, including twenty-six major ones."

35. Daly, *Empire on the Nile*, 194–201.

36. Sraïeb, *Le Collège Sadiki de Tunis, 1875–1956*; Goldthorpe, *An African Elite*; and July, *The Origins of Modern African Thought*.

37. Beshir, *Educational Development in the Sudan, 1898–1956*, 38–39.

38. SAD, 724/14/3: Sir Andrew Balfour Papers, magazine article, "The Eton of the Soudan: Gordon College at Khartoum," *Sphere*, November 12, 1904; Mangan, "Ethics and Ethnocentricity: Imperial Education in British Tropical Africa," 144.

39. Ibrahim, *Tarikh al-ta'lim al-dini fi al-Sudan*

40. Until 1931, Sudan government officials received a "climate allowance" on top of their salaries for serving in climates below 12°N latitude.

41. Sanderson and Sanderson, *Education, Religion, and Politics in Southern Sudan, 1899–1964*.

42. See Spaulding and Kapteijns, "The Orientalist Paradigm in the Historiography of the Late Precolonial Sudan."

43. Sanderson, "The Development of Girls' Education in the Northern Sudan, 1898–1960."

44. Iliffe, *Africans*, 223.

45. Young, *The Politics of Cultural Pluralism*.

46. Brubaker, *Citizenship and Nationhood in France and Germany*, x–xi; and Anderson, *Imagined Communities*.

47. Featherstone, *Undoing Culture*, 81.

48. Nandy, *The Intimate Enemy*, 3.

49. On the politics of authenticity in the postcolonial Sudan, see Hale, *Gender Politics in Sudan*, 6–7.

50. The Nubians of the far north, who do not speak Arabic as their first language, are an exceptional and in many ways ambiguous case. Many Nubian males achieved Arabic fluency and obtained advanced educations to such an extent that they were able to compete for and secure prominent government jobs in the colonial and postcolonial periods. They became part of the political mainstream without losing a sense of their distinct Nubian identity (see Hale, "The Changing Ethnic Identity of Nubians in an Urban Milieu").

51. Niblock, *Class and Power in the Sudan*, 147–58.

52. Lesch, *The Sudan*, 34–35.

53. Sirr al-Khatm al-Khalifa, interview with author. In 1950 Sirr al-Khatm al-Khalifa, then an Education Department official (and years later, Prime Minister), went to Juba to begin implementing these Arabicization policies.

54. Cited in Sandell, *English Language in Sudan*, 66. See also ch. 4, "Conflict and Peace in the South," 69–91, regarding these controversial policies.

55. Ruay, *The Politics of Two Sudans*, 72.

56. For a discussion of "everyday history" in European contexts, see Lüdtke, *The History of Everyday Life*.

57. SAD, 764/9/48: J. G. S. MacPhail Papers, copy of "Instructions for the Registration and Filing of Correspondence in the Provinces," published by the Sudan government (Khartoum: The Sudan Printing Press, 1923).

58. Perhaps the most meticulous keeper of records was Sir Reginald Wingate, whose papers, upon his death, filled up the billiard room, nursery, writing room, and even chauffeur's quarters of his Scottish estate (see Daly, *The Sirdar*, 3–4).

59. The most important British archive for Sudan materials is Durham University's Sudan Archive, which holds the papers of over 250 men and women who lived or worked in the Anglo-Egyptian Sudan. This work also draws upon individual British collections at the University of London (SOAS), Edinburgh University, and the Wellcome Institute for the History of Medicine (London), as well as on missionary records of the Church Missionary Society, deposited at the University of Birmingham.

60. Daly and Forbes, *The Sudan*; Graham-Brown, *Images of Women*. A useful methodological discussion of photography in the service of history is Forlacroix, "La photographie au service de l'histoire d'Afrique."

61. Consider the case of two Northern Sudanese colonial employees who paid from their own pocket to have their books published. The first was Hamza al-Malik Tanbal, who spent £E25 to have his poetry anthology, *Diwan al-Tabi'a* published in Cairo in 1931. This information came out when a board of discipline was convened to investigate whether one of the poems in the volume amounted to libel, as some of his former Northern Sudanese co-workers alleged. According to his record sheet, this sum would have amounted to just over one

month's salary, for he was making £E252 a year (i.e., £E21 per month) in 1931 (NRO, Personnel 3A/6/13: File of Hamza al-Malik Tanbal, statement of accused in sub-file, "Trial by Board of Discipline: Hamza Eff. Malek Tambel Melek," July 1931, and Sudan Government Record of Service and History Sheet). The second was Muhammad Abd al-Rahim, who published his literary study, *Nafathat al-yara'* in 1936, while he was an accountant in Darfur Province. In his conclusion (p. 272), he thanks the Khartoum publishers profusely for having made the project affordable by agreeing to have him pay publishing costs after, and not before, the book came out. Both of these works represent important sources for the cultural history of the period (see Tanbal, *Diwan al-Tabi'a;* Abd al-Rahim, *Nafathat al-yara'*).

62. Classic studies include Abidin, *Tarikh al-thaqafa al-arabiyya fi al-Sudan, mundhu nash'atiha ila al-asr al-hadith;* and Najila, *Malamih min al-mujtama' al-sudani.*

63. Sharkey, "*Tabaqat* of the Twentieth-Century Sudan." For a biography of a Northern Sudanese woman (written in response to the gap in the literature), see Sharkey, "Two Sudanese Midwives."

64. It is no accident that one strong English-language study, combining poetry and history in its study of Egypt, was written by a professor of Arabic literature (see Khouri, *Poetry and the Making of Modern Egypt, 1882–1922*).

65. The social force of poetry has been especially great in non-literate or low-literacy societies, where its recitation has provided a vehicle for censure or public ridicule, for example, or for the preservation of historical memory (see Finnegan, *Oral Poetry*).

66. Cooper and Stoler, *Tensions of Empire,* vii–viii.

67. Gandhi, *Postcolonial Theory,* 4.

68. Ibn Khaldun, *The Muqaddimah,* 5.

69. U.S. Committee for Refugees, *World Refugee Survey 1998,* 95–96; Hamid, *Population Displacement in the Sudan,* 55–71.

70. Ibrahim, "Civil Society and Prospects of Democratization in the Arab World"; and Lesch, "The Destruction of Civil Society in the Sudan."

71. Tilly, "How Empires End."

2: BEING "BLACK," BEING "SUDANESE"

1. Lorcin, *Imperial Identities,* 13.

2. Lewis, *The Emergence of Modern Turkey,* 1, 239–93.

3. The root is *s–w–d. Aswad* is the singular, *sud* or *sudan* the plural.

4. Kurita, "The Role of the 'Negroid but Detribalized' People in Sudanese Society, 1920s–1940s," 3:107–20.

5. Cooper, *From Slaves to Squatters.*

6. Fisher and Fisher, *Slavery and Muslim Society in Africa;* Willis, *Slaves and Slavery in Muslim Africa,* vol. 1.

7. The historian L. Carl Brown recalls hearing about the following incident in the 1956–58 period when he was an American diplomat in Khartoum:

"Muhammad Ahmad Mahjoub was speaking in legislative assembly lauding the integration of all Sudanese and emphasizing that Sudanese north and south were brothers. Thereafter, a southern representative got up to speak and—as was the case with so many Sudanese from the South—did not have great competence in Arabic. Mahjoub turned irritably to his colleague and muttered, 'What's that *abd* (slave) trying to say?'" He adds, "This was told with great relish to me in the presence of several Sudanese at, I believe, the Sudanese Cultural Center, but like all such hearsay tales it may have been distorted in the telling. Still, it has verisimilitude." (L. Carl Brown, e-mail to the author, Princeton, September 14, 1999).

8. Collins, "Slavery in the Sudan in History."

9. Hill, *Egypt in the Sudan, 1820–1881*, 10–12; Johnson, "Sudanese Military Slavery from the Eighteenth to the Twentieth Century," 142–56; Bjørkelo, *Prelude to the Mahdiyya*, 78–80; Ewald, *Soldiers, Traders, and Slaves*.

10. Spaulding, "Slavery, Land Tenure, and Social Class in the Northern Turkish Sudan"; and Kapteijns and Spaulding, "History, Ethnicity, and Agriculture in the Sudan."

11. Lovejoy and Hogendorn, *Slow Death for Slavery*; Cooper, *From Slaves to Squatters*.

12. Sikainga, *Slaves into Workers*.

13. Hargey, "The Suppression of Slavery in the Sudan, 1898–1939."

14. The distinction between *Muslim* and *Arab* was, however, sometimes blurry to outsiders. One British missionary, writing about the Nuba Mountains in the early 1930s, classified Muslim Nubas as "Arabs" and animist Nubas as "pagans" (see Cash, *The Nubas Calling*, 11).

15. Sharkey, "Domestic Slavery in the Nineteenth- and Early Twentieth-Century Northern Sudan."

16. al-Shahi, "Proverbs and Social Values in a Northern Sudanese Village."

17. Powell, "Brothers along the Nile"; and Powell, "Colonized Colonizers."

18. Comyn, *Service and Sport in the Sudan*, 14.

19. Beshir, *Educational Development in the Sudan*; Sanderson and Sanderson, *Education, Religion, and Politics in Southern Sudan*.

20. Sharkey, "Christians among Muslims."

21. Beasley, *Before the Wind Changed*; Bedri, *The Memoirs of Babikr Bedri*, vol. 2; Sanderson, "The Development of Girls' Education."

22. See the figures provided in the annual reports of the Education Department, in *SGR*, 1908–1913.

23. SAD, 275/2/2: F. R. Wingate Papers, Cromer to Wingate, dated Cairo, February 3, 1904.

24. *GMCR*, 1904, p. 6.

25. Johnson, "The Structure of a Legacy."

26. CMS, G3 E P2: Report by Rev. R. MacInnes on his visit to the Soudan, November and December, 1903; Agreement with American Presbyterian Mission, April 1912; and Memorandum of Interview with C. R. Watson, Secretary

of the Presbyterian Church of North America, December 4, 1913. Also see Shields, *Behind the Garden of Allah*, 77–106.

27. SAD, 103/5/27–30: F. R. Wingate Papers, Wingate to Governor Bahr el Ghazal, dated November 21, 1904.

28. Santandrea, *A Popular History of Wau*, 125.

29. Negash, *Italian Colonialism in Eritrea, 1882–1914*, 68–69.

30. Potter, *India's Political Administrators, 1919–1983*, 117–18; McDonald and Stark, *English Education, Nationalist Politics, and Elite Groups in Maharashtra, 1885–1915*, 16–17.

31. I call them "primary-intermediate" schools to avoid some of the confusion caused by their change of name and status over time. Until the early 1930s, the small number of schools which stressed academic education were called "primary" schools (the Gordon Memorial College had its own "primary" component until 1924). After the 1930s, officials began to refer to these schools as "intermediate" schools. To make matters more confusing, they then began to use the term *primary* (or sometimes *elementary*) to refer to the *kuttabs*, schools which taught basic literacy and mathematics skills to children in the seven- to eleven-year-old group.

32. SAD, 780/7/1–6: N. R. Udal papers, address by N. R. Udal on the history of the Gordon Memorial College, Khartoum, 1952.

33. SAD, 682/14/1–134: E. G. Sarsfield-Hall Papers, "Autobiography of Angelo Capato (c. 1860–1937) who was in business in Khartoum for many years and received the O.B.E. in 1926," n.d. [c. 1930]; unpublished typescript. See SAD, 682/14/92–93, pp. 84–85, for the relevant passage.

34. CMS, G3 E P1: Sub-Committee Resolution, June 14, 1898; and précis of letter from F. F. Adeney, December 9, 1898; CMS, G3 E P2: Précis of letter from Rev. F. F. Adeney, dated Helouan, March 14, 1902; Shields, *Behind the Garden of Allah*, 88.

35. Coptic numbers probably dwindled even before the anti-Egyptian policies of the post-1924 period. Figures for student breakdowns by religion, available in the 1908–1913 annual reports, show that Christians were a small minority among students at the college in these years, representing approximately 7 percent of the student body (academic tracks) in 1909–10, compared to 17 percent in 1913–14 (calculated on the basis of information in the *SGR* for the 1909 edition, p. 294, and the 1913 edition, p. 247). The last reference that I have found to Christians at the college appears in a Church Missionary Society précis book. In 1921 its records mention a plan that the missionaries discussed for building a separate hostel for Christian students "who might otherwise be influenced by Mohammedanism" at the college (CMS, G3 E P3: "Sudan Mission Policy," adopted by Khartoum Station Committee of May 27th, 1921).

36. Annual Report of Upper Nile Province, in *SGR*, 1909, p. 798.

37. Henderson, *The Making of the Modern Sudan*, 396, 430, 445.

38. Even after their sons had entered the school, some Mahdist *amirs* were kept imprisoned or under house arrest for many years (Ibrahim, "The Policy of the Condominium Government towards the Mahdist Political Prisoners").

39. Kramer, "The Capitulation of the Omdurman Notables."

40. SAD, 100/6 [AR]: F. R. Wingate Papers, file of addresses of welcome and verses of praise (*qasidas*), in Arabic, composed in honor of the Sirdar and Governor-General, Wingate, dated 1900–1906, presented by Col. H. E. Hebbert.

41. A document which Governor-General Wingate marked as a "Dervish Who's Who" shows that the following sons of the Khalifa Abdullahi were engaged in government service by about 1914: Umar, in Finance; Hamza, Yahya, and Ibrahim, in Agriculture; Hasan, in Post and Telegraphs; Abd al-Salam, in Railways; and Abd al-Samad, in Stores. Other sons were still in school, destined for future government careers. (SAD, 106/2/1–12: F. R. Wingate Papers, "Nominal Roll of the Family of the Mahdi, Arranged According to the Groups in Which They Are Living at Present," n.d. [c. 1914]).

42. Echenberg, *Colonial Conscripts*, 15.

43. Examples of such allies include two men whose sons, coincidentally, both became sub-mamurs and well-known poets. These elders were Shaykh Salih Jibril (1853–1938), leader of the Camel Corps, head of an intelligence-collecting mission to Sultan Ali Dinar of Darfur in 1900–1901, and father of Tawfiq Salih Jibril (1897–1968); and al-Malik Tanbal Hamad (1840–1922), source of intelligence information on the Mahdist forces of Wad Nujumi in 1890, and father of Hamza al-Malik Tanbal (1897–1951). On Shaykh Salih Jibril, see PRO, FO 78/5096, Sudan Intelligence Report No. 79, February 9 to March 8, 1901; Jibril, *Diwan ufuq wa-shafaq*, 145; and Mikha'il, *Al-Sudan bayna ahdayn*, 150–51. On al-Malik Tanbal Hamad, see SAD, 100/17/3 [AR]: F. R. Wingate Papers, Arabic letter from al-Malik Tanbal Hamad to Wingate Bey, dated January 6, 1890; and al-Malik, *Usrat muluk Arqu fi tarikh al-Sudan*, 79–85.

44. See, e.g., NRO, Civsec Personnel II/2/17, petition nos. 1297, 1194, 1186, 1269.

45. NRO, Personnel 11A/1/1: File of Ahmad Mahmud Abu'l-Naja, dossier no. 13, "Application to become a sub-mamur," dated October 28, 1924.

46. NRO, Personnel 3C/1/1: File of Abd Allah Uthman. This file includes letters from the Governor of Kordofan Province, asking officials to provide this candidate with jobs, first as an *ushur* (tax) clerk, then as a gum weigher, and finally as a sub-mamur—the last in spite of his unusually low educational qualifications. The province governor intervened on his behalf "for the sake of his father," the retired Yuzbashi Uthman Eff. Sulayman (letter from Acting Governor Kordofan to Inspector, Northern Kordofan, Bara, dated El Obeid, October 16, 1919).

47. Abu'l-Azayim, *Sahharat al-kashif*, 54–60. By 1936, Sudanese newspapers were publishing lists of young men who passed the civil service examinations (SAD, 683/8/1–2: E. G. Sarsfield-Hall Papers, "al-Najihuna fi imtihan al-Sikritir al-Idari," in *al-Nil* [Khartoum], March 15, 1936).

48. SAD, 769/10/18–19: T. R. H. Owen Papers, "Sudan Days," a memoir of T. R. H. Owen's life in the Sudan, 1926–53, dated 1960–61.

49. When Babikr Badri became an inspector of government schools in 1919, he was sent to inspect the Kassala *kuttab* school. He later persuaded the Educa-

tion Department to give one of its teachers a raise. This man had previously been denied his raise, on the grounds that all his students who went on to Gordon College failed their Arabic examinations. Babikr pointed out that those failures had nothing to do with the man's teaching, but everything to do with the boys themselves, who had been nominated into the college as the sons of *nazirs* and *umdas*, without having had to enter by competitive examination like everyone else (Bedri, *Memoirs*, 2:245).

50. *GMCR*, 1932, p. 15. Reports do not mention the proportion of scholarships before the cuts.

51. Consider the 1908 report of the Governor of Berber Province, who noted that cultivators were averse to sending their sons to the Berber primary school because they felt that they should be working on the land instead. Most of the primary school's students were the sons of townspeople (Annual Report of Berber Province, in *SGR*, 1908, p. 621). On the representation of alumni children at the college by the early 1930s, see *GMCR*, 1934, p. 15.

52. *GMCR*, 1932, p. 15.

53. Bedri, *Memoirs*, 2:115–16; Annual Report of Blue Nile Province, in *SGR*, 1913, 1:52.

54. Annual Report of the Education Department, in *SGR*, 1907, p. 567.

55. See the 1907 and 1908 Annual Report of the Prisons Department, in *SGR*, 1908, p. 291, and *SGR*, 1909, p. 463.

56. Annual Report of the Prisons Department, in *SGR*, 1907, p. 722.

57. Annual Report of the Prisons Department, in *SGR*, 1908, p. 291.

58. Annual Report of the Prisons Department, in *SGR*, 1907, p. 722.

59. Ibrahim, *Tarikh al-ta'lim al-dini fi al-Sudan*, 357–63; and Warburg, "Religious Policy in the Northern Sudan: Ulama and Sufism, 1899–1918," 104.

60. Legal Secretary to Governor Khartoum Province, dated February 19, 1930, in NRO, Personnel 4C/1/1: File of Ahmad Abu'l-Qasim Hashim.

61. Note by Nigel G. Davidson, Legal Secretary, dated November 10, 1926, in NRO, Personnel 4C/1/1: File of Ahmad Abu'l-Qasim Hashim.

62. This *qadi* was Shaykh Abd Allah Dafa' Allah al-Turabi, father of Hasan al-Turabi, who became the spiritual leader of the National Islamic Front under the regime of General Umar Hasan al-Bashir, who came to power in a 1989 coup (NRO, Personnel 4A/7/16: File of Abd Allah Dafa' Allah al-Turabi).

63. Ahmad, *Qadaya al-ta'lim al-ahli fi al-Sudan*, 95.

64. Daly, *Empire on the Nile*, 340–95.

65. *GMCR*, 1936, p. 17.

66. These trends in regional representation persisted into the postcolonial era, as statistics show for Khartoum University (the post-1956 successor of Gordon College) in the 1969–70 academic year (see El Tayeb, *The Students' Movement in the Sudan, 1940–1970*, 22).

67. *GMCR*, 1926–39, 1941–44.

68. By 1930, Darfur had only one government *kuttab*, or "Elementary Vernacular School," with 120 boys; by 1936, this number had risen to three government *kuttabs*, with 365 boys—and still no girls' *kuttabs* (*SGED*, 1930, p. 68;

SGED, 1936, pp. 34, 38–39; see also Abu Sinn, *Mudhakkirat Abi Sinn an mudiriyyat Dar Fur,* 182–83).

69. Kapteijns, *Mahdist Faith and Sudanic Tradition,* 227.

70. Boustead, *The Wind of Morning,* 119–20.

71. Okier, "Education Amongst the Beja."

72. Since ancient times, many Nubian men have migrated seasonally to seek work. In the nineteenth and twentieth centuries, they went to Egypt and Khartoum as highly paid servants in European households, thereby developing fluency in Arabic and often in English. As a non-Arabic-speaking Sudanese group, their marked success in education, business, and government has been exceptional (Hale, "The Changing Ethnic Identity of Nubians"; Adams, *Nubia,* 61). Moreover, British stereotypes about Nubians tended to be very positive, comparable in some respects to French attitudes towards the Berbers or "Kabyles" in Algeria (see Lorcin, *Imperial Identities*).

73. Cohen, *The Politics of Elite Culture,* xvi.

74. See Sudan government annual reports, *SGR,* for the years 1902–13 (including Education Department reports); separately published education reports of *SGED* for the years 1929–30, 1935, 1937–38, 1948; and Gordon College reports, *GMCR,* for the years 1904–45. Breakdowns according to ethnicity are not available in all of these reports. For example, the Gordon College reports only begin to provide information on ethnicity from 1926.

75. SAD, 769/10/18–19: T. R. H. Owen Papers, "Sudan Days," a memoir of T. R. H. Owen's life in the Sudan, 1926–53, dated 1960–61.

76. *SGED,* 1930.

77. On the format and authorship of documents, see Messick, *The Calligraphic State.*

78. Reliable birth dates were not always available, particularly before 1898, when the new regime began to encourage the keeping of systematic birth and death records. Hence, birth dates, as they appear in many files, are approximations.

79. *Jins* (plural *ajnas*) is a broad term and can denote "kind, sort, variety, species, class, genus; category; sex (male, female); gender (*gram.*); race; nation" (Wehr, *A Dictionary of Modern Written Arabic,* 141). The British often used the term to mean "nationality," which, to them, also meant "tribe."

80. This Issawi Bey would have been the father or uncle of Charles Issawi, the economic historian of the Middle East. Charles Issawi's father, Elias, worked for the Sudan government, and so did two of his father's younger brothers, Emile and Michel (Charles Issawi, interview with author).

81. Hamad, *Mudhakkirat Khidir Hamad,* 23.

82. NRO, Personnel 5A/2/8: File of Khidir Hamad. This file is also the source for his graduation date.

83. Hamad, *Mudhakkirat Khidir Hamad,* 22–23.

84. Hasan, *Al-Shillukh.*

85. Khidir does not specify the year in which this encounter with Blackley

took place, nor is it clear from his personnel file (NRO, Personnel 5A/2/8). The encounter probably occurred in the early 1930s.

86. Hamad, *Mudhakkirat Khidir Hamad*, 23–24.

87. SAD, 275/2/2: F. R. Wingate Papers, Cromer to Wingate, dated [Cairo,] February 3, 1904.

88. Hill, *Egypt in the Sudan*.

89. See Wehr, *A Dictionary of Modern Written Arabic*, 1098.

90. See Wehr, *A Dictionary of Modern Written Arabic*, 1079–80.

91. SAD, 275/2/2: F. R. Wingate Papers, Cromer to Wingate, dated [Cairo,] February 3, 1904.

92. E.g., Adam Da'ud Mandil, who was born in Omdurman in 1898, was classified as a *muwallad* in his personnel file when his service began in 1909. He does not have the typical Egyptian-Sudanese background of a *muwallad*, but the complexity of his background must have defied any other terminology. His mother is recorded as being of Turkish "nationality" and his father of Algerian "nationality." His own nationality came to be classified in post-1920 correspondence as "Sudanese," although he explained in one document that he was married to an "Egyptian" woman whose permanent home was in Cairo. In fact, Adam came from a family that was Jewish in background (although he is not identified as ethnically Jewish in any of the documents). On the contrary, his service sheet lists him as "Moslem," suggesting that his family was from the Masalma group made up of those who had been forced to convert to Islam during the Mahdist period (NRO, Personnel 5A/1/3: File of Adam Da'ud Mandil; on the Sudanese Jews and their identity, see Kramer, "The Death of Basiyouni").

93. Egyptian salaries were considerably higher because they included expatriation bonuses (Murqus, *Tatawwur nizam al-idara fi al-Sudan fi ahd al-hukm al-thuna'i al-awwal, 1899–1924*, 315).

94. NRO, Personnel 1D/1/3: File of Yahya al-Fadli, letter from W.L.A. dated March 10, 1934; unsigned note dated May 3, 1934; letter from Yahia El Fadli to Financial Secretary, dated Khartoum, May 3, 1934; pension authority forms dated April 7, 1934, and May 8, 1934.

95. Consider two more cases of men who were granted a "Sudanese" label so that they could qualify for job advancement: (1) Abd al-Fattah al-Maghribi, borne of a Tunisian father and Sudanese mother; and (2) Da'ud Iskandar, an Egyptian Christian (Copt). The former became a mathematics instructor at Gordon Memorial College, the latter a medical doctor (NRO, Personnel 15A/7/29: File of Abd al-Fattah al-Maghribi; and NRO, Personnel 1A/2/4: File of Da'ud Iskandar; both files contain paperwork in which officials debate their "nationality").

96. SAD, 275/2/2: F. R. Wingate Papers, Cromer to Wingate, dated [Cairo,] February 3, 1904; Currie's statement was quoted in this letter.

97. Taha, *Al-Sudan lil-Sudaniyyin*.

98. Regarding the Unionists, see Warburg, *Islam, Nationalism, and Communism in a Traditional Society*, 67–89.

99. Osman, "The Effendia and Concepts of Nationalism in the Sudan," 122–

25. On the Funj, see Spaulding, *The Heroic Age in Sinnar*; and McHugh, *Holymen of the Blue Nile*. According to another historian, some had suggested the name "Sennar," or even "Nubia," to distinguish the country from the French Soudan, which only adopted the name "Mali" after its independence in 1960 (Abdel Rahim, *Imperialism and Nationalism in the Sudan*, 1).

100. Garrett is referring to the Governor's-General cup that the team won in 1924.

101. SAD, 479/8/12: R. C. Garrett Papers, "History of Football in the Sudan," by R. C. Garrett, 1949 (completed before his retirement from the Stores and Ordnance Department).

102. Regarding the term *subaltern*, see Prakash, "Subaltern Studies as Postcolonial Criticism." The phrase *subaltern elite* is my own.

103. Spivak, "Can the Subaltern Speak?"

104. Kurita, *Ali Abd al-Latif wa thawrat 1924*.

105. al-Kid, "Al-Effendiyya wa-mafhum al-qawmiyya fi al-thalathin sana allati a'qabat al-fath fi al-Sudan, 1898–1928," 71. The history of Mawrada District is discussed in Ali, *Shakhsiyyat amma min al-Mawrada*, although this book does not mention the Ashri brothers.

106. Muhammad's article on translating appeared in *al-Fajr*, October 2, 1934; Abd Allah's poem appeared in *al-Fajr*, June 2, 1934.

107. NRO, Personnel 2B/1/4: File of Abd Allah Ashri al-Siddiq, letter from H. MacMichael to Major R. G. Archibald, Director, Wellcome Tropical Laboratories, dated Khartoum, October 11, 1933.

108. NRO, Personnel 2B/1/4: File of Abd Allah Ashri al-Siddiq, "Sudan Government Record of Service and History Sheet."

109. Osman, "The Effendia and Concepts of Nationalism in the Sudan," 138.

110. al-Kid, "Al-Effendiyya wa-mafhum al-qawmiyya," 71–73; and Osman, "The Effendia and Concepts of Nationalism in the Sudan," esp. ch. 5, 136–53. Khalid Husayn al-Kid and Khalid H. A. Osman are the same person.

111. A survey of this biographical literature appears in Sharkey, "*Tabaqat*," 17–34.

3: EDUCATION, ACCULTURATION, AND NATIONALIST NETWORKS

1. Lugard, *The Dual Mandate*, 617. The book was first published in 1922.

2. Chaudhuri, *The Autobiography of an Unknown Indian*, 143.

3. E.g., Zartman, *Elites in the Middle East*; Goldthorpe, *An African Elite*.

4. Meanwhile, in the same period but at the other end of the spectrum (on the level of mass rather than elite politics), researchers considered power, and the lack of it, from a Marxist perspective. Studies of peasants and popular resistance stood on the flip side of elite studies and were the "Third World" analogue of working-class history. A seminal inspirational text was Frantz Fanon's *The Wretched of the Earth*, a tract that dwelt on violent struggle and decolonization

in the Algerian context. Its counterpart in "First World" history was E. P. Thompson's *The Making of the English Working Class*.

5. Hunt, *The New Cultural History*; Grossberg, Nelson, and Treichler, *Cultural Studies*.

6. Fox, *Nationalist Ideologies and the Production of National Cultures*, 10.

7. Said, *Culture and Imperialism*, xiv.

8. Featherstone, *Undoing Culture*, 81.

9. See ibid.; and Appadurai, "Disjuncture and Difference in the Global Cultural Economy."

10. Annual Report of the Education Department, in *SGR*, 1907, pp. 585–86.

11. Renan, "What Is a Nation?," 52.

12. Dirks, Foreword to *Colonialism and Its Forms of Knowledge*.

13. *GMCR*, 1916, p. 13. D. H. Hibbert, who began his Education Department career in 1929 and rose to become Director of Education from 1950 to 1954, was in 1933 "the Tutor in charge of the grounds" and an obvious gardening enthusiast (*GMCR*, 1933, p. 15; and Bell, Dee, et al., *Sudan Political Service, 1899–1956*, 55, s.v. Denys Heseltine Hibbert; gardening details also come from Gordon College reports for 1934 and 1935).

14. In 1932 the workshops merged with the Omdurman Technical School. The military academy closed in 1924 after uprisings that led to the evacuation of the Egyptian Army and the creation of the Sudan Defence Force.

15. E.g., Artin, *England in the Sudan*, 16–18; Dugmore, *The Vast Sudan*, 56.

16. Baedeker, *Egypt and the Sudan*, 456.

17. al-Tum, *Dhikrayat wa-mawaqif fi tariq al-haraka al-wataniyya al-sudaniyya, 1914–1969*, 9.

18. Holmedal, "The Gordon Memorial College at Khartoum," 67.

19. Wingate, "The Story of the Gordon College and Its Work," 589; an offprint of this article (with different pagination) appears in SAD, 442/13: Rudolf von Slatin Papers.

20. Wingate, "The Story of the Gordon College and Its Work," 601.

21. Tignor, *Modernization and British Colonial Rule in Egypt, 1882–1914*, 102; Reid, *Cairo University and the Making of Modern Egypt*, 18–19.

22. PRO, FO 371/10080, Selby, Foreign Office, to Archer, Governor-General of the Sudan, dated [London,] April 27, 1925.

23. SAD, 724/14/3: Sir Andrew Balfour Papers, magazine article, "The Eton of the Soudan: Gordon College at Khartoum," *Sphere*, November 12, 1904; see also Mangan, "Ethics and Ethnocentricity," 138–71, esp. 144.

24. Lugard, *The Dual Mandate*; Mrinalini Sinha, *Colonial Masculinity*.

25. Mangan, *The Games Ethic and Imperialism*; and Mangan, "Britain's Chief Spiritual Export."

26. Wingate, "The Story of the Gordon College and Its Work," 601.

27. Atiyah, *An Arab Tells His Story*, 138.

28. Hamad, *Mudhakkirat Khidir Hamad*, 19; *GMCR*, 1919, p. 15.

29. *SGED*, 1929, p. 18.

30. *SGED*, 1929, p. 19.

31. *GMCR*, 1925, p. 19.

32. V. L. Griffiths mentioned that he tried to abolish the "Old Testament" style of corporal punishment which was so common in Northern Sudanese schoolrooms when he began to reform elementary education at Bakht er Ruda in the 1930s. "The European staff of three [at Bakht er Ruda] thought that there was too much of it: one of us wanted to abolish it altogether. This was more than the Sudanese staff responsible for the boarding-houses could face. But we agreed on a considerable reduction" (Griffiths, *An Experiment in Education*, 109).

33. Holmedal, "The Gordon Memorial College," 67. One historian claims that the British abolished flogging in schools in 1947 only to woo or appease the Northern Sudanese (Abdel Rahim, *Imperialism and Nationalism*, 122).

34. *GMCR*, 1933, p. 29.

35. MacDonald, *Sons of the Empire*; and Warren, "Citizens of the Empire."

36. *GMCR*, 1917, p. 8. According to the report, a troop had already started in the railway town of Atbara.

37. SAD, 780/5/15: N. R. Udal Papers, "The Boy Scout Association Warrant for N. R. Udal of Gordon College Khartoum, to act as Chief Commissioner for the Sudan," dated Imperial Headquarters London, March 2, 1927; and *SGED*, 1929, p. 39. See also SAD, 304/5/14–15: E. C. L. Flavell Papers, "The Boy Scout Movement in the Three Towns," reprinted from *The Sudan Daily Herald*, December 30, 1933; and "Scouting in Khartoum: Continued Progress in 1934," reprinted from *The Sudan Daily Herald* [January 1935].

38. SAD, 778/8/38: N. R. Udal Papers, group photograph of Gordon College Boy Scouts, seated with Withers, Crowfoot, and Udal [c. 1919].

39. SAD, 304/5/19: E. C. L. Flavell Papers, program, Omdurman Technical School, Scout Display, January 4, 1939; SAD, 304/5/15: E. C. L. Flavell Papers, "Scouting in Khartoum: Continued Progress in 1934," reprinted from *The Sudan Daily Herald* [January 1935].

40. al-Tum, *Dhikrayat*, 13.

41. Bell, *Shadows on the Sand*, 39. In some jobs, horsemanship was an official category for job evaluations; see, e.g., NRO, Personnel 3A/6/13: File of Hamza al-Malik Tambal, "Annual Confidential Report on Officials of the Sudan Government," dated Dueim, November 2, 1925. Similar motives to please British officials prompted some Northern Sudanese officials to take up tennis (Najila, *Dhikrayati fi al-badiya*, 10).

42. SAD, 479/8/1–260: R. C. Garrett Papers, "History of Football in the Sudan," by R. C. Garrett, 1949.

43. SAD, 479/8/1–260: R. C. Garrett Papers, "History of Football in the Sudan," by R. C. Garrett, 1949; Hawley, *Sandtracks in the Sudan*, 95.

44. Little has been written about sports in the Sudan. For some details on children's sports, see Rakha, *Al'ab sudaniyya*.

45. Chaudhuri, *Culture in the Vanity Bag*, 58.

46. Lugard, *The Dual Mandate*, 79–80.

47. Metcalf, *Ideologies of the Raj*, 106.

48. Miller, *On Nationality*, 30.

49. Griffiths, *An Experiment in Education*, 6.

50. Ibid., 5.

51. Cohn, *Colonialism and Its Forms of Knowledge*, 106–62.

52. Al-Dardiri was, in fact, unusual among Northern Sudanese for retaining the tarbush of his college days as a lifelong article of daily apparel, long after it had gone out of vogue. He explained, "My desire to wear the tarbush after my studies was owing to the following factors: first, for Sudanese wearing Western clothes there was no official headgear; second, my dissatisfaction with wearing a hat (*al-burnayta*) because it was the headgear of Europeans; third, the tarbush is an Islamic headgear, and it is possible to wear it at prayertime also. Added to that is the fact that I cannot stand what others do by leaving the head bare, for traditional and health reasons" (Uthman, *Mudhakkirati, 1914–1958*, 5).

53. SAD, 869/1/1, "Miscellaneous Small Donations," and tinted postcard of boys lined up at the front of Gordon Memorial College, pre-1914, donated by Mr. B. C. Bloomfield.

54. Uthman, *Mudhakkirati*, 6, and photograph facing p. 7.

55. *al-Fajr*, April 1, 1935, pp. 830–33. A set of photographs taken at the college between 1906 and 1915 shows this mix: many boys wear suits and bowties with tarbushes, while others, the *qadis*, have donned robes and turbans (SAD, 778/10/1–215: N. R. Udal Papers, album of photographs covering N. R. Udal's early career at Gordon College, 1906–15).

56. Abdullahi A. Ibrahim makes this point strongly in "Manichaean Delirium."

57. On the invention of tradition, see Hobsbawm and Ranger, *The Invention of Tradition*.

58. PRO, FO 371/10880, enclosure 1, Archer to Allenby, dated Khartoum, April 27, 1925, in Allenby to Chamberlain, memorandum on the general situation of the Sudan, dated Cairo, May 9, 1925.

59. Deng and Daly, *Bonds of Silk*, 102.

60. SAD, 795/2/1–30: R. C. Stevenson Papers, Sudan Government, "Regulations for Elementary Vernacular Schools (Kuttabs)," 1929, carbon copy.

61. SAD, 778/13/24: N. R. Udal Papers, group photograph, Gordon College boys, dated 1930.

62. For comparative African examples on clothing and its ambiguous modes of resistance, see Hendrickson, *Clothing and Difference*.

63. Bashiri, *Ruwwad al-fikr al-sudani*, 51–53, 276–81. "The junior translator Abdullah Wagiallah, . . . an avowed nationalist who never wore European clothes," served with H. B. Arber at El Obeid in 1928 (SAD, 736/2/1–27: H. B. Arber Papers, memoirs of H. B. Arber's life in the Sudan Political Service, from 1928 to 1954).

64. The Malja' al-Qirsh orphanage school had a program structured to produce goods that the Sudan might otherwise import, using local materials to make woven cotton cloth, cane chairs, straw brooms, leather slippers, and more (*al-Fajr*, July 16, 1935, pp. 1101–8, progress report on *Malja' al-Qirsh*). Ahmad

Khayr was an active supporter of the idea of producing local cotton weave—Sudanese *dammur* cloth (see the biographical entry on Ahmad Khayr in al-Hasan, *Rijal wa-mawaqif fi al-haraka al-wataniyya*, 6–18).

65. Hamad, *Mudhakkirat Khidir Hamad*, 23. As an A.D.C. in Kordofan, C. A. E. Lea saved his thoughts for his diary, remarking of a newly arrived *effendi* official in 1931, "He appeared pleasant-mannered, but a townsman and wearing European clothes!" (Lea, *On Trek in Kordofan*, 17). On the luxurious fabrics (silk and wool) of the graduates, see the column "A Word from the Editor" on "Graduates' Day," in *al-Fajr*, April 1, 1935.

66. This term, *effendyism*, appears, e.g., in the papers of Mabel Wolff at Durham (see SAD, 582/3/4, M. E. Wolff, Inspectress of Midwives, to Director, Sudan Medical Service, dated Omdurman, June 16, 1932).

67. SAD, 659/4/1–7: K. D. D. Henderson Papers, Monthly Diary, Central and Eastern Districts, Darfur, dated May 1934.

68. SAD, 606/4/87–89, 90–91: E. A. Balfour Papers, Balfour to his mother, two letters dated Singa, January 18, 1934, and Singa, January 25, 1934.

69. Hendrickson, *Clothing and Difference*, 13.

70. Hawley, *Sandtracks*, 26.

71. This very feature—their Europeanness—evoked envy or resentment among their contemporaries who had studied at the Ma'had al-Ilmi, an institute of Islamic studies that was the neglected stepdaughter of higher education during the Anglo-Egyptian period. Viewed in the aftermath of the 1989 coup, which brought an Islamist regime to power, it appears that independence ended the struggle between Britons and *effendis* but ignited a new one between *effendis* and *shaykhs* (Ibrahim, "Manichaean Delirium").

72. Badawi, *A Short History of Modern Arabic Literature*, 1.

73. Sharkey, "A Century in Print"; Ayalon, *The Press in the Arab Middle East*, 11–20; Anderson, *Imagined Communities*.

74. Sarkar, *Writing Social History*, 160, and more generally, ch. 5, "The City Imagined: Calcutta of the Nineteenth and Early Twentieth Centuries," 159–85.

75. Sharkey, "A Century in Print," 542.

76. SAD, 606/5/45–46: E. A. Balfour Papers, Balfour to his mother, dated Gordon College, October 9, 1936. The spare-time reading of students included such authors as Kipling, Conan Doyle, and Rider Haggard (Bashiri, *Ruwwad al-fikr al-sudani*, 268).

77. al-Tayyib, *Muhadarat fi al-ittijjahat al-haditha fi al-nathr al-arabi*, 53–54.

78. Annual Report of the Education Department in Sudan Government, *SGR*, 1907, p. 581.

79. Osman, "The Effendia and Concepts of Nationalism in the Sudan," 119–21, 129–30; Deng and Daly, *Bonds of Silk*, 104.

80. Najila, *Malamih min al-mujtama' al-sudani*, 58–65; Mahjub, *Nahwa al-ghad*, 222–23. Fu'ad al-Khatib published an anthology of poetry, *Diwan al-Khatib*, and a play set to verse, *Fath al-Andalus*.

81. SAD, 724/14/3: Sir Andrew Balfour Papers, magazine article, "The Eton of the Soudan: Gordon College at Khartoum," *Sphere*, November 12, 1904.

82. Hamad, *Mudhakkirat Khidir Hamad*, 25–26.

83. For theoretical insights, see Ong, *Orality and Literacy*.

84. *SGED*, 1929, p. 60.

85. See, e.g., Deng and Daly, *Bonds of Silk*, 122–23; Ahmad, *Jamal Muhammad Ahmad*, 25.

86. Sirr al-Khatm al-Khalifa, interview with author.

87. al-Tum, *Dhikrayat*, 10.

88. SAD, 606/5/43–44, 45–46: E. A. Balfour Papers, Balfour to his mother, dated Khartoum, October 3, 1936; and Balfour to his mother, dated Gordon College, October 9, 1936.

89. al-Tum, *Dhikrayat*, 10–11.

90. Isma'il al-Atabani, interview with author.

91. Isma'il al-Atabani, interview with author; Osman, "The Effendia and Concepts of Nationalism in the Sudan," 129–32.

92. Badawi, *A Critical Introduction to Modern Arabic Poetry* , esp. 14–67.

93. For classic examples of Sudanese reformist poetry, see al-Banna, *Diwan al-Banna*, vol. 1.

94. Ali, *Shakhsiyyat amma min al-Mawrada*, 20–21.

95. Isma'il al-Atabani, interview with author.

96. Abd al-Rahman Abu Zayd, interview with author; Qasim Badri, interview with author.

97. On the European context, see Berger et al., *Ways of Seeing*, 84; and Sontag, *On Photography*, 94–95; on the Sudanese context, see Abusabib, "The Impact of Islam on African Art."

98. Najila, *Malamih min al-mujtama' al-sudani*, 62–63.

99. See Geary, "Photographs as Materials for African History"; Edwards, *Anthropology and Photography, 1860–1920*.

100. Killingray and Roberts, "An Outline History of Photography in Africa (to c. 1940)," 12.

101. On the violent metaphors of photography, see Sontag, *On Photography*, 14–15.

102. Pictures of the Khalifa's corpse on the battlefield had the same function; see the conquest-related pictures in Daly and Forbes, *The Sudan*, 28–41, 143.

103. MacKenzie, *Imperialism and Popular Culture*; James R. Ryan, *Picturing Empire*. On the Boer War in particular, see Humphries, *Victorian Britain through the Magic Lantern*, 160.

104. Coombes, *Reinventing Africa*, 214. E.g., the Hadendowa man, popularized as the noble fighting "Fuzzy Wuzzy" of Rudyard Kipling's poem, is featured as the sixth in a set of eight "Human Races" in an instructional slide for British schoolchildren (Humphries, *Victorian Britain through the Magic Lantern*, 34); one can identify the Beja "type" by his hairstyle. The slide in question was produced in Nuremburg for a British market around 1900.

105. SAD, 778/10/1–215: N. R. Udal Papers, album of photographs covering N. R. Udal's early career at Gordon College, 1906–15, 1929.

106. Uthman, *Mudhakkirati*, photograph facing p. 7 from the year 1912; SAD, 778/13/1–27: N. R. Udal Papers, album of photographs, chiefly from N. R. Udal's service at Gordon College, 1925–45, including formal class pictures.

107. Department and district staff photographs are scattered through the papers in the Sudan Archive in Durham.

108. Slowly, Northern Sudanese women started to have their portraits done, too, though the pictures were seldom published. A couple of exceptions were made for female singers, though the photographs in question are of uncertain dating (Ya'qub, *Sudaniyyat fi salunatal-adab*, 41; Mikha'il, *Al-Sudan bayna ahdayn*, 251).

109. Mikha'il, *Shu'ara' al-Sudan*.

110. For a discussion of this trend (using mainly American examples), see Hunter, *Image and Word*.

111. Cartoons began to appear in the periodical *al-Sudan al-Jadid* after its founding in 1943 (Babiker, *Press and Politics in the Sudan*, 47). They probably appeared around the same time in monographs. Certainly, they were in use by the early 1950s, as shown by the caricatures accompanying biographical entries in Abd al-Qadir, *Shakhsiyyat min al-Sudan*.

112. Humphries, *Victorian Britain through the Magic Lantern*.

113. *GMCR*, 1915, p. 16; *GMCR*, 1919, p. 15; *GMCR*, 1929, p. 35. It is possible that the school may have obtained some of its slides from the Colonial Office Visual Instruction Committee (COVIC), although the Sudan's anomalous legal status as an Anglo-Egyptian "condominium," and not as a British "colony," would have precluded its active participation in this effort. COVIC was "an Empire-wide scheme of lantern-slide lectures and illustrated textbooks to instruct, first, the children of Britain about their Empire and, second, the children of the Empire about the 'Mother Country' " (Ryan, *Picturing Empire*, ch. 6, "Visual Instruction," 183–213).

114. Symes, *Tour of Duty*, 19–21.

115. Anderson, *Imagined Communities*, esp. 24–36.

116. *GMCR*, 1918, p. 16; *GMCR*, 1920, p. 18; *GMCR*, 1921, p. 16.

117. *GMCR*, 1929, p. 35.

118. SAD, A69/1–47: E. G. Sarsfield-Hall Papers, album of photographs, "The Cinema Industry of Khartoum, 1929–1936," presented to E. G. Sarsfield-Hall by G. Licos, cinema proprietor, 1936. On the "talkie," see Cook, *A History of Narrative Film*, 233–43.

119. A reference to Indian films appears in Mavrogordato, *Behind the Scenes*, 94.

120. *al-Fajr*, September 1, 1934, pp. 307–8.

121. For movie titles, see the billboards photographed in SAD, A69/1–47: E. G. Sarsfield-Hall Papers, album of photographs, "The Cinema Industry of Khartoum, 1929–1936," presented to E. G. Sarsfield-Hall by G. Licos, cinema proprietor, 1936; and the advertisements pasted in SAD, 629/1/1–239: V. H. G.

Vokes Papers, book of newspaper cuttings from *The Sudan Daily Herald*, as well as theatre notices and programs, 1929–42.

122. Film review in *al-Fajr*, July 16, 1934, pp. 182–85; film review in *al-Fajr*, February 1, 1935, pp. 749–53; praise poem by al-Tayyib Abd al-Qadir titled "Grita, Kawkab al-alam al-sati'," in *al-Fajr*, May 1, 1935, p. 901.

123. Short story signed "Rudolf Valentino," in *al-Nahda*, November 29, 1931, pp. 20–21.

124. SAD, 707/15/1–22: P. B. E. Acland Papers, P. B. E. Acland's personal memoirs and resumé of career in the Sudan, n.d.

125. The story refers here to the extreme form of female genital cutting, widespread in the Northern Sudan, commonly known as Pharaonic circumcision or infibulation. The main character implies a preference instead for the significantly more moderate practice of clitoridectomy. Regarding this issue, see Gruenbaum, *The Female Circumcision Controversy*.

126. Abd Allah Umar Abu Shama, "Khaybat al-amal," *al-Nahda*, November 15, 1931.

127. E.g., see the letter written on behalf of Khidir Hamad and Qasim al-Mahdi: N. R. Udal, Warden of Gordon College, to Financial Secretary, dated December 24, 1928, in NRO, Personnel 5A/2/8: File of Khidir Hamad.

128. In 1936 fifty-five students passed the examination for civil service jobs ("al-Najihuna fi imtihan al-Sikritir al-Idari," in *al-Nil* newspaper, March 15, 1936, in SAD, 683/8/1–2: E. G. Sarsfield-Hall Papers).

129. El Tayeb, *The Students' Movement in the Sudan*, 31. Only after the Depression did educators discuss the possibility of training Gordon College students for the private sector, though this never became a mission of the school (*GMCR* 1929, p. 23; Daly, *Imperial Sudan*, 111–12).

130. SAD, 185/1/132–39: F. R. Wingate Papers, text of speech delivered by Wingate at the Gordon College Old Boys' Celebration, King George's Day, dated January 17, 1913.

131. *al-Fajr*, April 1, 1935, pp. 830–33.

132. SAD, 778/13/1–5: N. R. Udal Papers, photographs, Sudan Schools Club tea party, 1930. The "Sudan Schools Club" in the caption implies attendance only of alumni belonging to the Omdurman and Khartoum Graduates Clubs. After 1919, to keep numbers manageable, the government restricted attendance to graduates based in Khartoum.

133. SOAS, A. J. Arkell Papers, file 21, folios 2–29, "Handing over notes: Southern District, White Nile Province, Period Covered October 1926-November 1929"; Duncan, *The Sudan's Path to Independence*, 50–51.

134. Abu'l-Azayim, *Sahharat al-kashif*, 47. It is hard to fix dates in Abu'l-Azayim's stream-of-consciousness account; however, since he mentions the attendance of Isma'il al-Atabani at the club, this tense mood at the club must date to the period between 1935 and 1939, when Isma'il al-Atabani was posted in Wad Medani as an accountant in the government's Agricultural Research Service (NRO, Personnel 7B/1/3: File of Isma'il al-Atabani).

135. Duncan, *The Sudan's Path to Independence*, 50–51.

136. Isma'il al-Atabani, interview with author.

137. Uthman, *Mudhakkirati*, 13–15.

138. PRO, FO 371/11613, [Sudan] Secret Intelligence Report No. 3, signed R. Davies, Acting Director of Intelligence, dated Khartoum May 25, 1926; and Abu Hasabu, *Factional Conflict in the Sudanese National Movement, 1918–1948*, esp. ch. 3, "Genesis of Factional Conflict: the Sudan Schools' Graduates Club, 1918," pp. 31–44. On sectarianism and nationalist politics in general, see Warburg, *Islam, Nationalism, and Communism in a Traditional Society*, esp. chs. 1 and 2, pp. 21–89; and Woodward, *Sudan*.

139. See Fadwa Abd al-Rahman Ali Taha, Introduction to *Al-Sudan lil-Sudaniyyin*, 8.

140. Najila, *Malamih min al-mujtama' al-sudani*, 277–85.

141. The "information order" is a central theme in Bayly, *Empire and Information*.

142. Consider Hasan Najila's first encounter with a camel and car on his way to take a job as a teacher in rural Kordofan (Najila, *Dhikrayati fi al-badiya*, 7–21); see also Sharkey, "Arabic Literature and the Nationalist Imagination in Kordofan," 170.

143. Daly, *Imperial Sudan*, 94.

144. In 1942 Abd al-Fattah al-Maghribi, a mathematics teacher at Gordon College, conferred with the Financial Secretary in the office of the Director of Education, via a "telephonic conversation," to discuss his petition for a motorcycle allowance (NRO, Personnel 15A/7/29: File of Abd al-Fattah al-Maghribi, letter from A. F. Maghrabi to Director of Education, May 11, 1942).

145. See, e.g., SAD, 427/5/1–194: R. S. Savile Papers, diary, January 1 to December 31, 1902, with trek notes for Gedaref area and Kassala. In Savile's diary, arrivals or delays of mail earn consistent mention. Letter-writing also features prominently in the diaries of C. A. E. Lea, *On Trek in Kordofan*. British officials devoted vast amounts of their free time to writing letters. Historians have benefited, mainly through the papers deposited at the Sudan Archive in Durham, and through collections such as Henderson, *The Making of the Modern Sudan*, and Foley, *Letters to Her Mother*.

146. Bridget Acland, the wife of P. B. E. Acland, recalled getting mail deliveries by camel post in Khashm el Ghirba in the late 1920s, and by airplane in Geteina (a stop on the Khartoum–Lagos air route) after c. 1935 (SAD, 777/15/1–13: P. B. E. Acland Papers, "Impression of the Sudan," unpublished memoir by Mrs. Bridget Susan Acland of her life in the Sudan, n.d.). On airmail, see Corbyn, "The Administration of the Sudan in 1937," 283.

147. Daly, *Imperial Sudan*, 94–95.

148. Hamza al-Malik Tanbal, e.g., finished an essay in Managil on August 11, 1927. It appeared in the August 17 issue of the newspaper *Hadarat al-Sudan* (Tanbal, *Al-Adab al-sudani wa-ma yajibu an yakuna alayhi*).

149. *al-Nahda*, October 11, 1931, pp. 22–23.

150. This theme is elaborated in Sharkey, "Arabic Literature and the Nationalist Imagination in Kordofan."

151. Collins, *Shadows in the Grass.*
152. Bell, *Shadows on the Sand,* 61.
153. PRO, FO 371/14653, memorandum, "Notes on a Short Visit to the Sudan, August 7–24, 1930," by W. H. B. Mack, dated Foreign Office, December 2, 1930.
154. Griffiths, *An Experiment in Education,* 5.
155. Foucault, *The Order of Things,* xix.
156. Sarkar, *Writing Social History,* 13, 283.
157. Khayr, *Kifah jil.*

4: THE MECHANICS OF COLONIAL RULE

1. They demonstrated this power first during the conquest and, later, during occasional "pacification" campaigns or punitive patrols led against unruly "natives" (Headrick, *The Tools of Empire*).
2. Willis, *The Upper Nile Province Handbook,* 51.
3. Robinson, "Non-European Foundations of European Imperialism"; and Crowder, *West Africa under Colonial Rule,* 70–71.
4. Young, *The African Colonial State in Comparative Perspective,* 1.
5. Woodruff, *The Men Who Ruled India,* 11.
6. Potter, *India's Political Administrators,* 57–59; Heussler, *Yesterday's Rulers*; Mangan, "The Education of an Elite Imperial Administration."
7. On the ethos of the British colonial official, see Potter, *India's Political Administrators,* 67–77; Mangan, *The Cultural Bond*; and Mangan, *The Games Ethic and Imperialism.*
8. Kirk-Greene, "The Thin White Line," 40; Blunt, *The I.C.S.,* 91–92.
9. Kirk-Greene, "The Thin White Line," 44. The "lone D.C." was featured as a stock player in colonial histories and memoirs. Examples of variations on this theme, from the memoirs of Sudan Political Service officials, include Jackson, *Sudan Days and Ways,* 28–29; and Duncan, *The Sudan's Path to Independence,* 23.
10. Woodruff, *The Men Who Ruled India,* 349.
11. Orwell, "Shooting an Elephant."
12. Kirk-Greene, "The Thin White Line," 36.
13. Sikka, *The Civil Service in India.*
14. Ajayi, "The Development of Secondary Grammar School Education in Nigeria," 527.
15. July, *The Origins of Modern African Thought,* 110–29, and *passim*; Kimble, *A Political History of Ghana,* 61–124.
16. For the British Empire, the list of such institutions is long. West African examples include Fourah Bay College in Sierra Leone (which had links to the University of Durham); Achimota College in the Gold Coast; and Kings College Lagos in Nigeria. Makerere College in Uganda, the counterpart of Gordon College in Khartoum, is the most prominent East African example. Egypt had not only the independent Victoria College in Alexandria, but, from 1908, Cairo Uni-

versity. India had a host of institutions: the universities of Bombay, Calcutta, and Madras, founded in 1826; the independent Aligarh College (a reformist Muslim institution); and several prestigious schools at the secondary level. For comparative examples, see Altbach and Kelly, *Education and the Colonial Experience*.

17. Forster, *A Passage to India*, 16.

18. Breuilly, *Nationalism and the State*, 49.

19. E.g., Roy, *The Civil Service in India*; Misra, *The Bureaucracy in India*; Singh, *The Civil Service in India (1858–1947)*; Shukla, *Indianisation of All-India Services and Its Impact on Administration*; and Sikka, *The Civil Service in India*.

20. A classic work of the early postcolonial era, conveying a sense of both optimism and heroism, is Hodgkin, *Nationalism in Africa*. Hodgkin only alluded to the connection between colonial employment and nationalism, by pointing out the importance of professional clubs and Old Boys Associations as centers for the exchange of nationalist ideas.

21. Cooper and Stoler, *Tensions of Empire*.

22. Anderson, *Imagined Communities*, 53–56.

23. Kirk-Greene, *The Sudan Political Service*, 1. For an Indian comparison, see O'Malley, *The Indian Civil Service, 1601–1930*, 1–2.

24. Early in 1932 the Sudan Government tallied 949 men and women in British classified (pensioned) staff; at the end of 1932 Depression-related retrenchments had reduced that number to 642. These figures include the elite corps of the Sudan Political Service as well as less-exalted beings working for the railways, customs, medical service, etc. The number of classified British officials present in the Sudan at any given time would have been lower than the stated figures, because many were able to take annual leaves, which in the case of S.P.S. officials were as long as three months. These figures did not include unclassified (non-pensioned) Britons working in the country on fixed contracts (PRO, FO 371/16107, Loraine to Simon, dated Cairo, April 9, 1932; and PRO, FO 371/17021, Maffey to Loraine, dated Khartoum, January 10, 1933).

25. Daly, *Imperial Sudan*, 3, 85, 175.

26. E.g., whereas Gordon College students accounted for 13.6 percent of government school-goers in 1907, they represented only 1.6 percent of the whole in 1926 (Annual Report of the Education Department, in *SGR*, 1907; and *GMCR*, 1926). In calculating the 1907 figure, I excluded the students of the technical school (or "Industrial Workshop") which was housed on Gordon College grounds. In other words, I used a figure for Gordon College students that included academic-track students only. For the 1926 figures, the Gordon College proportion would be even smaller were one to include students at the semi-independent schools, namely the Maʻhad al-Ilmi (Islamic Institute), the Ahfad schools run by Babikr Badri, and the Omdurman *Ahliyya* school.

27. MacMillan, "The Importance of the Educated African." The Nigerian intellectual, Nnamdi Azikiwe, published a rebuttal as Ben N. Azikiwe ("How Shall We Educate the African?").

28. Annual Report of the Education Department, in *SGR*, 1905, pp. 47–49.

29. Annual Report of the Education Department, in *SGR*, 1908.

30. *GMCR*, 1912.

31. By 1929, out of 534 graduates of the secondary-school program (excluding the primary-school component of the school's early years), there were 498 in government service, 18 dead, 13 in the private sector, and 5 out of country (*GMCR*, 1929, p. 23).

32. Hamad, *Mudhakkirat Khidir Hamad*, 21.

33. Daly, *Imperial Sudan*, 167.

34. *The New Shorter Oxford English Dictionary* (Oxford: Clarendon Press, 1993), s.v. "Indianization," "Nigerianization," "Kenyanization."

35. Change in Sudanization patterns is not as dramatic for labor-intensive jobs or for positions requiring low levels of literacy (such as steamer transport or police work), where Sudanese employees had already predominated from the early years of the regime. By 1907, e.g., more than 75 percent of the staff of the Steamers Department (2,177 out of a total 2,876 employees) was already Sudanese (Annual Report of the Steamers Department, in *SGR*, 1907, p. 807).

36. *GMCR*, 1930.

37. Daly, *Empire on the Nile*.

38. Currie, "The Educational Experiment in the Anglo-Egyptian Sudan, 1900–33"; and Wingate, "Sir James Currie's Life and Work."

39. Annual Report of the Education Department, in *SGR*, 1904, p. 36.

40. Annual Report of the Education Department, in *SGR*, 1906, p. 215.

41. Two examples of older men hired to serve the new Anglo-Egyptian regime include Muhammad Umar al-Banna (c. 1847–1919), a poet of the Mahdi later hired as a *qadi* and Inspector of Shari'a courts; and Muhammad Abd al-Rahim (1878–1966), a Mahdist state clerk (and independent historian) who was later hired as an accountant (O'Fahey, *Arabic Literature of Africa*, 1:339; and Karrar, Ibrahim, and O'Fahey, "The Life and Writings of a Sudanese Historian."

42. *GMCR*, 1918.

43. Murqus, *Tatawwur nizam al-idara fi al-Sudan*, 314–15.

44. SAD, 281/3/53–54: F. R. Wingate Papers, Currie to Wingate, dated Khartoum, September 6, 1907.

45. Annual Report of the Finance Department, in *SGR*, 1905, p. 285.

46. *GMCR*, 1908.

47. Warburg, *The Sudan under Wingate*, 132; Warburg, "Religious Policy in the Northern Sudan," 104.

48. Annual Report of the Sudan Surveys Department, in *SGR*, 1909, p. 558.

49. Vatikiotis, *The History of Modern Egypt*, 262–72.

50. PRO, FO 371/4984, Keown-Boyd to Allenby, dated Khartoum, March 14, 1920 (Keown-Boyd Report).

51. Great Britain, *Report of the Special Mission to Egypt*, 1921 (Milner Report), in SAD, 162/6/10: F. R. Wingate Papers.

52. Daly, *Empire on the Nile*, 290.

53. *GMCR*, 1922.

54. PRO, FO 371/10049, Allenby to MacDonald, "Memorandum on the

Future Status of the Sudan," dated Cairo, June 1, 1924; Mynors, "A School of Administration in the Anglo-Egyptian Sudan."

55. al-Jamal, "Athar thawrat 1919 fi Misr ala thawrat 1924 fi al-Sudan"; Diyab, *Al-Alaqat al-misriyya al-sudaniyya, 1919–1924.*

56. Abdin, *Early Sudanese Nationalism, 1919–1925.*

57. Sanderson emphasized the economic and generational factors in his Introduction to *The Memoirs of Babikr Bedri*, 2:70–74; Daly points out the job dissatisfaction factor, notably over Sudanese military commissions and over salaries, in Daly, *Empire on the Nile*, 294, 297.

58. Najila, *Malamih min al-mujtama' al-sudani*, 203–6.

59. A classic exposition of this view is found in Najila, *Malamih min al-mujtama' al-sudani.* Many of the papers delivered at the conference on the history of the nationalist movement in the Sudan, held at the University of Khartoum in January 1986, develop this theme. Some of the Arabic papers were published in al-Safi, *Al-Haraka al-wataniyya fi al-Sudan*; some of the English papers were published in El Safi, *The Nationalist Movement in the Sudan.*

60. Abdin, *Early Sudanese Nationalism*, 3.

61. The range in social backgrounds among the participants of the 1924 events comes through in British intelligence reports and trial proceeding for that year (see, e.g., PRO, FO 371/10050, details on the trials of demonstrators at Khartoum, in More, Sudan Agent, to the First Secretary of the Residency [Ramleh], dated Cairo, July 9, 1924, and July 13, 1924).

62. Petitions of loyalty from notables from the Blue Nile Province, Dongola Province, and elsewhere appear in PRO, FO 371/10050. An earlier petition of loyalty is found in PRO, FO 371/6303, Red Sea Nazirs and Sheikhs to Governor, Red Sea Province [undated English translation c. 1921].

63. PRO, FO 371/10050, enclosure 3, "The Political Situation," on the two camps of the Sudan intelligentsia, by C. A. Willis, Director of Intelligence, dated Khartoum, June 16, 1924.

64. SAD, 479/7/5–52: Major P. D. Mulholland Papers, scheme "E" for the evacuation of Egyptian elements in the Egyptian Army from the Sudan, [Summer] 1924; PRO, FO 371/10080, Allenby to Foreign Office, dated Cairo, March 15, 1925.

65. al-Fiki, *Tarikh quwat difa' al-Sudan*; and Salih, "The British Administration in the Nuba Mountains Region of the Sudan, 1900–1956," 242–75.

66. Bakheit, "British Administration and Sudanese Nationalism, 1919–1939," 80–81.

67. Warburg, *Islam, Nationalism, and Communism*, 93–94.

68. Daly, *British Administration and the Northern Sudan, 1917–1924*, 188–229; Bakheit, "British Administration and Sudanese Nationalism," 65–66; Sanderson, Introduction to *The Memoirs of Babikr Bedri*, 2:72–74.

69. Robinson, "Non-European Foundations of European Imperialism."

70. PRO, FO 371/10051, appendix on the League of the White Flag [typescript], by C. A. Willis, Director of Intelligence, dated Khartoum, July 20, 1924; see also Mikha'il, *Al-Sudan bayna ahdayn*, 150–51.

71. PRO, FO 371/10053, telegram, Hakimam to Stack, dated London, September 17, 1924; and PRO, FO 371/10053, Wasey Sterry, Acting Governor General, to Acting High Commissioner, dated Khartoum, September 7, 1924.

72. PRO, FO 371/13127, Secret Intelligence Report no. 22, signed J. C. Penney for the Director of Intelligence, dated Khartoum, July 15, 1928.

73. NRO, Personnel 3A/5/10: File of Tawfiq Salih Jibril. Biographical information on Tawfiq Salih Jibril, his brother Muhammad Salih Jibril, and his father Shaykh Salih Jibril also comes from the editors' commentary in Jibril, *Diwan ufuq wa-shafaq*, 5–15, 143–49; and from Muhammad Uthman Yasin, *Al-Sha'ir Tawfiq Salih Jibril*.

74. On the life and writings of Muddaththir Ibrahim al-Hajjaz, see O'Fahey, *Arabic Literature of Africa*, 1:293–97.

75. PRO, FO 371/10053, testimony taken from Ali Ahmed Saleh by E. N. Corbyn, dated September 19, 1924.

76. PRO, FO 371/10880, White Flag League Conspiracy: Result of Trial, in P. Munro, Governor of Khartoum Province, to the Director of Intelligence, dated [Khartoum,] April 6, 1925.

77. Bedri, *The Memoirs of Babikr Bedri*, 2:309–10.

78. NRO, Personnel 3A/1/1, File of Ibrahim Badri. Most of the materials from this file appear to be missing; the file only contains complimentary materials from the end of Ibrahim Badri's career.

79. Ibrahim, *Assaulting with Words*, 10, 22–23.

80. PRO, FO 371/10050, petition signed by the leading inhabitants of Omdurman, translation dated Omdurman, June 10, 1924.

81. EUL, MS Gen 1899: Reginald Davies Papers, Diary, 1920–36.

82. The young Gordon Memorial College generation did not disappear from these lists because in the mid-1920s there were few of them in positions of authority. However, elder Sudanese employees (including *qadis*) disappeared, as did Lebanese and Egyptian employees (including Gordon Memorial College schoolteachers, high-ranking departmental clerks, etc.). From 1925 to 1935 the staff lists became an essentially British preserve, contrasting with earlier reports (e.g., issues for 1919), and with the reports that emerged once Sir Stewart Symes became governor-general in 1935. The Sudan Archive at the University of Durham holds copies of the *Quarterly List of the Sudan Government* for the years between 1919 and 1940.

83. PRO, FO 371/13875, Lloyd to Chamberlain, dated Cairo, April 30, 1929.

84. Douglas H. Johnson, "From Military to Tribal Police."

85. Bakheit, "British Administration and Sudanese Nationalism," 145.

86. Consider SAD, 777/14/1–32: P. B. E. Acland Papers, copy of handing-over notes on Butana District by P. B. E. Acland for H. M. Watt, dated November 1931. Acland compares the Butana district staffs in 1925 and 1930; reductions are clear for both administrative staff and police. Plans were also afoot to abolish the post of mamur at Khashm el Girba during 1931. On mamur cutbacks, see SAD, 716/1/31–34: A. W. M. Disney Papers, "A Note on Sub-Inspectors," Civil Secretary's Office, dated September 21, 1939 (marked "Secret").

87. SOAS, A. J. Arkell Papers, file 21, folio 3, "Handing over notes, Southern District, White Nile Province, Period Covered October 1926–November 1929."

88. Hamad, *Mudhakkirat Khidir Hamad*, 32–36.

89. SAD, 241/7/101–4: F. R. Wingate Papers, notes of Gordon Memorial College meeting (draft of minutes), typescript dated [London,] September 28, 1927.

90. Maffey feared the subversive potential of Egyptians in the Sudan (SAD, 584/8/44–47: H. A. MacMichael Papers, Maffey to MacMichael, dated Rugby, October 1, 1932; see also PRO, FO 371/14609, "Note on the Sudan from the Reconquest to the Present Time," memorandum by J. Murray, dated Foreign Office, [London,] April 3, 1930).

91. PRO, FO 371/14609, "Note on the Sudan from the Reconquest to the Present Time," by J. Murray, dated Foreign Office, [London,] April 3, 1930; and SAD, 641/10/2–3: J. Longe Papers, approximate list of past mamurs and sub-mamurs for Eastern Kordofan District [c. 1939]). Until 1924, all the mamurs of Eastern Kordofan District were Egyptian; after 1924, they were all Sudanese.

92. PRO, FO 371/14650, memorandum on the Condominium Agreement and on Sudanese progress toward self-administration, with appendices giving numbers, salaries, and grades of Sudanese officials according to department [typescript], 1930, folios 347–49. The report specifies that most of those included in these figures were graduates of "Gordon College, the Primary Schools or the Instructional Workshops." I use the term *primary-intermediate* here instead of *primary* to refer to those schools which adopted "intermediate" status in the 1930s. I use this term to distinguish these "primary schools" from the Elementary Vernacular Schools, or *kuttabs*, which were sometimes called "primary" schools in later years.

93. *GMCR*, 1926.

94. SAD, G/S 1096: Ali Badri Papers (uncatalogued), "Obituary for Ali Bedri," by Dr. A. M. Halim, Khartoum [c. 1987]; SAD, 555/10/2–4: Papers of the Gordon Memorial College Trust, "The Kitchener School of Medicine, Khartoum: Short Report on the School's Activities for the Year 1934"; SAD, 570/11/12–14: Papers of the Gordon Memorial College Trust, "Medical Staff Graduated from the Kitchener School of Medicine" [1928–44]; and Squires, *The Sudan Medical Service*, 77–78.

95. In 1932, e.g., one of the program's first graduates, Ali Badri (a son of Babikr Badri), went to Omdurman Civil Hospital to become the first Sudanese senior medical officer (*hakimbash*), joining the ranks of Lebanese doctors in this post (SAD, G/S 1096: Ali Badri Papers [uncatalogued], "Sirat D. Ali Badri," by Babikr Ali Badri, dated January 1987; and "Obituary for Ali Bedri," by Dr. A. M. Halim, Khartoum [c. 1987]).

96. *GMCR*, 1924, p. 17.

97. NRO, Personnel 1C/1/2: File of Yusuf Badri, Pridie, Director Sudan Medical Service, to Financial Secretary, dated Khartoum, February 16, 1939.

98. NRO, Personnel 15A/7/29: File of Abd al-Fattah al-Maghribi, Sudan

Government Record of Service and History Sheet; and N. R. Udal, for Director of Education, to Financial Secretary, dated February 29, 1928.

99. *GMCR*, 1929.

100. PRO, FO 371/17021, Maffey to Loraine, dated Khartoum, January 10, 1933.

101. PRO, FO 371/10880, Allenby to Foreign Office, dated Cairo, March 15, 1925.

102. PRO, FO 371/16107, Loraine to Simon, dated Cairo, April 9, 1932.

103. PRO, FO 371/16107, Loraine to Simon, dated Cairo, April 9, 1932.

104. PRO, FO 371/16107, Maffey to Loraine, copy of telegram dated Khartoum, December 22, 1931. Personnel files in the National Records Office in Khartoum show the patterns of these abatements (see, e.g., NRO, Personnel 2A/3/8: File of Musa al-Hilu; NRO, Personnel 3A/3/5: File of Ahmad al-Shinqiti; and NRO, Personnel 5A/1/3: File of Adam Da'ud Mandil).

105. PRO, FO 371/16107, Foreign Office minute on salaries of officers and officials in the Sudan, in reply to a question posed in Parliament by Major General Sir Alfred Knox, dated May 10, 1932; and PRO, FO 371/16107, Knox to Simon, dated London, June 1, 1932. I am extrapolating the 12th parallel as the definition of "Southernness" on the basis of NRO personnel files, some of which record service south of the 12th parallel in a separate section of the Record of Service and History Sheet (see, e.g., NRO, Personnel 3A/1/2: File of Abu Bakr Uthman Arbab; this Gordon Memorial College graduate served the regime from 1914 to 1951, beginning his career as a clerk and ending as the chairman of the Jonglei Investigation Team [for the Jonglei Canal project]).

106. SAD, 414/3/1–4: T. R. H. Owen Papers, Owen to his mother, dated El Dueim, January 3, 1931.

107. PRO, FO 371/16107, Maffey to Loraine, dated [Khartoum,] February 9, 1932.

108. El Mahdi, *A Short History of the Sudan*, 137–38. More thorough coverage of this strike appears in Maqar, "Mawqif al-idara fi al-Sudan min nahwa al-haraka al-wataniyya khilala al-harbayn al-alamiyyatayn fi al-fitra min 1914 ila 1947"; see the section entitled "Idrab talabat kulliyat Ghurdun amm 1931, asbabuhu wa-nata'ijuhu ala mustaqbal al-haraka al-wataniyya al-sudaniyya," 391–407.

109. al-Tum, *Dhikrayat*, 12.

110. PRO, FO 371/16107, Maffey to Loraine, dated [Khartoum,] February 9, 1932.

111. PRO, FO 371/16107, Foreign Office minute on "Retrenchment in the Sudan," by Peterson, dated [London,] January 15, 1932.

112. PRO, FO 371/16107, Maffey to Loraine, dated [Khartoum,] February 9, 1932.

113. In 1932, e.g., the college released all seven of the school's remaining Lebanese teachers; five of these returned to Lebanon, two went into business in Khartoum, and all were replaced by Northern Sudanese (*GMCR*, 1932).

114. Information on Yusuf Najjar comes from correspondence with the

niece and sister of the one-time Sudan intelligence officer, Edward Atiyah (Jurdak and Shami, letter to author). According to the *Quarterly List of the Sudan Government* for October 1, 1931, Yusuf Najjar retired on November 19, 1931. For reminiscences on the career of Muhammad Salih al-Shinqiti, see SAD, 722/10/1–12: A. R. C. Bolton Papers, "The Sudan Political Service," a memoir by A. R. C. Bolton, dated February 28, 1982.

115. SAD, 641/10/1–42: J. Longe Papers, Notes on Eastern Kordofan District, Vol. II, 1935–1939.

116. SAD, 541/7/1–32: J. Winder Papers, "Fifty Years On," an account by John Winder of his service in the Opari/Kajo-Kaji District of Mongalla Province, dated November 1979. The regime soon abandoned the idea of coffee cultivation entirely (see Daly, *Imperial Sudan*, 91, 100).

117. Daly, *Imperial Sudan*, 8–46; and Bakheit, "British Administration and Sudanese Nationalism," 236–73.

118. Symes, *Tour of Duty*, esp. ch. 9, "The Anglo-Egyptian Sudan (1934–40)," 211–32; see also Daly, *Imperial Sudan*, 45.

119. Daly, *Imperial Sudan*, 13.

120. SAD, 448/3/6–8: J. A. Gillan Papers, memorandum, "Substitution of British A.D.C.s by Natives," by J. A. Gillan, Civil Secretary, dated June 14, 1934 (marked "Secret").

121. SAD, 716/1/31–34: A. W. M. Disney Papers, "A Note on Sub-Inspectors," Civil Secretary's Office, dated September 21, 1939 (marked "Secret").

122. In 1938, e.g., the British A.D.C. disappeared from Umm Ruwaba district in Eastern Kordofan (SAD, 641/10/1–42: J. Longe Papers, Notes on Eastern Kordofan District, Vol. II, 1935–39).

123. SAD, 448/3/6–8: J. A. Gillan Papers, memorandum, "Substitution of British A.D.C.s by Natives," by J. A. Gillan, Civil Secretary, dated June 14, 1934 (marked "Secret").

124. This restriction applied even in the 1940s when Northern Sudanese officials were granted the title of Assistant District Commissioner (SAD, 797/6/21: L. M. Buchanan Papers, Buchanan to Crawford, dated Merowe, January 22, 1944).

125. SAD, 641/12/1–44: J. Longe Papers, Handing-over notes, Eastern Kordofan, by J. Longe, dated February 1937.

126. Daly, *Imperial Sudan*, 18.

127. This Egyptian was named Mustafa Nada (SAD, 797/4/48: L. M. Buchanan Papers, Buchanan to Luce, dated Merowe, July 13, 1942; and SAD, 797/5/5–6: L. M. Buchanan Papers, Robertson for Civil Secretary to Financial Secretary, dated Khartoum, January 3, 1943).

128. SAD, 716/1/31–34: A. W. M. Disney Papers, "A Note on Sub-Inspectors," Civil Secretary's Office, dated September 21, 1939 (marked "Secret").

129. SAD, 716/1/20–25: A. W. M. Disney Papers, note by A. W. M. Disney on the use of Sub-Inspectors in the administration, dated November 11, 1934. In an attached note, Douglas Newbold, Civil Secretary of the Sudan Government from 1939 to 1945, agreed.

130. SAD, 799/15/1–64: S. L. Milligan Papers, Sudan Government, "Technical Training of Sudanese: Report of a Committee Appointed by His Excellency the Governor-General," dated Khartoum, July 15, 1935. This report is preserved in the papers of Milligan (Director of the Survey Department from 1927 to 1937) because he was a member of the committee.

131. "Al-Najihuna fi imtihan al-Sikritir al-Idari," in al-Nil newspaper, March 15, 1936, in SAD, 683/8/1–2: E. G. Sarsfield-Hall Papers. Sarsfield-Hall kept this issue because it includes a cover article on a farewell tea party in honor of his retirement.

132. SAD, 414/8/12–15, T. R. H. Owen to his father, dated [Khartoum,] February 2, 1937.

133. Daly, Imperial Sudan, 16.

134. Beshir, Educational Development in the Sudan, 141.

135. Sudan Government, Report of Lord De La Warr's Educational Commission, 1937; Daly, Imperial Sudan, 111–12.

136. GMCR, 1941.

137. GMCR, 1938; GMCR, 1936, p. 26.

138. GMCR, 1942.

139. Isma'il al-Atabani, interview with author; and NRO, Personnel 7B/1/3: File of Isma'il al-Atabani.

140. PRO, FO 371/10049, Allenby to MacDonald, "Memorandum on the Future Status of the Sudan," dated Cairo, June 1, 1924; and SAD, 716/1/31–34: A. W. M. Disney Papers, "A Note on Sub-Inspectors," Civil Secretary's Office, dated September 21, 1939 (marked "Secret").

141. Mynors, "A School of Administration in the Anglo-Egyptian Sudan," 24–26.

142. SAD, 414/8/18–20: T. R. H. Owen Papers, T. R. H. Owen to his father, dated [Khartoum,] March 8, 1937.

143. PRO, FO 371/20886: "Notes on the Near East by the Intelligence Officer, Khartoum, July–August 1937" (Appendix to S.M.I.S. [sic] no. 43, August 1937), by Edward Atiyah, dated Khartoum, August 25, 1937.

144. SAD, 762/11/38: J. G. S. MacPhail Papers, copy extracts from the Renk monthly diary by Abd al-Salam Effendi Abd Allah, Mamur Renk, describing his visit to Britain in 1937; SAD, 764/7/26–30: J. G. S. MacPhail Papers, MacPhail to his mother, dated Malakal, October 8, 1937.

145. NRO, Personnel 1A/3/6: File of Ali Badri, sub-dossier no. 3, promotion form and letters signed by Pridie, Director Sudan Medical Service, March 1937.

146. NRO, Personnel 4A/5/12: File of al-Dardiri Muhammad Uthman, letter from M. E. C. Pumphrey, Assistant Sudan Agent in London, to Legal Secretary Khartoum, dated London, April 11, 1947.

147. NRO, Personnel 1A/1/2: File of Dr. al-Tijani Muhammad al-Mahi.

148. Hamad, "Sudan Notes and Records and Sudanese Nationalism, 1918–1956," 255. I have drawn the biographical details from Bashiri, Ruwwad al-fikr al-sudani.

149. Griffiths, Sudan Courtesy Customs.

150. Gifford and Louis, *The Transfer of Power in Africa*; Morris-Jones and Fischer, *Decolonisation and After*; Goldberg, "Decolonisation and Political Socialisation with Reference to West Africa," 663–77.

151. Daly, *Imperial Sudan*, 143.

152. C. G. Davies, Governor, Upper Nile Province, to Financial Secretary, dated Malakal, December 29, 1944, in NRO, Personnel 3A/1/1: File of Ibrahim Badri. On Ibrahim Badri himself, see Bashiri, *Ruwwad al-fikr al-sudani*, 24–26.

153. Daly, *Imperial Sudan*, 154.

154. For a parallel with India, see Potter, *India's Political Administrators*, 63.

155. Daly, *Imperial Sudan*, 144–45.

156. SAD, 815/10/8–20: R. M. Cooper Papers, memoirs by R. M. Cooper on his career in the Sudan, undated transcript [1983].

157. SAD, 815/13/1–20: P. P. Bowcock Papers, memoirs by P. P. Bowcock of his service in the Sudan from 1951 to 1955, undated typescript.

158. SAD, 815/10/8–20: R. M. Cooper Papers, memoirs by R. M. Cooper on his career in the Sudan, undated transcript [1983].

159. Austin, "The Transfer of Power," 19.

160. SAD, 517/8/32–33: J. W. Robertson Papers, Robertson to Scott, dated Khartoum, December 12, 1943.

161. E.g., SAD, 777/8/1–20: T. H. B. Mynors Papers, memoirs of T. H. B. Mynors's service in the Sudan, dated March 1982.

162. Shafiq, *Hawliyyat Misr al-siyasiyya*, 183–86.

163. SAD, 745/10/1–24: D. Vidler Papers, "Fallen Angels, 1956–1989: Their Story," by Denis Vidler [1989]; and Bell and Kirk-Greene, *The Sudan Political Service, 1902–1952*.

164. SAD, 815/2/1–20: E. J. Bickersteth Papers, memoirs of E. J. Bickersteth concerning his career in the Sudan Political Service from 1938 to 1955, typescript dated April 16, 1982.

165. SAD, 711/18/8: D. M. H. Evans Papers, photograph, Sudanese mamur at Nyala in Dar Fur [c. 1954].

166. GMCR, 1944.

167. GMCR, 1929, 23.

5: LIFE AND THE REGIME

1. Roberts, *The Colonial Moment in Africa*.

2. Cooper, "Conflict and Connection."

3. Guha, Introduction to *A Subaltern Studies Reader, 1986–1995*.

4. Rodney, *How Europe Underdeveloped Africa*.

5. Davidson, *The Black Man's Burden*.

6. Prakash, "Subaltern Studies as Postcolonial Criticism," 1475–90.

7. Rushdie, *Midnight's Children*, 7; Guha, Introduction to *A Subaltern Studies Reader*.

8. Guha, Introduction to *A Subaltern Studies Reader*, xi.

9. Two important works, representing each of these strands, were Robinson,

"Non-European Foundations of European Imperialism," and Ranger, "Connexions between 'Primary Resistance' Movements and Modern Mass Nationalism in East and Central Africa."

10. Ranger, "Making Northern Rhodesia Imperial," 349.

11. Ranger, "The Inventing of Tradition in Colonial Africa," 211–12.

12. Jankowski and Gershoni, *Rethinking Nationalism in the Arab Middle East*; Khalidi, *Palestinian Identity*; Zerubavel, *Recovered Roots*.

13. Schmid, "Decentering the 'Middle Kingdom' "; Lee, "Modernity, Legality, and Power in Korea under Japanese Rule"; and Eckert, "Exorcising Hegel's Ghosts."

14. Chatterjee, *The Nation and Its Fragments*.

15. A classic study of Arab nationalism reflecting the Great Men approach is Hourani, *Arabic Thought in the Liberal Age, 1798–1939*.

16. On the interaction of imperialisms, consider, e.g., Brown, *International Politics and the Middle East*; and Ravindiran, "Discourses of Empowerment."

17. The pathbreaker was Said, *Orientalism*.

18. Middle Eastern products of these trends include Mitchell, *Colonising Egypt*; and Douglas and Malti-Douglas, *Arab Comic Strips*. South Asian examples include Bhabha, *Nation and Narration*; Chatterjee, *Nationalist Thought and the Colonial World*; and Viswanathan, *Masks of Conquest*. African examples include Allman, *The Quills of the Porcupine*; and Burke, *Lifebuoy Men, Lux Women*.

19. Timothy Brook asks a similar question in his essay, "Collaborationist Nationalism in Occupied Wartime China."

20. Guha, Introduction to *A Subaltern Studies Reader*, xviii. See also Guha, *Dominance without Hegemony*.

21. Amin al-Tum Satti, interview with author.

22. Atiyah, *An Arab Tells His Story*, 158.

23. See, e.g., Wellcome Institute, General Collections, J. A. Simons Papers, GC/125/A, letter from C. G. Dupuis, Governor Darfur Province, to Director, Sudan Medical Service, re: Transfer of Dispensaries to Native Administration, April 9, 1931.

24. Macdonald and Wright, *"Da Kitab,"* page b.

25. SAD, 290/3/43–51: F. R. Wingate Papers, Clayton to Wingate, dated March 6, 1910.

26. Hamad, *Mudhakkirat Khidir Hamad*, 21.

27. See, e.g., SAD, 741/3/16–34: J. H. R. Orlebar Papers, memoirs of T. W. Davidson's life as a senior medical officer, Sudan Defence Force, from 1925 to 1931 (n.d.).

28. Forster, *A Passage to India*, 42–43.

29. Deng and Daly, *Bonds of Silk*, 114.

30. See, e.g., SAD, 210/1/1–148: C. A. Willis Papers, diary for life and work in Kordofan, December 1907 to December 1908; Lea, *On Trek in Kordofan*; and Cruickshank, *The Kindling Fire*.

31. On British praise for Northern Sudanese colleagues, see, e.g., SAD,

736/2/1–27: H. B. Arber Papers, memoirs of H. B. Arber's life in the Sudan Political Service, from 1928 to 1954 (n.d.); SAD, 797/8/16–56: L. M. Buchanan Papers, L. M. Buchanan's memoirs of his career, 1928 to 1954, dated May 10, 1982; SAD, 541/7/1–32: J. Winder Papers, "Fifty Years On," an account by John Winder of his service in Opari/Kajo-Kaji District of Mongalla Province, dated November 1979.

32. Deng and Daly, *Bonds of Silk.* For a letter of appreciation written to R. E. H. Baily years later (after his retirement to Britain) by a man whom Baily had pointed out as a "lad of promise" and had recommended for the Sub-Mamurs Training Program, see SAD, 533/3/46–49: R. E. H. Baily Papers, Hashim El Khalifa Mohammed, mamur of Wad Medani, to Baily, dated Wad Medani, August 26, 1945. Another gracious letter from a Northern Sudanese is SAD, 533/3/56: R. E. H. Baily Papers, Daud El Khalifa to Baily, n.d. (post-1956; written on paper with a Republic of the Sudan letterhead).

33. One historian of the Indian Civil Service suggested that "a clear distinction must be made . . . between a *generalized* sense of racial superiority [on the part of Britons] and relations between *individuals*" (Potter, *India's Political Administrators,* 80).

34. The case of Tawfiq Salih Jibril stands out in this regard (see Sharkey, "Arabic Literature and the Nationalist Imagination in Kordofan," esp. 167–69).

35. See Chapter 4 for a more detailed discussion of the 1924 uprisings, which considers their causes, participants, aims, and effects.

36. PRO, FO 371/10053, profile of Ali Ahmed Saleh, forwarded along with a letter from Wasey Sterry to Stack, dated Khartoum, August 28, 1924.

37. PRO, FO 371/10053, testimony of Ali Ahmed Saleh, recorded on September 21, 1924.

38. PRO, FO 371/10053, testimony of Ali Ahmed Saleh, recorded on August 23, 1924.

39. Bashiri, *Ruwwad al-fikr al-sudani,* 18–20.

40. Simpson for Director of Education to Financial Secretary, dated [Khartoum,] January 1, 1915; Simpson for Director of Education to Director General, Medical Department, dated [Khartoum,] December 29, 1915; Medical Certificate for Temporary Service and Apprentices, signed Crispin, dated Khartoum, December 29, 1915; and Director of Post and Telegraphs, "Conditions of Service of Arafat Eff. Mohamed," dated June 6, 1916, all in NRO, Personnel 5A/4/14: File of Arafat Muhammad Abd Allah.

41. *GMCR,* 1910, pp. 14–15.

42. Simpson to Moir, Director, Post and Telegraphs Department, dated Gordon Memorial College, May 8, 1918, in NRO, Personnel 5A/4/14: File of Arafat Muhammad Abd Allah.

43. PRO, FO 371/11613, [Sudan] Secret Intelligence Report No. 1, signed R. Davies, Acting Director of Intelligence, dated Khartoum, March 18, 1926. Arafat spent only a brief time writing in Egyptian papers. Unable to eke out a livelihood in Egyptian journalism, he took a job as an English-language translator for the British Petroleum Company in the Sinai, and later for the Gellatly-Hankey

Company in Jidda. He then returned to the Sudan and started producing the journal *al-Fajr* in 1934 (see the entry on Arafat in Bashiri, *Ruwwad al-fikr al-sudani*, 246–48).

44. His Sudan Government Record of Service and Appointment sheet notes that he was "struck off the Service, in accordance with Section 32 Officials Discipline Ordinance 1912, for absenting himself from duty for a period exceeding 15 days," as of September 4, 1924.

45. The emphasis was his. See Arafat Mohammed to the Controller of Personnel, dated November 6, 1922, in NRO, Personnel 5A/4/14: File of Arafat Muhammad Abd Allah.

46. PRO, FO 371/10039, Sudan Monthly Intelligence Report No. 361, August 1924, Appendix: "Account of Events Connected with Pro-Egyptian Propaganda in Various Parts of the Sudan during August, 1924."

47. Najila, *Malamih min al-mujtama' al-sudani*, 176.

48. PRO, Personnel 5B/2/6: File of Muhammad al-Mahdi al-Khalifa Abd Allah. The papers in his personnel file show that the government was reluctant to hire Muhammad al-Mahdi but eventually relented in 1922, after the eager youth spent a two-month translation apprenticeship at Kosti at his own expense—an unusual arrangement. The government then approached his brother, Muhammad al-Sayyid, about employment, but he declined on the grounds that he was comfortable and settled in his career as a cultivator. Although the regime imprisoned Muhammad al-Mahdi for his subversive activities in 1924, his file shows that they treated him remarkably well, insofar as they continued to pay him his monthly translator's salary of £E14 while he was awaiting trial in prison. For a comparison of the two brothers, see SAD, 661/4/48–65: K. D. D. Henderson Papers, "The Forgotten Generation," K. D. D. Henderson's personal recollections of certain survivors of the Mahdiya, manuscript, dated Durham 1979.

49. The major account is included in Najila, *Malamih min al-mujtama' al-sudani.*

50. Several literary salons were run by women during this period, and most of these women assumed the name of "Fawz" during their salon-business dealings (Ya'qub, *Sudaniyyat fi salunat al-adab*).

51. Farah, *Diwan Khalil Farah*, esp. 9–11. Ali al-Makk saw Khalil Farah's personnel file in the NRO (though it has since been declared missing) and noted that he had been fined twenty days' wages between 1913 and 1929 (his term of service) for showing up late to work.

52. Abdel Rahim, *Imperialism and Nationalism in the Sudan*, 111.

53. In 1995 a tribute to Khalil Farah, entitled "Khalil Farah: You Will Remain Immortal throughout the Passage of Time," appeared on the sixty-third anniversary of his death in 1932 (al-Fatih al-Tahir, "Khalil Farah . . . sa-tabqa khalidan ala marr al-dahr," *al-Sudan al-Hadith* (Khartoum), October 24, 1995, p. 7). Tributes to Khalil Farah also appear in the following: Bashiri, *Haqibat al-fann*, 37–43; and al-Shush, *Al-Shi'r al-hadith fi al-Sudan*, 1:100–27.

54. Members of the salon included Tawfiq Salih Jibril, Muhyi al-Din Jamal,

Ibrahim Badri, Sulayman Kisha, Khalil Farah, Makkawi Ya'qub, Hasan Najila, Ubayd Hajj al-Amin, al-Amin Ali Madani, Salih Abd al-Qadir, Khalaf Allah Khalid, Bashir Abd al-Rahman, and others. The major source on the group is Hasan Najila, who wrote a sort of literary group memoir in his *Malamih min al-mujtama' al-sudani* ("Glimpses of Sudanese Society"), published in 1964. Sources for members' names are Najila, *Malamih min al-mujtama' al-sudani*, 149–62; Jibril, *Diwan ufuq wa-shafaq*, 141; and Osman, "The Effendia," 49.

55. PRO, FO 371/7746, Sudan Monthly Intelligence Report No. 331, February 1922, Appendix, "Seditious Circulars in the Sudan."

56. Najila, *Malamih min al-mujtama' al-sudani*, 154, 164.

57. PRO, FO 371/10051, Memorandum Appendix on the League of the White Flag, by C. A. Willis, Director of Intelligence, typescript copy dated Khartoum, July 20, 1924; and PRO, FO 371/10052, Sudan Agency to Foreign Office, "Information regarding the activities of the League of the White Flag in El Obeid," dated Cairo, August 15, 1924.

58. PRO, FO 371/10905, Henderson, Acting High Commissioner, to Austen Chamberlain, memorandum, "Report on Political Agitation in the Sudan," dated Ramleh, June 27, 1925.

59. Bashiri, *Ruwwad al-fikr al-sudani*, 203–5.

60. PRO, FO 371/10053, Testimony of Ali Ahmed Saleh, dated August 19, 1924.

61. Bashiri, *Ruwwad al-fikr al-sudani*, 204.

62. Ibid., 181–83. A study of his life and poetry appears in Abd Allah, *Salih Abd al-Qadir*.

63. Najila, *Malamih min al-mujtama' al-sudani*, 108–22.

64. Ibid., 289.

65. PRO, FO 370/142, "On the press law in the Sudan," F. C. C. Balfour, Acting Director of Intelligence, to Sudan Agent, Cairo, dated Khartoum, September 24, 1921 (marked "Confidential"). As of 1921 there were three Northern Sudanese papers which submitted to censorship: *al-Sudan/The Sudan Times*, published in English and Arabic; *The Sudan Herald*, published in English and Greek; and *Hadarat al-Sudan*, published in Arabic. A fourth paper, produced by the Chamber of Commerce, was not censored.

66. The government had the right to demand a security fee up to £E100. Nevertheless, when Muhammad Abbas Abu'l-Rish applied to publish the journal *al-Nahda* in 1931, he was asked to pay only a single pound (£E1) (Salih, *al-Sihafa al-sudaniyya fi nisf qarn, 1903–1953*, ch. 9, on journalism and the law, 102–12, 119).

67. These editors were Muhammad Abbas Abu'l-Rish, of *al-Nahda*, who died in 1932, and Arafat Muhammad Abd Allah, of *al-Fajr*, who died in 1936.

68. Salih, *al-Sihafa al-sudaniyya fi nisf qarn*, 119–20.

69. Mikha'il, *Shu'ara' al-Sudan*, 128–35; and Bashiri, *Ruwwad al-fikr al-sudani*, 175–77. I have drawn his birth date from Mikha'il and his death date from Bashiri (believing that Mikha'il's suggested date of 1903 sounds more realistic than Bashiri's 1907).

70. NRO, Personnel 1D/1/3: File of Yahya al-Fadli, list of punishments on his "Sudan Government Record of Service and History Sheet." The reasons for his first trial in 1936 are provided in the personnel file, though they are not provided for the second trial in 1937. I am assuming that the second Board of Discipline trial is the one which Mahjub Umar Bashiri describes—although Bashiri claims that the penalty for publishing the article on sectarianism in *al-Fajr* was a fine of half a month's salary, not one week's salary, as the personnel file indicates (Bashiri, *Ruwwad al-fikr al-sudani*, 391).

71. NRO, Personnel 3A/6/13: File of Hamza al-Malik Tanbal, sub-file marked "Board of Discipline on Sub-Mamur Hamza Eff. Melik Tambal" [1931]; and Tanbal, *Diwan al-Tabi'a*.

72. R. J. Hillard for Civil Secretary to Mohammed Eff. Abdel Rahim, Accountant, Kuttum, Darfur Province, dated Khartoum, July 8, 1931: "With reference to your letter of 7.7.31 to Controller, Public Security Intelligence Branch I have to inform you that there is no objection to the publication of your book 'Nafathat El Yara, fil Adab wal Tarikh wal Igtimal' " [sic] (reproduced in Abd al-Rahim, *Nafathat al-yara'*, vi).

73. Ali, *Shakhsiyyat amma min al-Mawrada*, 27.

74. One item in Tawfiq Salih Jibril's poetry anthology is a telegram, made up of two short lines of poetry, that the poet sent to his friend, Hasan Najila, on the last day of 1949. In a footnote to his manuscript, Tawfiq Salih Jibril wrote that he, Ibrahim Badri, and Hasan Najila sometimes exchanged poem-telegrams (Jibril, *Diwan ufuq wa-shafaq*, 115).

75. NRO, Personnel 3A/5/10: File of Tawfiq Salih Jibril. The following documents from that file, all marked "Confidential," have been cited here: Governor, Blue Nile Province to Civil Secretary, dated Wad Medani, March 2, 1925; Acting Governor, Blue Nile Province to District Commissioner, Rufa'a, dated Wad Medani, October 13, 1926; handwritten initialed letter (sender's initials unintelligible—perhaps A. W.?) to H.C.J., dated August 1927; H. C. Jackson, Governor, Halfa Province, to Governor, Kordofan Province, dated Wadi Halfa, March 16, 1928; Sudan Government Confidential Report on Tawfiq Eff. Saleh Gibreil, signed D.C. of H.Q. for Governor, Kordofan Province, dated El Obeid, March 29, 1933.

76. NRO, Personnel 3A/5/10: File of Tawfiq Salih Jibril. Cited from this file here are Sudan Government Confidential Report on Tewfik Eff. Saleh Gibril, signed L. M. Buchanan for Governor, Northern Province, dated El Damer, November 16, 1948; and E. D. Arbuthnot, D.C. Shendi, to Governor, Northern Province, dated Shendi, June 21, 1950.

77. Yasin, *al-Sha'ir Tawfiq Salih Jibril*.

78. T. R. Blackley, D.C., memorandum on Tewfik Eff. Saleh Gibril, dated Kassala, November 5, 1938, in NRO, Personnel 3A/5/10: File of Tawfiq Salih Jibril.

79. Mr. Arthur would have been Allan J. V. Arthur, who served in Northern Province from 1951 to 1954 (Bell, Dee, et al., *Sudan Political Service, 1899–1956*, 79).

80. Najila, *Malamih min al-mujtama' al-sudani*, 161–62.

81. The year for this event must have been 1929 for that would have been the only occasion when Tawfiq and the D.C., Armstrong, overlapped on a King's Day (always held in January) in Kordofan (Jibril, *Diwan ufuq wa-shafaq*, 92–93). On Armstrong, see Bell, Dee, et al., *Sudan Political Service*, 32. The details of Tawfiq's service are in NRO, Personnel 3A/5/10: File of Tawfiq Salih Jibril.

82. Abu'l Azayim, *Sahharat al-kashif*, 47–48.

83. By contrast, the British A.D.C. or D.C. spent most of his time hearing cases and petitions; assessing taxes (as opposed to collecting them, as the mamur had to do); inspecting schools; directing the construction of roads, bridges, and buildings; and so on (see, e.g., Jackson, *Sudan Days and Ways*, 43–50). In a large town like El Obeid, capital of Kordofan Province, the A.D.C. was "Assistant Commandant of Police, controller of Province transport, peacemaker in inter-departmental quarrels, social secretary to the Governor, interviewer of all displeased with the Government, pacifier of the Head Accountant and the Storekeeper; in short, all things to all men" (Duncan, *The Sudan's Path to Independence*, 12).

84. Sudan Government, *The Sub-Mamur's Handbook*, in SAD, 678/1: C. A. E. Lea Papers.

85. SAD, 661/4/48–65: K. D. D. Henderson Papers, "The Forgotten Generation," personal recollections of certain survivors of the Mahdiya, manuscript, dated Durham, England, 1979.

86. Some accounts date from the period when the officials would have been Egyptians, i.e., from pre-1914, in the case of sub-mamurs, and from pre-1924, in the case of mamurs. In 1911, e.g., there was an attack on the sub-mamur at Jebel Feri, Fung Province: "The affair was precipitated by the ignorance of the natives and the action of the sub-Mamur in attempting to collect the tax in the absence of the local Mek" (PRO, FO 371/1111, Sudan Intelligence Report No. 198, January 1911).

87. PRO, WO 32/3537: Report on Operations in the Nuba Mountains, 1926. After these reprisals against the Nuba, the government recommended awarding several officials with medals. One Mulazim Awwal (1st Lieutenant) was even recommended for being made a Member of the Most Excellent Order of the British Empire. This file also includes lists of casualties. There were other reasons for revolt, too, sometimes arising from grave but avoidable misunderstandings. Such was the case, e.g., in 1915, near Kafia Kingi in Bahr el Ghazal Province, when the mamur and a troop of police burned down several huts in a village where an outbreak of cerebro-spinal meningitis had occurred. The mamur first secured the consent of the village leader for this precaution, but no one explained the measure to the villagers. Seeing their huts burnt for no apparent reason, the enraged villagers speared and killed a policeman. In reprisal the remaining police burned down 150 more huts and shot at least a dozen villagers (PRO, FO 371/2349, Sudan Intelligence Report No. 250, May 1915).

88. Mawut, "The Southern Sudan under British Rule, 1898–1924: The Constraints Reassessed," 77 n. 51.

89. Abu'l-Azayim, *Sahharat al-kashif*, 108–13.

90. "Mr. Hawkesworth" would have been either Desmond or Geoffrey Hawkesworth, twin brothers who were both posted in Blue Nile Province in the early 1940s, when this incident presumably occurred (Bell, Dee, et al., *Sudan Political Service, 1899–1956,* 49).

91. Abu'l-Azayim, *Sahharat al-kashif,* 162–65.

92. Dealing with witchcraft-related offenses was a tricky matter. See, e.g., SAD, 641/9/1–2: J. Longe Papers, "A Note on the Trial of Witchcraft Cases," by Howell Owen, Chief Justice, Sudan Government, typescript dated Khartoum, May 5, 1934; PRO, WO 106/232, Sudan Intelligence Report No. 178, May 1909; SAD, 414/7/1–3, 4–6: T. R. H. Owen Papers, two letters describing a witchcraft trial—T. R. H. Owen to his mother, dated Sinkat , January 14, 1936, and T. R. H. Owen to his father, dated Sinkat, January 27, 1936; "Two Murder Trials in Kordofan"; Yunis, "The Kuku and Other Minor Tribes of the Kajo Kaji District"; Ghawi, "Notes on the Law and Custom of the Jur Tribe in the Central District of the Bahr El Ghazal Province"; and SAD, K. H. J. Hayes Papers: box 1/1, Crimes 1900–30, court case, Sudan Government vs. Koko Konga and others (1945).

93. Hamad, *Mudhakkirat Khidir Hamad,* 33; and Bedri, *The Memoirs of Babikr Bedri,* 2:325. Islamic law forbids Muslim women from marrying outside the faith, although Muslim men are indeed allowed to marry Christian women. Islamic law also limits the number of wives a man may have to four.

94. Bashiri, *Ruwwad al-fikr al-sudani,* 298–301. Regarding another case, see Mawut, "The Southern Sudan under British Rule," 151.

95. Ali, *Shakhsiyyat amma min al-Mawrada,* 43.

96. In 1926, e.g., Babikr Badri went to inspect a school in the Nuba Mountains. He later recorded in his memoirs, "At our first mid-day stop I saw a sight which appalled me—twenty women carrying wood, and all stark naked, their ages being not less than twenty. This was the first time I had ever seen a woman, naked as the day her mother bore her, walking along a public road; later however I became accustomed to this disgraceful sight" (Bedri, *The Memoirs of Babikr Bedri,* 2:130).

97. Bell, *Shadows on the Sand,* 75.

98. SAD, A74/1–246: G. Bell Papers, photograph album covering Gawain Bell's service as an A.D.C. in the Eastern Jebels, Kordofan, 1933–37. Photographs 80 and 81 are labeled "Tea Party Rashad Nadi [Club]."

99. Jackson, *Sudan Days and Ways,* 39–40.

100. SAD, 759/11/1–68: E. A. Balfour Papers, memoirs of E. A. Balfour's life in the Sudan, from his early childhood in the Sudan (1909–13) to 1955, written c. 1981. On quinine injections, see also Bell, *Shadows on the Sand,* 56; and Henderson, *Set under Authority,* 23–25.

101. Medical records were at some point removed from the personnel files that are now in Khartoum's National Records Office, although files occasionally mention medical leave that was taken when officials came down with serious bouts of malaria and other diseases. Other sources include the memoirs of doctors such as Alexander Cruickshank, William Byam, and H. C. Squires, and doc-

tors' archival collections in the Sudan Archive in Durham and at the Wellcome Institute in London.

102. Staniforth, *Imperial Echoes*, 24, 132.

103. Cruickshank, *The Kindling Fire*, ch. 12, "Round the Bend," 168–76.

104. Senior Surgeon, Khartoum Hospital, to Governor, Khartoum Province, dated November 16, 1931, in NRO, Personnel 3A/6/13: File of Hamza al-Malik Tanbal. Hasan Najila, who met Hamza al-Malik Tanbal in Kordofan with an anti-locust campaign, said that he was not surprised to hear that Hamza had been removed from government service, because the government was looking for ways to make staff cutbacks at that time. Najila recalled that when the British D.C. at Soderi invited Northern Sudanese officials to tea, they were expected to come punctually. But one day, when Hamza was invited, he arrived late. The D.C. asked him if he had overslept, and Hamza replied that no, he had merely been reading a very good book. Hasan Najila suggests that Hamza's candor did not endear him to British officials (Najila, *Dhikrayati fi al-badiya*, 214).

105. SAD, 402/3/19: H. A. MacMichael Papers, spoof, "Proceedings of a Medical Board on XXX Effendi, a Clerk," unsigned, n.d.

106. Annual Report of the Posts and Telegraph Department, in *SGR*, 1907, p. 689.

107. PRO, FO 371/16107, Foreign Office minute on salaries of officers and officials in the Sudan, in reply to a question posed in Parliament by Major General Sir Alfred Knox, May 10, 1932. This document mentions the elimination of the climate allowance and the preferable weighting of Southern service on the pension. Government service south of the 12th parallel is listed, e.g., in the "Record of Service and History Sheet" for Adam Da'ud Mandil, in NRO, Personnel 5A/1/3: File of Adam Da'ud Mandil.

108. NRO, Personnel 3A/1/1: File of Ibrahim Badri. On Ibrahim Badri himself, see Bashiri, *Ruwwad al-fikr al-sudani*, 24–26.

109. Abu Salim and Hasan, Introduction to *Diwan ufuq wa-shafaq*, 8.

110. Jibril, *Diwan ufuq wa-shafaq*; see, e.g., pt. 1, 94, 132–33; pt. 2, 19–21, 22–24, 115, 121; pt. 3, 21–23, 121, 129; and pt. 4, 41, 51. There are comments on many of the poems in the anthology and these explain allusions to work-related people, places, and occasions.

111. Mikha'il, *Shu'ara' al-Sudan*, 115–27; NRO, Personnel 4B/2/4: File of Hasib Ali Hasib, Sudan Government Record of Service and History Sheet.

112. This story appeared anonymously in *al-Fajr* magazine, p. 1168, cited in Abidin, *Tarikh al-thaqafa al-arabiyya fi al-Sudan*, 341.

113. Tanbal, *Diwan al-Tabi'a*, 47–51; the quotation is from the footnote on p. 47.

114. This book remains in manuscript form and was never published (see Karrar, Ibrahim, and O'Fahey, "The Life and Writings of a Sudanese Historian," 125–36).

115. Abd al-Rahim, *Nafathat al-yara'*, iii.

116. Abdel Halim, "Native Medicines in the Northern Sudan"; and Bedri,

"Notes on Dinka Religious Beliefs in Their Hereditary Chiefs and Rain Makers."

117. Langley, *No Woman's Country*, 176.

118. Tanbal, *Diwan al-Tabi'a*; Bara is in Kordofan.

119. Ali, *Shakhsiyyat amma min al-Mawrada*, 24–34.

120. Khayr, *Kifah jil*; editions appeared in 1948, 1970, and 1991.

6: THE NATION AFTER THE COLONY

1. Weber, *Peasants into Frenchmen*; "Mexico's Indians: One Nation, or Many?"; McDowall, *A Modern History of the Kurds*.

2. Griffiths, *The Atlas of African Affairs*, 166–71.

3. An early example of this literature is Ranger, "Connexions between 'Primary Resistance' Movements and Modern Mass Nationalism"; a later example is Geiger, "Women and African Nationalism."

4. Brook and Schmid, "Introduction: Nations and Identities in Asia," 3–4.

5. Forty years later, a Southern Sudanese historian reflected, "In the eyes of Southerners self-government was simply a change of masters," which in its favoring of Northerners, "sent shock waves through the South." (Ruay, *The Politics of Two Sudans*, 72).

6. Renan, "What Is a Nation?," esp. 52–53.

7. Kohn, *Nationalism*, 9–10.

8. Anderson, Introduction to *Mapping the Nation*, 1; see also Anderson, *Imagined Communities*.

9. Miller, *On Nationality*, 24.

10. Gellner, *Nations and Nationalism*, 1, 43; Kedourie, *Nationalism*; Breuilly, *Nationalism and the State*, 1–2.

11. Renan, "What Is a Nation?," 52.

12. McCrone, *The Sociology of Nationalism*, viii.

13. Adapted from Miller, *On Nationality*, 25.

14. Contrast, e.g., the views of Seton-Watson, "Old and New Nations," and Conner, "When Is a Nation?"

15. Miller, *On Nationality*, 19; Gellner, *Nations and Nationalism*, 1, 43.

16. Guha, Introduction to *A Subaltern Studies Reader*, xi; Breckenridge and van der Veer, *Orientalism and the Postcolonial Predicament*. The phrase is not limited to South Asian studies; consider, e.g., Cutbill, "A Postcolonial Predicament," which studies Djibouti a country that is "virtually a city-state" (p. 20).

17. An excellent discussion of colonial border politics (including the Gambian demarcation) appears in Griffiths, *The African Inheritance*, ch. 8, "Political Boundaries," pp. 84–98. On Iraq, see Simon, "The Imposition of Nationalism on a Non-Nation State." On the pre-British Indian empires, see Wolpert, *A New History of India*, 64–66.

18. Roberts, *The Colonial Moment in Africa*.

19. Weber, *Peasants into Frenchmen*, 485.

20. Osterhammel, *Colonialism*, 68.

21. Miller, *On Nationality,* 25.

22. Luckham, *The Nigerian Military.*

23. Smith, *State and Nation in the Third World,* 28.

24. Austin, *Politics in Ghana, 1946–1960,* 40, 44, 47.

25. Woodward, *Sudan.*

26. Cohen, *The Politics of Elite Culture.*

27. Potter, *India's Political Administrators,* 117–18; McDonald and Stark, *English Education, Nationalist Politics, and Elite Groups in Maharashtra,* 16–17; Luhrmann, *The Good Parsi,* 37–38, 113.

28. Metz, *Sudan.* Of course, minor differences, rooted in family origins or ideologies, prevailed within this group, and these were sufficient to produce factional rivalries during and after the colonial era.

29. Many of these themes were discussed at a conference on "Literature and Nationalism in the Middle East and North Africa," held at the University of Edinburgh, July 10–13, 2000. Yasir Suleiman is preparing an edited collection of articles from this conference, which will include Sharkey, "Articulating the Nation."

30. For a critical view of the early nationalists as secularists, see Sidahmed, *Politics and Islam in Contemporary Sudan.*

31. Sharkey, "Arabic Literature and the Nationalist Imagination in Kordofan," 165–66, 171–75.

32. Tambal, *Al-Adab al-sudani wa-ma yajibu an yakuna alayhi,* 30.

33. See Chapter 2.

34. Years later, historians and literary analysts recognized this article as a landmark in the development of nationalism and Arabic literature in the Northern Sudan (see al-Shush, Introduction to *Al-Adab al-sudani wa-ma yajibu an yakuna alayhi;* al-Shush, *Al-Shi'r al-hadith fi al-Sudan,* 149–68; al-Nuwayhi, *Muhadarat an al-ittijahat al-shi'riyya fi al-Sudan,* 48; Sharkey, "Colonialism and the Culture of Nationalism in the Northern Sudan, 1898–1956," 2:285–90.

35. Abu Hasabu, *Factional Conflict in the Sudanese National Movement.*

36. Consider the debate in *al-Fajr* in 1935 between Muhammad Ahmad Mahjub, who wrote an essay titled "Sudanese Culture: Its Essence Must be Separate from Egyptian Culture," and the Egyptian writer Muhammad Abd al-Qadir Hamza, who wrote a rejoinder titled "Egyptian Literature and Sudanese Literature: The Mistake of Separating Them and the Necessity of Working to Consolidate Their Links" (*al-Fajr,* April 1, 1935, 857–64; *al-Fajr,* June 1, 1935, 1006–1009).

37. See Khayr, *Kifah jil,* 80–85; and Warburg, *Islam, Nationalism, and Communism in a Traditional Society,* 66, 94.

38. Tanbal, *Diwan al-Tabi'a.*

39. Abd al-Rahim, *Nafathat al-yara',* 119.

40. A brief survey of Sudanese "nature poetry," i.e., poetry with specific local Sudanese settings, appears in Badawi, *al-Shi'r al-hadith fi al-Sudan,* 567–77.

41. Muhammad Ahmad Mahjub, "Al-Shu'ur al-qawmi (wa-hajatuna

ilayhi)," *al-Nahda*, February 21, 1932; Muhammad Ahmad Mahjub, "Al-Shi'r al-qawmi," *al-Fajr*, September 16, 1934, pp. 329–32; Muhammad Ahmad Mahjub, "Wajib al-udaba' nahwa ummatihim wa-fannihim," *al-Fajr*, October 1, 1934, pp. 385–88. These appear in Mahjub, *Nahwa al-ghad*, 57–61, 113–16, and 117–20, respectively.

42. Ali Abd al-Rahman al-Amin, "Tarikh al-Sudan," *al-Nahda*, November 8, 1931, pp. 12–13. Regarding unsympathetic accounts, the author mentioned histories by the Lebanese Na'um Shuqayr and by the Egyptian Ibrahim Pasha Fawzi; he may have also been thinking of English-language works such as Richard A. Bermann's xenophobic history of the Mahdist movement, which was reviewed in *al-Nahda* two weeks later (see Shuqayr, *Tarikh al-Sudan al-qadim wa'l-hadith wa-jughrafiyatuhu*; Fawzi, *Kitab al-Sudan bayna yaday Ghurdun wa-Kitshinir*; and Bermann, *The Mahdi of Allah*).

43. Shibayka, *Al-Sudan abra al-qurun*. For his early history articles, see *al-Fajr*, July 16, 1934, pp. 166–68; and September 16, 1934, pp. 346–49. For his biography, see Abu Salim, *Udaba' wa-ulama' wa-mu'arrikhun fi tarikh al-Sudan*, 289–310.

44. Abidin, *Tarikh al-thaqafa al-arabiyya fi al-Sudan*, 165–75. According to Abidin, "Ibn Sudan" was probably Shaykh Abd al-Rahman Ahmad, a graduate of the Gordon College *qadi*'s section. These articles by "Ibn Sudan" appeared in *al-Nahda*, November 29, 1931, pp. 13–14; and *al-Nahda*, January 17, 1932, pp. 13–14.

45. A translation of the speech made by Sayyid Abd al-Rahman al-Mahdi is reported in *al-Nil* (see SAD, 657/4/26: Ina Beasley Papers); and a copy appears in *al-Nil*, July 22, 1944 (see SAD, 658/5/15: Ina Beasley Papers).

46. Sharkey, "Colonialism and the Culture of Nationalism," ch. 8, "The Other Half of Life: Women as a Battleground for Nationalism," 2:331–92.

47. Consider the history of Andalusia that appears in Abd al-Rahim, *Nafathat al-yara'*, 241–81. Note, too, that Muhammad Ahmad Mahjub published a poetry anthology called *al-Andalus al-mafqud* (Lost Andalusia). On the latter, see Abu Salim, *Udaba' wa-ulama' wa-mu'arrikhun fi tarikh al-Sudan*,

46. Mekki Shibayka wrote about the Seljuks in the Abbasid caliphate in *al-Fajr*, September 16, 1934, pp. 346–49. The figure of the Kurdish anti-Crusader, Salah al-Din al-Ayyubi, was also very popular; he served as the hero of at least one Northern Sudanese play in the early 1920s (see Najila, *Malamih min al-mujtama' al-sudani*, 287).

48. Abidin, *Tarikh al-thaqafa al-arabiyya fi al-Sudan*, 393. One leading poet who studied Kababish poetry and drew inspiration from it was Muhammad Sa'id al-Abbasi (1881–1959) (see Sami, *Al-Sha'ir al-sudani Muhammad Sa'id al-Abbasi*, 49; Abidin, *Tarikh al-thaqafa al-arabiyya fi al-Sudan*, 185–99, 239; and Sharkey, "Arabic Literature and the Nationalist Imagination," 175–78.

49. The author was Abd Allah Abd al-Rahman al-Amin al-Darir (1890–1964). For his biography, see Bashiri, *Ruwwad al-fikr al-sudani*, 229–31. On its place in the early history of monograph publication, see Sharkey, "Colonialism and the Culture of Nationalism," 2:301–2. A reference to the book of Abd Allah

Abd al-Rahman al-Amin (a.k.a., al-Darir), entitled *Diwan al-Uruba* appears in Mashru' Tarikh al-Haraka al-Wataniyya fi al-Sudan, *Bibliyughrafiya al-haraka al-wataniyya fi al-Sudan, 1919–1955*, vol. 2.

50. Hillelson, "Arabic Proverbs, Sayings, Riddles, and Popular Beliefs."

51. al-Fadli, Introduction to *Kitab al-arabiyya fi al-Sudan*, i.

52. *al-Nahda*, February 21, 1932; Mahjub, *Nahwa al-ghad*, 57–61.

53. Mahjub, *al-Haraka al-fikriyya fi al-Sudan*, in Mahjub, *Nahwa al-ghad*, 226.

54. Sandell, *English Language in Sudan*; Abu Bakr, "Language and Education in the Southern Sudan."

55. Muslim missionaries had been operating informally in parts of the South and in the Nuba Mountains during the colonial period, but after decolonization they gained greater freedom in operating and greater support from authorities. On Muslim proselytism in the Anglo-Egyptian era, see Nasr, *al-Idara al-baritaniyya wa'al-tabshir al-islami wa'al-masihi fi al-Sudan*.

56. Ruay, *The Politics of Two Sudans*, 98–101.

57. Khayr, *Kifah jil*, 184–85.

58. Ibid., 11.

59. Interest in African components of Sudanese identity was a postcolonial development. It was the consequence, perhaps, of the Sudan's membership in the Africa-wide Organization of African Unity (founded 1963), and the growth of university curricula in anthropology and folklore studies. A landmark study was Hasan, *Sudan in Africa*. This volume first appeared in 1971.

60. Mahjub, *al-Haraka al-fikriyya fi al-Sudan*, in Mahjub, *Nahwa al-ghad*, 212.

61. The phrase comes from the dedication page of Haddara, *Tayyarat al-shi'r al-arabi al-mu'asir fi al-Sudan*.

62. Warburg, *Historical Discord in the Nile Valley*, 139–40, citing al-Sadiq al-Mahdi, *Al-Islam wa-mas'alat janub al-Sudan*.

63. Bakheit, "British Administration and Sudanese Nationalism," 7–8. His thesis was never published in English, although it did appear in Arabic. See also Bakhit, *Al-Idara al-baritaniyya wa'l-haraka al-wataniyya fi al-Sudan, 1919–1939*.

64. Ibrahim, *Al-Fikr al-sudani*, 11–12. This book was first published in 1979, although the author notes in the Foreword that he wrote much of the text in 1965.

65. A survey of the historical discord between Northern and Southern Sudanese views appears in Warburg, *Historical Discord in the Nile Valley*; regarding the thought of Garang especially, see p. 149. Among the relevant works by Francis Mading Deng are *Seed of Redemption* and *Cry of the Owl*.

66. Harir, "Recycling the Past in the Sudan," 10–68. In *The Quills of the Porcupine*, Jean Allman makes a related argument about the continuing political relevance of Ashante identity in twentieth-century Ghana.

67. U.S. Committee for Refugees, "Country Report: Sudan."

68. Ibrahim, "Civil Society and Prospects of Democratization in the Arab

World," 35, Summary Table 1: "The Cost of Armed Conflicts in the Middle East and North Africa (MENA) Region, 1948–1992."

69. See, e.g., Wöndu and Lesch, Battle for Peace in Sudan, 29–37.

70. In the 1960s guerrilla fighters of the Anya-Nya (an organization whose name means "snake poison" in the Madi language, as a reflection of its lethal intentions vis-à-vis Northern administrators; see Ruay, The Politics of Two Sudans, 106) even reverted to colonial policies regarding language instruction in schools. "Far from the eyes and control of the Government," wrote one Northern linguist and educator, "the Anyanya were running their schools in the sixties in the jungles of the South," teaching local vernaculars at lower levels and only English to advanced students (Abu Bakr, "Language and Education in the Southern Sudan," 14–15).

71. Lesch, The Sudan, 47–48.

72. Chatterjee, The Nation and Its Fragments, 3.

73. Hobsbawm, "Ethnicity and Nationalism in Europe Today," 255.

74. Keane, Civil Society, 94–95.

75. Ibid., 102–12; Lesch, The Sudan; Hale, Gender Politics in Sudan. On civil society debates regarding the Middle East, see Norton, Civil Society in the Middle East; on civil society debates regarding Africa, see Comaroff and Comaroff, Civil Society and the Political Imagination in Africa.

76. Discussions of breakup frequently occurred at the annual meetings of the Sudan Studies Association (SSA) in the United States; the Nasir branch of the SPLM openly called for a two-state solution at the Abuja peace talks in 1992 (Wöndu and Lesch, Battle for Peace in Sudan, 35–36).

77. Ruay, The Politics of Two Sudans, 175.

78. Remarkably, in the Horn of Africa during the 1990s, two regions showed evidence of reverting to colonial borders: Eritrea (a former Italian colony), which won a war to secede from Ethiopia; and the region of the former British Somaliland, which, in the context of Somali state breakdown, achieved quasi-autonomy from its other half, the former Italian Somalia.

79. Leopold Senghor of Senegal and Kwame Nkrumah of Ghana both inveighed against the "Balkanization" of Africa (see Gardinier, "The Path to Independence in French Africa," 33 n. 3; and Griffiths, The Atlas of African Affairs, 76).

80. Griffiths, The Atlas of African Affairs, 66–69. African leaders dissolved the OAU in 2002 and replaced it with an African Union that claimed authority to intervene in the affairs of member countries in order to stop human rights abuses and war crimes. It remains to be seen whether this new organization will fulfill its mandate.

81. Hudson, Introduction to Middle East Dilemma: The Politics and Economics of Arab Integration; and Burrowes, "The Republic of Yemen," 187–213.

82. Sivan, "Arab Nationalism in the Age of the Islamic Resurgence."

CONCLUSION: THE COLONY AND THE NATION

1. Rene Malouf, telephone conversation with author. Mr. Malouf was born in Khartoum in 1924 and grew up in the Sudan. His father, Nicolas Khattar Malouf (1884–1958), a graduate of the American University of Beirut, had come to the Sudan to work as a doctor in the government medical service (1909–16) and later went into private practice.

2. Professor R. S. O'Fahey, conversation with author.

3. Daly, *Imperial Sudan*, 3.

4. Harir, "Recycling the Past in the Sudan," 10, citing Thomas, *Sudan*, 118–21.

5. Hyam, *Empire and Sexuality*, 158–59.

6. Boustead, *The Wind of Morning;* Collins, *Shadows in the Grass;* Beasley, *Before the Wind Changed;* Hawley, *Sandtracks in the Sudan.*

7. Tosh, *The Pursuit of History,* 5.

8. Renan, "What Is a Nation?"

9. Ibn Khaldun, *The Muqaddimah,* 5.

Bibliography

ARCHIVAL MATERIALS

Sudan Government Archives, Khartoum
National Records Office (NRO)

NRO PERSONNEL FILES

Listed below are the names of the government employees whose personnel files are cited in this book. Birth and death dates and schools attended (where known), professions, years of government service, and file numbers are listed. Sources for dates come from the personnel files but also from Mahjub Umar Bashiri, *Ruwwad al-fikr al-sudani*, and from SAD G/S 1096: "Sirat D. Ali Badri," obituary by Babikr Ali Badri, dated January 1987. Note that many of the men below pursued other careers (e.g., in journalism or business) after their years of service.

Arafat Muhammad Abd Allah (1897–1936):
    Clerk (Post and Telegraphs), served 1916–24
    Graduate of Gordon College
    NRO Personnel 5A/4/14

Muhammad al-Mahdi al-Khalifa Abd Allah (b. circa 1894):
    Temporary accountant, translator, served 1916–17, 1921–24
    Privately educated; did not attend government schools
    NRO Personnel 5B/2/6

Ahmad Mahmud Abu'l-Naja (b. circa 1890):
    Surveyor, served 1908–1945
    Graduate of Berber intermediate school
    NRO Personnel 11A/1/1

Abu Bakr Uthman Arbab (b. circa 1895):
    Clerk, translator, sub-mamur, mamur, served 1914–52
    Graduate of Gordon College
    NRO Personnel 3A/1/2

Isma'il al-Atabani (b. 1910):
    Accountant, served 1930–41
    Graduate of Gordon College
    NRO Personnel 7B/1/3

Ali Babikr Badri (1903–87):
    Teacher, medical doctor, served 1923–48
    Graduate of Gordon College and Kitchener School of Medicine
    NRO Personnel 1A/3/6

Ibrahim Yusuf Badri (1897–1962):
    Sub-mamur, mamur, Assistant District Commissioner, served 1923–50
    Graduate of Gordon College
    NRO Personnel 3A/1/1

Yusuf Babikr Badri (1912–95):
    Pharmacist, served 1937–43
    Graduate of Gordon College and the American University of Beirut
        (Chemistry and Pharmacy)
    NRO Personnel 1C/1/2

Yahya al-Fadli (1911–74):
    Translator (Medical Service, Financial Secretariat), served 1931–43
    Graduate of Gordon College
    NRO Personnel 1D/1/3

Khidir Hamad (1908–70):
    Clerk/typist (Financial Secretariat), served 1928–46
    Graduate of Gordon College
    NRO Personnel 5A/2/8

Ahmad Abu'l-Qasim Hashim (b. circa 1895):
    Teacher at Ma'had al-Ilmi, *qadi*, served 1922–c. 1942
    Graduate of al-Azhar, Cairo (*alamiyya* certificate)
    NRO Personnel 4C/1/1

Hasib Ali Hasib (b. circa 1898):
    Legal assistant (Shari'a courts), served 1920–29
    Graduate of Gordon College
    NRO Personnel 4B/2/4

Musa al-Khalifa Ali al-Hilu (b. circa 1890):
    Agriculturalist, served 1911–38
    Graduate of Egyptian agricultural schools (trained on the farms of

the Khedivial Agricultural Society near Tanta, while exiled with
Mahdist prisoners)
NRO Personnel 2A/3/8

Da'ud Iskandar (b. Assyut, 1900):
Teacher, medical doctor, served 1928–55
Graduate of Gordon College and Kitchener School of Medicine
NRO Personnel 1A/2/4

Tawfiq Salih Jibril (1897–1968):
Teacher, clerk, sub-mamur, served 1920–52
Graduate of Gordon College
NRO Personnel 3A/5/10

Abd al-Fattah al-Maghribi (1898–1990):
Mathematics teacher (Gordon Memorial College), served 1919–49
Graduate of Gordon College and the American University of Beirut (B.A.,
    Mathematics)
NRO Personnel 15A/7/29

al-Tijani Muhammad al-Mahi (1908–70):
Medical doctor, served 1935–c. 1954
Graduate of Gordon College and Kitchener School of Medicine
NRO Personnel 1A/1/2

Adam Da'ud Mandil (b. 1891):
Stevedor (Customs), translator, head clerk (*bashkatib*), served 1908–41
Graduate of Omdurman intermediate school
NRO Personnel 5A/1/3

Ahmad al-Shinqiti (b. circa 1899):
Clerk, sub-mamur, mamur, served 1923–52
Graduate of Omdurman intermediate school
NRO Personnel 3A/3/5

Abd Allah Ashri al-Siddiq (b. 1910):
Technical assistant to government entomologist (Agriculture and Forests),
    served 1935–36
Graduate of Gordon College
NRO Personnel 2B/1/4

Hamza al-Malik Tanbal (1897–1951):
Sub-mamur, served 1923–32
Graduate of Aswan intermediate school
NRO Personnel 3A/6/13

Abd Allah Dafa' Allah al-Turabi (b. circa 1896):
Clerk and legal assistant (Shari'a courts), *qadi*, served 1925–c. 1943
Graduate of Ma'had al-Ilmi, Omdurman (*alamiyya* certificate)
NRO Personnel 4A/7/16

Abd Allah Uthman (b. circa 1901):
    Ushur (herd tax) clerk, gum weigher, sub-mamur, mamur, Assistant
        District Commissioner, served 1919–57
    Attended Omdurman intermediate school for one year
    NRO Personnel 3C/1/1

Dardiri Muhammad Uthman (1896–1977):
    Teacher, sub-mamur, mamur, District Judge, High Court Judge, served
        1914–c. 1944
    Graduate of Gordon College
    NRO Personnel 4A/5/12

NRO Personnel Petitions
    NRO Personnel II/2/17: CIVSEC Petition Nos. 43, 1186, 1194, 1269, 1788,
        1297

University of Durham

SUDAN ARCHIVE (SAD)

Below is a list of collections from which items are cited in this book. Information is provided on the career track of individual donors, their dates of Sudan service, and, where known, their birth and death dates. In the listings, starting dates for careers in the Sudan Political Service refer to the date of first Sudan appointment rather than the date of acceptance into the service. A designation of S.P.S., standing for "Sudan Political Service," refers to participation in the elite, exclusively male and British civil administration of Assistant District Commissioners, District Commissioners, province governors, and policy makers. Most S.P.S. officials served in several provinces or positions during the course of their careers and rose through the ranks. The following auxiliary sources were useful in tracking dates: Durham University Library, *Summary Guide to the Sudan Archive* (Durham, 1996); G. Bell, B. D. Dee et al., comp., *Sudan Political Service, 1899–1956* (Oxford, c. 1957); and the collection of obituaries kept by Jane Hogan of Durham University's Sudan Archive.

P. B. E. Acland (1902–93)
    S.P.S., served 1925–42

H. B. Arber (1906–86)
    S.P.S., served 1928–54

R. E. H. Baily (1885–197?)
    S.P.S., served 1909–33

Andrew Balfour (1873–1931)
    Wellcome Tropical Laboratories, served 1902–13

E. A. Balfour (b. 1909)
S.P.S., served 1932–55

Ina M. Beasley (b. 1898)
Education Department, served 1939–49

G. W. Bell (1909–95)
S.P.S., served 1931–55

E. J. Bickersteth (b. 1915)
S.P.S., served 1938–55

A. R. C. Bolton (b. 1900)
S.P.S., served 1923–47

P. P. Bowcock
S.P.S., served 1951–55

L. M. Buchanan (b. 1906)
S.P.S., served 1929–54

R. M. Cooper (b. 1920)
S.P.S., served 1947–55

A. W. M. Disney (1903–79)
S.P.S., served 1927–53
Managing Director of Blue Nile Brewing Ltd. (Khartoum North), 1953–57

D. M. H. Evans (b. 1907)
S.P.S., served 1930–55

E. C. L. Flavell
Civil Secretariat, served 1920–40

R. C. Garrett
Finance Department, Military Transport Department of the Sudan Defence
Force, War Supplies Department, Stores and Ordnance Department,
served 1925–49

J. A. Gillan (1885–1981)
S.P.S., served 1909–39

K. H. J. Hayes
Legal Department, served 1939–53

K. D. D. Henderson (1903–88)
S.P.S., served 1927–53

P. P. Howell (1917–94)
S.P.S., served 1938–55

C. A. E. Lea (b. 1902)
S.P.S., served 1927–51

J. Longe (1903–87)
S.P.S., served 1926–53

H. A. MacMichael (b. 1882)
S.P.S., served 1905–34

J. G. S. MacPhail (b. 1900)
S.P.S., served 1923–47

S. L. Milligan (1887–1968)
Egyptian Army, Anglo-French Boundary Commission, Sudan Defence
Force, Sudan Survey Department, served 1919–37

P. D. Mulholland
Egyptian Army, Finance Department, Sudan Railways, War Supply Department, served 1922–44

T. H. B. Mynors (b. 1907)
S.P.S., served 1930–55

J. H. R. Orlebar (1907–89)
Sudan Defence Force, served 1933–43
Including the papers of T. W. Davidson (served Sudan Defence Force, 1925–
31), and A. D. Dodds-Parker (served S.P.S., 1931–39)

T. R. H. Owen (b. 1903)
S.P.S., served 1936–53

J. W. Robertson (1899–1983)
S.P.S., 1923–53

E. G. Sarsfield-Hall (b. 1886)
S.P.S., served 1909–36

R. V. Savile (b. 1873)
S.P.S., served 1902–23

R. von Slatin (1857–1932)
Inspector-General, 1900–14

R. C. Stevenson (1915–91)
Church Missionary Society, served 1937–59

N. R. Udal (1883–1964)
Education Department, served 1906–30
Personal and Political Advisor in the United Kingdom to Sayyid Abd
al-Rahman al-Mahdi, c. 1940s–1950s

D. Vidler (b. 1914)
S.P.S., served 1937–55

V. H. G. Vokes
Finance Department, then Public Relations Section of the Civil Secretary's Department, served 1925–49

C. A. Willis (b. 1881)
S.P.S., served 1905–31

J. Winder (1905–89)
S.P.S., served 1927–55

F. R. Wingate (1861–1953)
Governor-General, served 1899–1916

Mabel E. Wolff (c.1890–1981)
Matron of Midwifery Training School, later Inspectress of Midwives, served 1921–37

OTHER DURHAM COLLECTIONS CITED

Ali Badri (1903–87)
Education Department, later Sudan Medical Service, served 1923–48; Minister of Health, 1948–53; President, Sudan Red Cross (latterly Red Crescent), 1945–76; private practice doctor, 1954–57; pharmaceutical entrepreneur, 1962–87. Uncatalogued papers include miscellaneous photographs and obituaries.

Gordon Memorial College Trust
These papers date from 1899 to 1968 and include records of board meetings for the Gordon Memorial College at Khartoum.

Miscellaneous Small Donations
Including early picture postcards of Gordon College.

University of London
School of Oriental and African Studies Library (SOAS)

The Reverend Dr. A. J. Arkell Papers (Accession No. 210522)
A. J. Arkell (1898–1980); Sudan Political Service, later Sudan Government Archaeologist, served 1921–48

University of Birmingham
Church Missionary Society Archives (CMS)

Egyptian Mission Précis Books:
G3 E P1: Précis book, 1890–1901
G3 E P2: Précis book, 1901–12
G3 E P3: Précis book, 1912–26

University of Edinburgh
Manuscripts and Special Collections (EUL)

Reginald Davies Papers (EUL MS Gen 1899)
    Reginald Davies (b. 1897)
    Sudan Political Service, served 1921–45
    Sudan Agency (London), served 1946–55

Wellcome Institute for the History of Medicine, London
General Collections

J. A. Simons Papers (GC/125)
    Dr. John Antoine Simons (1900–71)
    Sudan Medical Service, served 1927–31

University of Bergen, Norway, Senter for Midtausten- og islamske studiar
(Centre for Middle Eastern and Islamic Studies)

Copies of the following journals:
    al-Nahda al-Sudaniyya (Khartoum), 1931–32
    al-Fajr (Khartoum), 1934–35

British Government Archives, London

Public Record Office (PRO)

Documents from the following files are cited:

FOREIGN OFFICE PAPERS

FO 78/5096	FO 371/10050	FO 371/13151
FO 370/142	FO 371/10051	FO 371/13875
FO 371/1111	FO 371/10052	FO 371/14609
FO 371/2349	FO 371/10053	FO 371/14650
FO 371/4984	FO 371/10080	FO 371/14653
FO 371/6303	FO 371/10880	FO 371/16107
FO 371/7746	FO 371/10905	FO 371/17021
FO 371/10039	FO 371/11613	FO 371/20886
FO 371/10049	FO 371/13127	

WAR OFFICE PAPERS

WO 32/3537
WO 106/232

GOVERNMENT AND INSTITUTIONAL PUBLICATIONS

The Gordon Memorial College at Khartoum. *Report and Accounts, 1904–45.*
Great Britain. *Report of the Special Mission to Egypt, 1921* (Milner Report).

Sudan Government. *Reports on the Finances, Administration and Condition of the Sudan,* 1902–13.

——. *Monthly Return of Our Senior Officials, Sudan Government, and British Officers Temporarily Employed in Sudan Government Service,* 1914–18.

——. *Quarterly List of the Sudan Government* (staff lists), 1919–40.

——. *The Sub-Mamur's Handbook.* Khartoum: McCorquodale and Co., 1926.

——. *Report of a Commission of Inspection on the Gordon Memorial College, Khartoum, February* 1929.

——. *Annual Reports of the Education Department,* 1929–30, 1935, 1937–38, 1948.

——. *Education in the Northern Sudan: Report of a Committee Appointed by His Excellency the Governor-General,* 1934.

——. *Report of Lord De La Warr's Educational Commission,* 1937.

——. *Half Yearly List of the Sudan Government* (staff lists), 1941–42.

——, Education Department. *Regulations and Syllabus of Studies for Elementary Vernacular Schools,* 1926.

——. *Codes of Regulations for Primary Schools and Syllabus of the Primary Course of Study,* n.d. (c. 1926?).

Sudan Republic. *Ministry of Education Annual Report,* 1956–57.

JOURNALS

al-Fajr (Khartoum), 1934–35.
al-Nahda (Khartoum), 1931–32.
Sudan Notes and Records, from vol. 1, 1918.

INTERVIEWS AND PERSONAL COMMUNICATIONS

The book includes citations from the following individuals who shared information with the author in interviews, conversations, or letters:

Abu Zayd, Dr. Abd al-Rahman. Interview with author, Omdurman, Sudan, October 23, 1995.
Vice-Chancellor, Omdurman Ahlia University; former Vice-Chancellor, University of Juba.

al-Atabani, Isma'il. Interview with author, Omdurman, Sudan, October 30, 1995.
Major figure in the nationalist literary circles of the 1930s; active figure in establishing the Graduates Congress; contributor to *al-Nahda* and *al-Fajr* literary magazines; editor-in-chief of the daily newspaper, *Sawt al-Sudan* (1941–44); founder and editor-in-chief of the daily non-sectarian newspa-

per, *al-Ra'y al-Amm* (1945–70); graduate of Gordon College (1930); served as an accountant in the Sudan Government (1930–41).

Badri, Dr. Qasim. Interview with author, Omdurman, Sudan, October 25, 1995.
President, Ahfad University for Women; son of Yusuf Badri; grandson of Babikr Badri.

Brown, Professor L. C. E-mail letter to author, September 14, 1999.
Historian of the modern Middle East; former U.S. diplomat to the Republic of Sudan, 1956–58.

Hawley, Sir Donald. Letter to author, August 4, 1997.
Served Sudan Defence Force and Sudan Political Service, 1941–55.

Issawi, Professor Charles. Conversation with author, Princeton, New Jersey, September 25, 1996; letter to author, August 26, 1997.
Economic historian of the Middle East; son of Emile Issawi, a Sudan government employee.

Jurdak, Muna Shami, in cooperation with her mother, Najla Shami. Letter to author, August 14, 1996.
Niece of Edward Atiyah and granddaughter of Salim Atiyah, both of whom served as directors of intelligence in the Sudan government.

al-Khalifa, Sirr al-Khatm. Interview with author, Khartoum, Sudan, October 19, 1995.
Government-employed educator; teacher at Bakht er Ruda (1938–50); Ministry of Education, school inspector and director of Arabicization policies in Southern education, based at Juba (1950–60); Prime Minister (1964); ambassador to Italy (1965–67) and the United Kingdom (1968–71); publisher of educational books and magazines for children (1985–89); Chancellor of Omdurman Ahlia University; graduate of Gordon College (1936).

Malouf, René. Telephone conversation with author, February 12, 1997.
Son of Dr. Nicholas Khattar Malouf (1884–1958), who served in the Sudan Medical Service from 1909 to 1916.

O'Fahey, R. S. Conversation with author in Bergen, Norway, September 1994.
Historian of Sudan and of the Arabic and Islamic cultures of Africa.

al-Tum Satti, Amin. Interview with author, Omdurman, Sudan, October 27, 1995.
Former Umma Party chairman; Minister of Defense (1957); parliamentary representative for Amintago (1955–56); secretary-general of the Graduates Club of Port Sudan (1937–40); Graduates Congress politician; secretary-general of the Graduates Congress committee for the Eastern Sudan (1939–40); graduate of Gordon College (1934); served as an estimator in the Customs Department of the Sudan government (1935–46).

OTHER WORKS

*An asterisk indicates that the author, whether British, Sudanese, Egyptian, or Syrian/Lebanese, is known to have worked in the Sudan during the 1898–1956 period (in most cases, as government employees; in a few cases, as missionaries), or to have attended Gordon College. Works thus marked include memoirs, apologias, historical studies, and poetry anthologies.

*Abbas, Mekki. *The Sudan Question: The Dispute over the Anglo-Egyptian Condominium, 1884–1952.* London: Faber and Faber, 1952.

Abd Allah, Awatif Umar. *Salih Abd al-Qadir: Hayatuhu wa-shi'ruhu.* Beirut: Dar al-Jil, 1991.

Abd al-Qadir, Yahya Muhammad., *Shakhsiyyat min al-Sudan: Asrar wara' al-rijal.* 3 vols. Khartoum: Dar al-Sudaniyya lil-kutub, 1952, 1955, 1956.

*Abd al-Rahim, Muhammad. *Nafathat al-yara': Al-adab wa'l-tarikh wa'l-ijtima'.* Khartoum: Sharikat al-Tab' wa'l-Nashr, 1936.

*Abdel Halim, Ahmed Effendi. "Native Medicines in the Northern Sudan." *Sudan Notes and Records* 22 (1939): 27–48.

Abdel Rahim, Muddathir. *Imperialism and Nationalism in the Sudan.* Khartoum: Khartoum University Press, 1986.

Abdin, Hasan. *Early Sudanese Nationalism, 1919–1925.* Khartoum: Khartoum University Press, 1985.

Abdul-Hai. *Conflict and Identity: The Cultural Poetics of Contemporary Sudanese Poetry.* Institute of African and Asian Studies, Seminar Paper no. 26. Khartoum: Khartoum University Press, 1976.

Abidin, Abd al-Majid. *Tarikh al-thaqafa al-arabiyya fi al-Sudan, mundhu nash'atiha ila al-asr al-hadith: Al-din, al-ijtima', al-adab.* 2d ed. Beirut: Dar al-Thaqafa, 1967.

Abu Bakr, Yusuf al-Khalifa. "Language and Education in the Southern Sudan." In *Directions in Sudanese Linguistics and Folklore,* edited by Sayyid H. Hurreiz and Herman Bell, 13–18. Khartoum: Khartoum University Press, 1975.

Abu Hasabu, Afaf Abdel Majid. *Factional Conflict in the Sudanese National Movement, 1918–1948.* Khartoum: Graduate College, University of Khartoum, 1985.

Abu'l-Azayim, Muhammad. *Sahharat al-kashif.* Beirut: Dar Maktabat al-Hilal, n.d.

Abusabib, Mohamed. "The Impact of Islam on African Art: The Case of the Sudan." In *Islamic Art and Culture in Sub-Saharan Africa,* edited by Karin Ådahl and Berit Sahlström, 139–48. Uppsala: Acta Universitatis Upsaliensis, 1995.

Abu Salim, Muhammad Ibrahim. *Tarikh al-Khartum.* 3d ed. Beirut, Dar al-Jil, 1991.

———. *Udaba' wa-ulama' wa-mu'arrikhun fi tarikh al-Sudan.* Beirut: Dar al-Jil, 1991.

Abu Salim, Muhammad Ibrahim and Muhammad Salih Hasan. Introduction to *Diwan ufuq wa-shafaq*, by Tawfiq Salih Jibril, 5–15. Beirut: Dar al-Jil.

*Abu Sinn, Ali Abd Allah. *Mudhakkirat Abi Sinn an mudiriyyat Dar Fur.* Khartoum: Dar al-Watha'iq, 1968.

Adams, William Y. *Nubia: Corridor to Africa.* Princeton, N.J.: Princeton University Press, 1977.

Ajayi, J. F. Ade. "The Development of Secondary Grammar School Education in Nigeria." *Journal of the Historical Society of Nigeria* 2, no. 4 (1963): 517–35.

*Ahmad, Jamal Muhammad. *Jamal Muhammad Ahmad: Rasa'il wa-awraq khassa.* Edited by Uthman Muhammad al-Hasan, Introduction by al-Tayyib Salih. Beirut: Dar al-Jil, 1992.

Ahmad, Su'ad Abd al-Aziz. *Qadaya al-ta'lim al-ahli fi al-Sudan.* Khartoum: Khartoum University Press, 1991.

Ali, Haydar Ibrahim, ed. *Al-Tanawwu' al-thaqafi wa-bina' al-dawla al-wataniyya fi al-Sudan.* Cairo: Markaz al-Dirasat al-Sudaniyya, 1995.

Ali, Mirghani Hasan. *Shakhsiyyat amma min al-Mawrada.* Omdurman: Omdurman Islamic University, n.d.

Allman, Jean Marie. *The Quills of the Porcupine: Asante Nationalism in an Emergent Ghana.* Madison: University of Wisconsin Press, 1993.

Altbach, Philip G., and Gail P. Kelly, eds. *Education and the Colonial Experience.* 2d rev. ed. New Brunswick, N.J.: Transaction Books, 1984.

*al-Amin [al-Darir], Abd Allah Abd al-Rahman. *Diwan al-Uruba.* Cairo: Dar al-Fikr al-Arabi, 1962.

*Amir, al-Tijani. *Al-Sudan tahta al-hukm al-thuna'i (1898–1918).* Cairo: Markaz al-Dirasat al-Siyasiyya wa'l-Istratijiyya bil-Ahram, 1979.

Anderson, Benedict. *Imagined Communities: Reflections on the Origin and Spread of Nationalism.* Rev. ed. London: Verso, 1991.

———. Introduction to *Mapping the Nation*, edited by Gopal Balakrishnan, 1–16. London: Verso, 1996.

Anderson, David M., and David Killingray. "Consent, Coercion, and Colonial Control: Policing the Empire, 1830–1940." In *Policing the Empire: Government, Authority, and Control, 1830–1940*, edited by David M. Anderson and David Killingray, 1–15. Manchester: Manchester University Press, 1991.

Appadurai, Arjun. "Disjuncture and Difference in the Global Cultural Economy." In *Global Culture: Nationalism, Globalization, and Modernity*, edited by Mike Featherstone, 295–310. London: Sage, 1990.

*Archer, Geoffrey. *Personal and Historical Memoirs of an East African Administrator.* Edinburgh: Oliver and Boyd, 1963.

Artin, Yacoub Pasha. *England in the Sudan.* Translated by George Robb. London: Macmillan, 1911.

*Atiyah, Edward. *An Arab Tells His Story: A Study in Loyalties.* London: John Murray, 1946.

———. *Black Vanguard.* London: Peter Davies, 1952.

Austin, Dennis. *Politics in Ghana, 1946–1960.* London: Oxford University Press, 1964.

————. "The Transfer of Power: Why and How." In *Decolonisation and After: The British and French Experience,* edited by W. H. Morris-Jones and Georges Fischer, 3–34. London: Frank Cass, 1980.

Ayalon, Ami. *The Press in the Arab Middle East: A History.* New York: Oxford University Press, 1995.

Azikiwe, Ben N. "How Shall We Educate the African?" *Journal of the African Society* 33, no. 131 (1934): 143–51.

Babiker, Mahjoub Abd al-Malik. *Press and Politics in the Sudan.* Graduate College Publications, no.14. Khartoum: University of Khartoum, 1985.

Babiker, Yousif Omer. "The Al-Fajr Movement and Its Place in Modern Sudanese Literature." Ph.D. diss., University of Edinburgh, 1979.

Badawi, Abduh. *Al-Shi'r al-hadith fi al-Sudan.* Cairo: Al-Majlis al-A'la li-Ri'ayat al-Funun wa'l-Adab wa'l-Ulum al-Ijtima'iyya, 1964.

Badawi, M. M. *A Critical Introduction to Modern Arabic Poetry.* Cambridge: Cambridge University Press, 1975.

————. *A Short History of Modern Arabic Literature.* Oxford: Clarendon Press, 1993.

Baedeker, Karl. *Egypt and the Sudan: Handbook for Travellers.* 8th rev. ed. Leipzig: Karl Baedeker, 1929.

Bakheit, G. M. A. "British Administration and Sudanese Nationalism, 1919–1939." Ph.D. diss., Cambridge University, 1965.

*Bakhit, Ja'far Muhammad Ali. *Al-Idara al-baritaniyya wa'l-haraka al-wataniyya fi al-Sudan, 1919–1939.* Translated by Hinri Riyad. 3d ed. Khartoum: al-Matbu'at al-arabiyya lil-ta'lif wa'l-tarjama, 1987.

Balakrishnan, Gopal , ed. *Mapping the Nation.* Introduction by Benedict Anderson. London: Verso, 1996.

*al-Banna, Abd Allah Muhammad Umar. *Diwan al-Banna.* Edited by Ali al-Makk. Vol. 1. Khartoum: Khartoum University Press, 1976.

Barbour, K. M. *The Republic of the Sudan: A Regional Geography.* London: University of London Press, 1961.

Bashiri, Mahjub Umar. *Ruwwad al-fikr al-sudani.* Beirut: Dar al-Jil, 1991.

————. *Haqibat al-fann: Shu'ara' wa-fannanun.* Khartoum: Mu'assasat Ishraqa lil-Nashr wa'l-Tawzi' wa'l-I'lam, 1994.

Bayly, C. A. *Empire and Information: Intelligence Gathering and Social Communication in India, 1780–1870.* Cambridge: Cambridge University Press, 1996.

*Beasley, Ina. *Before the Wind Changed: People, Places, and Education in the Sudan.* Edited by Janet Starkey. Oxford: Oxford University Press, 1992.

*Bedri, Babikr. *The Memoirs of Babikr Bedri.* Vol. 2. Translated and edited by Yusuf Bedri and Peter Hogg. London: Ithaca Press, 1980.

*Bedri, Ibrahim Effendi. "Notes on Dinka Religious Beliefs in Their Hereditary Chiefs and Rain Makers." *Sudan Notes and Records* 22 (1939): 125–32.

*Bell, Gawain. *Shadows on the Sand: The Memoirs of Sir Gawain Bell.* London: C. Hurst and Co., 1983.

*Bell, G., B. D. Dee, et al. *Sudan Political Service, 1899–1956.* Introduction by Harold MacMichael. Oxford: Oxonian Press, n.d.

Bell G. W., and A. H. M. Kirk-Greene. *The Sudan Political Service, 1902–1952: A Preliminary Register of Second Careers.* Oxford: St. Antony's College, 1989.

Berger, John, et al. *Ways of Seeing.* London: British Broadcasting Corporation and Penguin Books, 1988.

Bermann, Richard A. *The Mahdi of Allah: The Story of the Dervish Mohammed Ahmed.* Introduction by Winston Churchill. New York: Macmillan, 1932.

*Beshir, Mohamed Omer. *Educational Development in the Sudan, 1898–1956.* Oxford: Clarendon Press, 1969.

Bhabha, Homi, ed. *Nation and Narration.* London: Routledge, 1990.

Billig, Michael. *Banal Nationalism.* London: Sage, 1995.

Bjørkelo, Anders. *Prelude to the Mahdiyya: Peasants and Traders in the Shendi Region, 1821–1885.* Cambridge: Cambridge University Press, 1989.

Blunt, Edward. *The I.C.S.: The Indian Civil Service.* London: Faber and Faber, 1937.

Boehmer, Elleke. *Colonial and Postcolonial Literature: Migrant Metaphors.* Oxford: Oxford University Press, 1995.

*Bousfield, Leonard. *Sudan Doctor.* London: Christopher Johnson, 1954.

*Boustead, Hugh. *The Wind of Morning.* London: Chatto and Windus, 1971.

Breckenridge, Carol A., and Peter van der Veer, eds. *Orientalism and the Postcolonial Predicament: Perspectives on South Asia.* Philadelphia: University of Pennsylvania Press, 1993.

Breuilly, John. *Nationalism and the State.* 2d ed. Manchester: Manchester University Press, 1993.

Brook, Timothy. "Collaborationist Nationalism in Occupied Wartime China." In *Nation Work: Asian Elites and National Identities,* edited by Timothy Brook and Andre Schmid, 159–90. Ann Arbor: University of Michigan Press, 2000.

Brook, Timothy, and Andre Schmid, eds. *Nation Work: Asian Elites and National Identities.* Ann Arbor: University of Michigan Press, 2000.

———. "Introduction: Nations and Identities in Asia." In *Nation Work: Asian Elites and National Identities,* edited by Timothy Brook and André Schmid, 1–16. Ann Arbor: University of Michigan Press, 2000.

Brown, L. Carl. *International Politics and the Middle East: Old Rules, Dangerous Game.* Princeton, N.J.: Princeton University Press, 1984.

Brubaker, Rogers. *Citizenship and Nationhood in France and Germany.* Cambridge, Mass.: Harvard University Press, 1992.

Burke, Timothy. *Lifebuoy Men, Lux Women: Commodification, Consumption, and Cleanliness in Modern Zimbabwe.* Durham: Duke University Press, 1996.

Burrowes, Robert D. "The Republic of Yemen: The Politics of Unification and Civil War, 1989–1995." In *Middle East Dilemma: The Politics and Economics of Arab Integration,* edited by Michael C. Hudson, 187–213. New York: Columbia University Press, 1999.

*Byam, William. *The Road to Harley Street*. London: Geoffrey Bles, 1963.
*Cash, W. Wilson. *The Nubas Calling: A Challenge to Pioneer Missionary Adventure among Sudan Hill Tribes*. London: Church Missionary Society, 1933.
Chatterjee, Partha. *Nationalist Thought and the Colonial World: A Derivative Discourse?* London: Zed Books, 1986.
———. *The Nation and Its Fragments: Colonial and Postcolonial Histories*. Princeton, N.J.: Princeton University Press, 1993.
Chaudhuri, Nirad C. *The Autobiography of an Unknown Indian*. New York: Macmillan, 1951.
———. *Culture in the Vanity Bag*. Bombay: Jaico Publishing House, 1976.
Churchill, Winston Spencer. *The River War: An Historical Account of the Reconquest of the Soudan*. 2 vols. London: Longmans, Green, 1900.
Cohen, Abner. *The Politics of Elite Culture: Explorations in the Dramaturgy of Power in a Modern African Society*. Berkeley: University of California Press, 1981.
Cohn, Bernard S. *Colonialism and Its Forms of Knowledge: The British in India*. Princeton, N.J.: Princeton University Press, 1996.
Collins, Robert O. *Shadows in the Grass: Britain in the Southern Sudan, 1918–1956*. New Haven, Conn.: Yale University Press, 1983.
———. "Slavery in the Sudan in History." *Slavery and Abolition* 20, no. 3 (1999): 69–95.
Comaroff, John L., and Jean Comaroff, eds. *Civil Society and the Political Imagination in Africa: Critical Perspectives*. Chicago: University of Chicago Press, 1999.
*Comyn, D. C. E. *Service and Sport in the Sudan: A Record of Administration in the Anglo-Egyptian Sudan, with Some Intervals of Sport and Travel*. London: John Lane, 1911.
Conner, Walker. "When Is a Nation?" In *Nationalism*, edited by John Hutchinson and Anthony D. Smith, 154–59. Oxford: Oxford University Press, 1994.
Cook, David A. *A History of Narrative Film*. New York: W. W. Norton, 1981.
Coombes, Annie E. *Reinventing Africa: Museums, Material Culture, and Popular Imagination in Late Victorian and Edwardian England*. New Haven, Conn.: Yale University Press, 1994.
Cooper, Frederick. *From Slaves to Squatters: Plantation Labor and Agriculture in Zanzibar and Coastal Kenya, 1890–1925*. New Haven, Conn.: Yale University Press, 1980.
———. "Conflict and Connection: Rethinking Colonial African History." *The American Historical Review* 99, no. 5 (1994): 1516–45.
Cooper, Frederick, and Ann Laura Stoler, eds. *Tensions of Empire: Colonial Cultures in a Bourgeois World*. Berkeley: University of California Press, 1997.
*Corbyn, E. N. "The Administration of the Sudan in 1937." *Journal of the Royal African Society* 38, no. 151 (1939): 281–88.
Crowder, Michael. *West Africa under Colonial Rule*. Evanston, Ill.: Northwestern University Press, 1968.

*Cruickshank, Alexander. *The Kindling Fire: Medical Adventures in the Southern Sudan*. London: Heinemann, 1962.

———. *Itchy Feet—A Doctor's Tale*. Ilfracombe, U.K.: Arthur H. Stockwell, 1991.

Cudsi, Alexander Solon. "The Rise of Political Parties in the Sudan, 1936–1946." Ph.D. diss., SOAS, University of London, 1978.

*Currie, James. "The Educational Experiment in the Anglo-Egyptian Sudan, 1900–33." Parts 1 and 2. *The Journal of the African Society* 33, no. 133 (1934): 361–71, 34, no. 134 (1935): 41–59.

Cutbill, Catherine Christine. "A Postcolonial Predicament: Imagining Djibouti." Ph.D. diss., University of Virginia, 1994.

*al-Darir, Abd Allah Abd al-Rahman al-Amin. *Kitab al-arabiyya fi al-Sudan*. Beirut: Dar al-Kitab al-Lubnani, 1967.

Daly, M. W. *British Administration and the Northern Sudan, 1917–1924: The Governor-Generalship of Sir Lee Stack in the Sudan*. Istanbul: Nederlands Historisch-Archaeologisch Instituut, 1980.

———. *Empire on the Nile: The Anglo-Egyptian Sudan, 1898–1934*. Cambridge: Cambridge University Press, 1986.

———. *Imperial Sudan: The Anglo-Egyptian Condominium, 1934–1956*. Cambridge: Cambridge University Press, 1991.

———. *The Sirdar: Sir Reginald Wingate and the British Empire in the Middle East*. Philadelphia: American Philosophical Society, 1997.

Daly, M. W., and L. E. Forbes. *The Sudan: Photographs from the Sudan Archive, Durham University Library*. Caught in Time: Great Photographic Archives. Reading, U.K.: Garnet Publishing, 1994.

Davidson, Basil. *The Black Man's Burden: Africa and the Curse of the Nation-State*. New York: Random House, 1992.

*Davies, Reginald. *The Camel's Back: Service in the Rural Sudan*. London: John Murray, 1957.

Deng, Francis Mading. *Seed of Redemption: A Political Novel*. New York: Lilian Barber Press, 1986.

———. *Cry of the Owl*. New York: Lilian Barber Press, 1989.

Deng, Francis Mading, and M. W. Daly. *Bonds of Silk: The Human Factor in the British Administration of the Sudan*. East Lansing: Michigan State University Press, 1989.

Dirks, Nicholas B., ed. *Colonialism and Culture*. Ann Arbor: University of Michigan Press, 1992.

———. Foreword to *Colonialism and Its Forms of Knowledge: The British in India*, by Bernard S. Cohn. Princeton, N.J.: Princeton University Press, 1996.

Diyab, Ahmad Ibrahim. *Al-Alaqat al-misriyya al-sudaniyya, 1919–1924*. Cairo: al-Hay'a al-Misriyya al-Amma lil-Kitab, 1985.

Douglas, Allen and Fedwa Malti-Douglas. *Arab Comic Strips: Politics of an Emerging Mass Culture*. Bloomington: Indiana University Press, 1994.

*Dugmore, A. Radclyffe. *The Vast Sudan*. London: Arrowsmith, 1926.

*Duncan, J. S. R. *The Sudan: A Record of Achievement.* Edinburgh: William Blackwood and Sons, 1952.

———. *The Sudan's Path to Independence.* Foreword by Sir Knox Helm. Edinburgh: William Blackwood and Sons, 1957.

Durham University Library. *Summary Guide to the Sudan Archive.* Durham: Durham University Library, 1995.

Eagleton, Terry. *The Idea of Culture.* Oxford: Blackwell Publishers, 2000.

Echenberg, Myron. *Colonial Conscripts: The Tirailleurs Sénégalais in French West Africa, 1857–1960.* Portsmouth, N.H.: Heinemann, 1991.

Eckert, Carter J. "Exorcising Hegel's Ghosts: Toward a Postnationalist Historiography of Korea." In *Colonial Modernity in Korea*, edited by Gi-Wook Shin and Michael Robinson, 363–78. Cambridge, Mass.: Harvard University Asia Center, 1999.

Edwards, Elizabeth, ed. *Anthropology and Photography, 1860–1920.* New Haven, Conn.: Yale University Press, 1992.

El Mahdi, Mandour. *A Short History of the Sudan.* Oxford: Oxford University Press, 1984.

El Tayeb, Salah El Din El Zein. *The Students' Movement in the Sudan, 1940–1970.* Khartoum: Khartoum University Press, 1971.

Ewald, Janet J. *Soldiers, Traders, and Slaves: State Formation and Economic Transformation in the Greater Nile Valley, 1700–1885.* Madison: University of Wisconsin Press, 1990.

*al-Fadli, Yahya. Introduction to *Kitab al-arabiyya fi al-Sudan*, by Abd Allah Abd al-Rahman al-Amin al-Darir. Beirut: Dar al-Kitab al-Lubnani, 1967.

Fanon, Frantz. *The Wretched of the Earth.* Translated by Constance Farrington. New York: Grove Weidenfeld, 1963.

*Farah, Khalil. *Diwan Khalil Farah*, edited by Ali al-Makk. Khartoum: Khartoum University Press, 1977.

Fawzi, Ibrahim. *Kitab al-Sudan bayna yaday Ghurdun wa-Kitshinir.* Cairo: Idarat Jaridat al-Mu'ayyid, 1901.

Featherstone, Mike. *Undoing Culture: Globalization, Postmodernism, and Identity.* London: Sage, 1995.

*al-Fiki, Abd al-Rahman. *Tarikh quwat difa' al-Sudan.* Khartoum: al-Dar al-Sudaniyya, 1971.

Finnegan, Ruth. *Oral Poetry: Its Nature, Significance, and Social Context.* Cambridge: Cambridge University Press, 1977.

Fisher, Allan G. B., and Humphrey J. Fisher. *Slavery and Muslim Society in Africa.* London: C. Hurst and Co., 1970.

*Foley, Helen. *Letters to Her Mother: War-Time in the Sudan, 1938–1945.* Castle Cary, U.K.: Castle Cary Press, 1992.

Forlacroix, Christian. "La photographie au service de l'histoire d'Afrique." *Cahiers d'Études Africaines* 10 (1970): 125–43.

Forster, E. M. *A Passage to India.* New York: Harcourt, Brace, 1924.

Foucault, Michel. *The Order of Things: An Archaeology of the Human Sciences.* New York: Vintage Books, 1973.

Fox, Richard G., ed. *Nationalist Ideologies and the Production of National Cultures.* Washington, D.C.: American Anthropological Association, 1990.

Gandhi, Leela. *Postcolonial Theory: A Critical Introduction.* New York: Columbia University Press, 1998.

Gardinier, David E. "The Path to Independence in French Africa: Recent Historiography." *Africana Journal* 15 (1990): 15–38.

Geary, Christraud M. "Photographs as Materials for African History: Some Methodological Considerations." *History in Africa* 13 (1986): 89–116.

Geiger, Susan. "Women and African Nationalism." *Journal of Women's History* 2, no. 1 (1990): 227–44.

Gellner, Ernest. *Nations and Nationalism.* Ithaca, N.Y.: Cornell University Press, 1983.

*Ghawi, Jad Boutros. "Notes on the Law and Custom of the Jur Tribe in the Central District of the Bahr El Ghazal Province." *Sudan Notes and Records* 7 (1924): 71–81.

Gifford, Prosser, and William Roger Louis, eds. *The Transfer of Power in Africa: Decolonization 1940–1960.* New Haven, Conn.: Yale University Press, 1982.

*Gillan, Angus. "Sudan Anecdotage: Extracts from a talk given to the Supper Club on 19th February 1939 just before he retired as Civil Secretary," *Sudan Diocesan Review* (1971): 15–18.

Goldberg, Melvin. "Decolonisation and Political Socialisation with Reference to West Africa." *The Journal of Modern African Studies* 24, no. 4 (1986): 663–77.

Goldthorpe, J. E. *An African Elite: Makerere College Students, 1922–1960.* Foreword by Julius Nyerere. Nairobi: Oxford University Press, 1965.

Goody, Jack. *The Power of the Written Tradition.* Washington, D.C.: Smithsonian Institution Press, 2000.

Graham-Brown, Sarah. *Images of Women: The Portrayal of Women in Photography of the Middle East, 1860–1950.* New York: Columbia University Press, 1988.

Gramsci, Antonio. *The Prison Notebooks: Selections.* Translated by Quintin Hoare and Geoffrey Nowell-Smith. New York: International Publishers, 1971.

Griffiths, Ieuan Ll. *The Atlas of African Affairs.* 2d ed. London: Routledge, 1995.

———. *The African Inheritance.* London: Routledge, 1995.

Griffiths, V. L. *Sudan Courtesy Customs: A foreigner's guide to polite phrases in common use amongst the sophisticated Arabic-speaking population of the Northern Sudan.* Khartoum: Sudan Government, 1936.

———. *An Experiment in Education: An account of the attempts to improve the lower stages of boys' education in the Moslem Anglo-Egyptian Sudan, 1930–1950.* London: Longmans, Green, 1953.

Grossberg, Laurence, Cary Nelson, and Paula A. Treichler, ed. *Cultural Studies.* New York: Routledge, 1992.

Gruenbaum, Ellen. *The Female Circumcision Controversy: An Anthropological Perspective.* Philadelphia: University of Pennsylvania Press, 2001.

Guha, Ranajit. *Dominance without Hegemony: History and Power in Colonial India.* Cambridge, Mass.: Harvard University Press, 1997.

———. Introduction to *A Subaltern Studies Reader, 1986–1995,* edited by Ranajit Guha. Minneapolis: University of Minnesota Press, 1997.

Haddara, Muhammad Mustafa. *Tayyarat al-shiʿr al-arabi al-muʿasir fi al-Sudan.* Beirut: Dar al-Thaqafa, 1972.

Hag El Safi, Mahasin Abdelgadir, ed. *The Nationalist Movement in the Sudan.* Proceedings of the Conference on the Nationalist Movement in the Sudan, held on 8–15 January 1986. Khartoum: Khartoum University Press, 1989.

Hajj al-Safi, Mahasin Abd al-Qadir, ed. *Al-Haraka al-wataniyya fi al-Sudan: Thawrat 1924.* Khartoum: Khartoum University Press, 1992.

Hale, Sondra. *Gender Politics in Sudan: Islamism, Socialism, and the State.* Boulder, Colo.: Westview Press, 1996.

Hale, Sondra Dungan. "The Changing Ethnic Identity of Nubians in an Urban Milieu: Khartoum, Sudan." Ph.D. diss., University of California at Los Angeles, 1979.

Hamad, Bushra. "Sudan Notes and Records and Sudanese Nationalism, 1918–1956." *History in Africa* 22 (1995): 239–70.

*Hamad, Khidir. *Mudhakkirat Khidir Hamad: Al-Haraka al-wataniyya al-sudaniyya, al-Istiqlal wa-ma baʿdahu.* N.p.: Matbaʿat Sawt al-Khalij, 1980.

Hamid, Gamal Mahmoud. *Population Displacement in the Sudan: Patterns, Responses, Coping Strategies.* New York: Center for Migration Studies, 1996.

*Hamilton, J. A. de C., ed. *The Anglo-Egyptian Sudan from Within.* Foreword by Sir Stewart Symes. London: Faber and Faber, 1935.

al-Hardallu, Ibrahim. *Al-Ribat al-thaqafi bayna Misr waʾl-Sudan.* Khartoum: Khartoum University Press, 1977.

Hargey, Taj. "The Suppression of Slavery in the Sudan, 1898–1939." D.Phil. thesis, University of Oxford, 1981.

Harir, Sharif. "Recycling the Past in the Sudan." In *Short-Cut to Decay: The Case of the Sudan,* edited by Sharif Harir and Terje Tvedt, 10–68. Uppsala, Sweden: Nordiska Afrikainstitutet, 1994.

al-Hasan, Mustafa Muhammad. *Rijal wa-mawaqif fi al-haraka al-wataniyya.* N.p., n.d. [Khartoum, 198?].

Hasan, Yusuf Fadl. *Al-Shillukh: Asluha wa-wazifatuha fi Sudan wadi al-Nil al-awsat.* 2d ed. Khartoum: Khartoum University Press, 1989.

———, ed. *Sudan in Africa.* Studies presented to the First International Conference sponsored by The Sudan Research Unit, 7–12 February 1968. 2d ed. Khartoum: Khartoum University Press, 1985. (1st ed., 1971.)

*Hawley, Donald. *Sandtracks in the Sudan.* Wilby, U.K.: Michael Russell, 1995.

Headrick, Daniel R. *The Tools of Empire: Technology and European Imperialism in the Nineteenth Century.* New York: Oxford University Press, 1981.

*Henderson, K. D. D. *The Making of the Modern Sudan: The Life and Letters of Sir Douglas Newbold, K.B.E.* Introduction by Margery Perham. London: Faber and Faber, 1953.

———. *Set under Authority.* Somerset, U.K.: Castle Cary Press, 1987.

*Henderson, K. D. D., and T. R. H. Owen, eds. *Sudan Verse*. London: Chancery Books, 1963.

Hendrickson, Hildi, ed. *Clothing and Difference: Embodied Identities in Colonial and Post-Colonial Africa*. Durham: Duke University Press, 1996.

Heussler, Robert. *Yesterday's Rulers: The Making of the British Colonial Service*. Syracuse, N.Y.: Syracuse University Press, 1963.

*Hill, Richard. *Egypt in the Sudan, 1820–1881*. London: Oxford University Press, 1959.

———. *Sudan Transport: A History of Railway, Marine, and River Services in the Republic of the Sudan*. London: Oxford University Press, 1965.

*Hillelson, S. "Arabic Proverbs, Sayings, Riddles, and Popular Beliefs." *Sudan Notes and Records* 4 (1921): 76–86.

Hobsbawm, Eric J. "Ethnicity and Nationalism in Europe Today." In *Mapping the Nation*, edited by Gopal Balakrishnan, 255–66. London: Verso, 1996.

Hobsbawm, Eric, and Terence Ranger, eds. *The Invention of Tradition*. Cambridge: Cambridge University Press, 1983.

*Hodgkin, Robin A. *Sudan Geography*. London: Longmans, Green, 1951.

Hodgkin, Thomas. *Nationalism in Africa*. London: Frederick Muller, 1968.

Holmedal, Bjarne Osvald. "The Gordon Memorial College at Khartoum: Agent of British Imperialism or Cradle of Independence?" Cand. Philol. thesis, University of Bergen (Norway), 1988.

Holt, P. M., and M. W. Daly. *A History of the Sudan*. 5th ed. London: Longman, 2000.

Hourani, Albert. *Arabic Thought in the Liberal Age, 1798–1939*. Cambridge: Cambridge University Press, 1962.

Hudson, Michael C. Introduction to *Middle East Dilemma: The Politics and Economics of Arab Integration*, edited by Michael C. Hudson, 1–32. New York: Columbia University Press, 1999.

Hudson, Michael C., ed. *Middle East Dilemma: The Politics and Economics of Arab Integration*. New York: Columbia University Press, 1999.

Humphries, Steve. *Victorian Britain through the Magic Lantern*. London: Sidgwick and Jackson, 1989.

Hunt, Lynn, ed. *The New Cultural History*. Berkeley: University of California Press, 1989.

Hunter, Jefferson. *Image and Word: The Interaction of Twentieth-Century Photographs and Texts*. Cambridge, Mass.: Harvard University Press, 1987.

Hyam, Ronald. *Empire and Sexuality: The British Experience*. Manchester, U.K.: Manchester University Press, 1991.

Hyslop, John. *Sudan Story*. London: Naldrett Press, 1952.

Ibn Khaldun. *The Muqaddimah: An Introduction to History*. Translated by Franz Rosenthal, edited and abridged by N. J. Dawood. Princeton, N.J.: Princeton University Press, 1969.

Ibrahim, Abdullahi Ali. *Assaulting with Words: Popular Discourse and the Bridle of Shari'ah*. Evanston: Northwestern University Press, 1994.

———. "Manichaean Delirium: Islam and Colonialism in Sudan." Work in progress, 1999–2000.

Ibrahim, Hasan Ahmed. "The Policy of the Condominium Government towards the Mahdist Political Prisoners." *Sudan Notes and Records* 55 (1974): 33–45.

Ibrahim, Muhammad al-Makki. *Al-Fikr al-sudani: Usuluhu wa-tatawwuruhu.* 2d ed. N.p.: Matba'at Aru al-Tijariyya, 1989. (1st ed., 1979)

Ibrahim, Saad Eddin. "Civil Society and Prospects of Democratization in the Arab World." In *Civil Society in the Middle East*, edited by Augustus Richard Norton, 27–54. Vol. 1. Leiden: E. J. Brill, 1995.

Ibrahim, Yahya Muhammad. *Tarikh al-ta'lim al-dini fi al-Sudan.* Beirut: Dar al-Jil, 1987.

Iliffe, John. *Africans: The History of a Continent.* Cambridge: Cambridge University Press, 1995.

*Jackson, H. C. *Sudan Days and Ways.* London: Macmillan, 1954.

———. *Behind the Modern Sudan.* Foreword by Sir Harold MacMichael. London: Macmillan, 1955.

al-Jamal, Shawqi Ata Allah. "Athar thawrat 1919 fi Misr ala thawrat 1924 fi al-Sudan." In *al-Haraka al-wataniyya fi al-Sudan: Thawrat 1924*, edited by Mahasin Abd al-Qadir Hajj al-Safi, 114–58. Khartoum: Khartoum University Press, 1992.

Jankowski, James, and Israel Gershoni, eds. *Rethinking Nationalism in the Arab Middle East.* New York: Columbia University Press, 1997.

Jarvis, C. S. *Oriental Spotlight.* London: John Murray, 1946.

*Jibril, Tawfiq Salih. *Diwan ufuq wa-shafaq.* Edited by Muhammad Ibrahim Abu Salim and Muhammad Salih Hasan. Vols. 1–4. Beirut: Dar al-Jil, 1991.

Johnson, Douglas H. "Sudanese Military Slavery from the Eighteenth to the Twentieth Century." In *Slavery and Other Forms of Unfree Labour*, edited by Leonie Archer, 142–56. London: Routledge, 1988.

———. "The Structure of a Legacy: Military Slavery in Northeast Africa." *Ethnohistory* 36, no. 1 (1989): 72–88.

———. "From Military to Tribal Police: Policing the Upper Nile Province of the Sudan." In *Policing the Empire: Government, Authority, and Control, 1830–1940*, edited by David M. Anderson and David Killingray, 151–67. Manchester: Manchester University Press, 1991.

July, Robert W. *The Origins of Modern African Thought: Its Development in West Africa during the Nineteenth and Twentieth Centuries.* London: Faber and Faber, 1968.

Kapteijns, Lidwien. *Mahdist Faith and Sudanic Tradition: The History of the Masalit Sultanate 1870–1930.* London: Kegan Paul, 1985.

Kapteijns, L. and J. Spaulding. "History, Ethnicity, and Agriculture in the Sudan." In *The Agriculture of the Sudan*, edited by G. M. Craig, 84–100. Oxford: Oxford University Press, 1991.

Karrar, Ali Salih, Yahya Muhammad Ibrahim, and R. S. O'Fahey. "The Life and Writings of a Sudanese Historian: Muhammad Abd al-Rahim (1878–1966)." *Sudanic Africa: A Journal of Historical Sources* 6 (1995): 125–36.

Keane, John. Civil Society: Old Images, New Visions. Stanford, Calif.: Stanford University Press, 1998.

Kedourie, Elie. Nationalism. Rev. ed. London: Hutchinson University Library, 1961.

Keun, Odette. A Foreigner Looks at the British Sudan. London: Faber and Faber, 1930.

Khalidi, Rashid. Palestinian Identity: The Construction of Modern National Consciousness. New York: Columbia University Press, 1997.

*al-Khatib, Fu'ad. Diwan al-Khatib. 192?, reprint, Cairo: Dar al-Ma'arif, 1959.

———. Fath al-Andalus. 2d ed. Damascus: Matba'at Ibn Zaydun, 1931.

*Khayr al-Muhami, Ahmad. Kifah jil: Tarikh harakat al-khirrijin wa-tatawwuriha fi al-Sudan. Introduction by Muddaththir Abd al-Rahim. 3d ed. Khartoum: Khartoum University Press, 1991. (1st ed., 1948)

Khouri, Mounah A. Poetry and the Making of Modern Egypt, 1882–1922. Leiden: E. J. Brill, 1971.

al-Kid, Khalid Husayn. "Al-Effendiyya wa-mafhum al-qawmiyya fi al-thalathin sana allati a'qabat al-fath fi al-Sudan, 1898–1928." Majallat al-dirasat al-sudaniyya 12, no. 1 (1992): 44–76.

Killingray, David, and Andrew Roberts. "An Outline History of Photography in Africa (to c. 1940)." In Photographs as Sources for African History, papers presented at a workshop held at the School of Oriental and African Studies, London, May 12–13, 1988, edited by Andrew Roberts, 9–24. London: SOAS, 1988.

Kimble, David. A Political History of Ghana: The Rise of Gold Coast Nationalism. Oxford: Clarendon Press, 1963.

Kirk-Greene, A. H. M. "The Thin White Line: The Size of the British Colonial Service in Africa." African Affairs 79, no. 314 (1980): 25–44.

———. The Sudan Political Service: A Preliminary Profile. Oxford: N.p., 1982.

———. "Nationalism in the Non-Nationalist Literature: The Case of the Sudan Political Service." In The Nationalist Movement in the Sudan, edited by Mahasin Abdelgasir Hag El Safi, 322–84. Khartoum: Khartoum University Press, 1989.

———. Nationalism and Arcadianism in the Sudan: The Janus Factor in the Political Service Memoirs. Oxford: n.p., 1993.

Kirk-Greene, Anthony. "Imperial Administration and the Athletic Imperative: The Case of the District Officer in Africa." In Sport in Africa: Essays in Social History, edited by William J. Baker and James A. Mangan, 81–113. New York: Africana Publishing Company, 1987.

———. "Badge of Office: Sport and His Excellency in the British Empire." In The Cultural Bond: Sport, Empire, Society, edited by J. A. Mangan, 178–200. London: Frank Cass, 1992.

*Kisha, Sulayman. Suq al-dhikrayat. Vol. 1. Khartoum: Sharikat al-Tab' wa'l-Nashr, 1963.

Kohn, Hans. Nationalism: Its Meaning and History. Princeton, N.J.: D. Van Nostrand, 1955.

Kramer, Robert S. "The Capitulation of the Omdurman Notables." *Sudanic Africa: A Journal of Historical Sources* 3 (1992): 41–55.

———. "The Death of Basiyouni: A Meditation on Race, Religion, and Identity in the Sudan." Paper presented at the Fifteenth Annual Meeting of the Sudan Studies Association, Alexandria, Virginia, 10–12 May 1996.

Kurita, Yoshiko. "The Role of the 'Negroid but Detribalized' People in Sudanese Society, 1920s–1940s." In vol. 3 of *Papers of the Second International Sudan Studies Conference,* held at the University of Durham (U.K.), 8–11 April 1991, 107–20. Durham: University of Durham, 1991.

———. "The Language of Class and the Language of Race in Modern Sudanese Politics." In *Al-Tannawu' al-thaqafi wa-bina' al-dawla al-wataniyya fi al-Sudan,* edited by Haydar Ibrahim Ali, 76–92. Cairo: Markaz al-Dirasat al-Sudaniyya, 1995.

———. *Ali Abd al-Latif wa thawrat 1924: Bahth fi masadir al-thawra al-sudaniyya.* Translated by Majdi al-Na'im, introduction by Muhammad Sa'id al-Qaddal. Cairo: Markaz al-Dirasat al-Sudaniyya, 1997.

Langley, Michael. *No Woman's Country: Travels in the Anglo-Egyptian Sudan.* New York: Philosophical Library, 1951.

Lavin, Deborah, ed. *The Condominium Remembered: Proceedings of the Durham Sudan Historical Records Conference, 1982.* 2 vols. Durham, U.K.: Centre for Middle Eastern and Islamic Studies, University of Durham, 1991.

*Lea, C. A. E. *On Trek in Kordofan: The Diaries of a British District Officer in the Sudan, 1931–1933.* Edited by M. W. Daly. Oxford: Oxford University Press, 1994.

Lee, Chulwoo. "Modernity, Legality, and Power in Korea under Japanese Rule." In *Colonial Modernity in Korea,* edited by Gi-Wook Shin and Michael Robinson, 21–51. Cambridge, Mass.: Harvard University Asia Center, 1999.

Lenin, V. I. *Imperialism: The Highest Stage of Capitalism.* Moscow: Foreign Languages Publishing House, 1920.

Lesch, Ann Mosely. "The Destruction of Civil Society in the Sudan." In *Civil Society in the Middle East,* edited by Augustus Richard Norton, 153–91. Vol. 2. Leiden: E. J. Brill, 1995.

———. *The Sudan: Contested National Identities.* Bloomington: Indiana University Press, 1998.

Lewis, Bernard. *The Emergence of Modern Turkey.* 2d ed. Oxford: Oxford University Press, 1968.

Lorcin, Patricia M. E. *Imperial Identities: Stereotyping, Prejudice, and Race in Colonial Algeria.* London: I. B. Tauris, 1995.

Lovejoy, Paul E., and Jan S. Hogendorn. *Slow Death for Slavery: The Course of Abolition in Northern Nigeria, 1897–1936.* Cambridge: Cambridge University Press, 1993.

Luckham, Robin. *The Nigerian Military: A Sociological Analysis of Authority and Revolt, 1960–67.* Cambridge: Cambridge University Press, 1971.

Lüdtke, Alf, ed. *The History of Everyday Life: Reconstructing Historical Expe-*

riences and Ways of Life. Translated by William Templer. Princeton, N.J.: Princeton University Press, 1995.

Lugard, F. D. *The Dual Mandate in British Tropical Africa.* Edinburgh: William Blackwood and Sons, 1922.

Luhrmann, T. M. *The Good Parsi: The Fate of a Colonial Elite in a Postcolonial Society.* Cambridge, Mass.: Harvard University Press, 1996.

Macaulay, Thomas Babington. "Government of India: A Speech Delivered in the House of Commons on the 10th of July, 1833." In vol. 8 of *The Works of Lord Macaulay Complete*, edited by Lady Trevelyan, 111–42. New York: Longmans, Green, 1897.

MacDonald, Robert H. *Sons of the Empire: The Frontier and the Boys Scout Movement, 1890–1918.* Toronto: University of Toronto Press, 1993.

*Macdonald, R. S., and Mary Wright, comps. *"Da Kitab": A Sudanese Colloquial Grammar.* Edited by J. Spencer Trimingham. Cairo: The Society for Promoting Christian Knowledge for The Church Missionary Society, Northern Sudan, 1939.

MacKenzie, John M., ed. *Imperialism and Popular Culture.* Manchester: Manchester University Press, 1986.

*MacMichael, Harold. *The Anglo-Egyptian Sudan.* London: Faber and Faber, 1934.

MacMillan, W. M. "The Importance of the Educated African." *Journal of the African Society* 33, no. 131 (1934): 137–42.

al-Mahdi, al-Sadiq. *Al-Islam wa-mas'alat janub al-Sudan.* Omdurman: Matba'at al-Tamaddun, 1985.

*Mahjub, Muhammad Ahmad. *Al-Haraka al-fikriyya fi al-Sudan: Ila ayna yajibu an tattajjiha?* Khartoum: al-Matba'a al-Tijariyya al-Jadida, 1941.

———. *Al-Andalus al-mafqud.* Beirut, 1969.

———. *Nahwa al-ghad.* Khartoum: Khartoum University Press, 1970.

*Mahjub, Muhammad Ahmad, and Abd al-Halim Muhammad. *Mawt dunya.* 2d ed. Khartoum: Khartoum University Press, 1986.

al-Malik, Sharaf al-Din Muhammad Hamad. *Usrat muluk Arqu fi tarikh al-Sudan: Nabdha atifiyya.* N.p., 1990.

Mamdani, Mahmood. *Citizen and Subject: Contemporary Africa and the Legacy of Late Colonialism.* Princeton, N.J.: Princeton University Press, 1996.

Mangan, J. A. "The Education of an Elite Imperial Administration: The Sudan Political Service and the British Public School System." *International Journal of African Historical Studies* 15, no. 4 (1982): 671–99.

———. *The Games Ethic and Imperialism: Aspects of the Diffusion of an Ideal.* Harmondsworth, U.K.: Viking, 1986.

———. "Britain's Chief Spiritual Export: Imperial Sport as Moral Metaphor, Political Symbol, and Cultural Bond." In *The Cultural Bond: Sport, Empire, Society*, edited by J. A. Mangan, 1–10. London: Frank Cass, 1992.

———, ed. *The Cultural Bond: Sport, Empire, Society.* London: Frank Cass, 1992.

Mangan, James A. "Ethics and Ethnocentricity: Imperial Education in British Tropical Africa." In *Sport in Africa: Essays in Social History,* edited by William J. Baker and James A. Mangan, 138–71. New York: Africana Publishing Company, 1987.

Maqar, Hilmi Jirjis Ghubriyal. "Mawqif al-idara fi al-Sudan min nahwa al-haraka al-wataniyya khilala al-harbayn al-alamiyyatayn fi al-fitra min 1914 ila 1947." Ph.D. diss., Cairo University, 1976.

*Martin, Percy F. *The Sudan in Evolution: A Study of the Economic, Financial, and Administrative Conditions of the Anglo-Egyptian Sudan.* Foreword by General Sir F. Reginald Wingate. London: Constable and Co., 1921.

Mashru' Tarikh al-Haraka al-Wataniyya fi al-Sudan. *Bibliyughrafiya al-haraka al-wataniyya fi al-Sudan, 1919–1955.* Vol. 2. Khartoum: Ma'had al-Dirasat al-Ifriqiyya wa'l-Asyawiyya, Jami'at al-Khartum, 1985.

*Mavrogordato, Jack. *Behind the Scenes: An Autobiography.* Tisbury, U.K.: Element Books Limited, 1982.

Mawut, Lazarus Leek. "The Southern Sudan under British Rule, 1898–1924: The Constraints Reassessed." Ph.D. diss., University of Durham, 1995.

McCrone, David. *The Sociology of Nationalism.* London: Routledge, 1998.

McDonald, Ellen E., and Craig M. Stark. *English Education, Nationalist Politics, and Elite Groups in Maharashtra, 1885–1915.* Occasional Paper, no. 5. Berkeley: Center for South and Southeast Asia Studies, University of California, 1969.

McDowall, David. *A Modern History of the Kurds.* London: I. B. Tauris, 1996.

McHugh, Neil. *Holymen of the Blue Nile: The Making of an Arab-Islamic Community in the Nilotic Sudan, 1500–1850.* Evanston, Ill.: Northwestern University Press, 1994.

Messick, Brinkley. *The Calligraphic State: Textual Domination and History in a Muslim Society.* Berkeley: University of California Press, 1993.

Metcalf, Thomas R. *Ideologies of the Raj.* Vol. 3, *The New Cambridge History of India,* pt. 4, *The Indian Empire and the Beginning of Modern Society.* Cambridge: Cambridge University Press, 1994.

Metz, Helen Chapin, ed. *Sudan: A Country Study.* Washington, D.C.: Library of Congress, 1991.

"Mexico's Indians: One Nation, or Many?" *The Economist,* 20–26, January 2001, pp. 33–34.

*Mikha'il, Sa'd. *Shu'ara' al-Sudan.* Cairo: Matba'at Ramsis, 1924.

———. *Al-Sudan bayna ahdayn: Ittifaqiyyat 1899—mu'ahadat 1936.* Minya: al-Matba'a al-Khayriyya, n.d. [c. 1940].

Miller, David. *On Nationality.* Oxford: Clarendon Press, 1995.

Misra, B. B. *The Bureaucracy in India: An Historical Analysis of Development up to 1947.* Delhi: Oxford University Press, 1977.

Mitchell, Timothy. *Colonising Egypt.* Cambridge: Cambridge University Press, 1988.

Morris-Jones, W. H., and Georges Fischer, eds. *Decolonisation and After: The British and the French Experience.* London: Frank Cass, 1980.

Murqus, Yuwaqim Rizq. *Tatawwur nizam al-idara fi al-Sudan fi ahd al-hukm al-thuna'i al-awwal, 1899–1924.* Cairo: Hay'at al-misriyya al-amma lil-kutub, 1984.

*Mynors, T. H. B. "A School of Administration in the Anglo-Egyptian Sudan." *Journal of African Administration* 2, no. 2 (1950): 24–26.

*Najila, Hasan. *Malamih min al-mujtama' al-sudani.* 3d ed. Beirut: Dar Maktabat al-Hayat, 1964.

———. *Dhikrayati fi al-badiya.* Beirut: Dar Maktabat al-Hayat, 1964.

Nandy, Ashis. *The Intimate Enemy: Loss and Recovery of Self under Colonialism.* Delhi: Oxford University Press, 1983.

Nasr, Ahmad Abd al-Rahim. *Al-Idara al-baritaniyya wa'l-tabshir al-islami wa'l-masihi fi al-Sudan: Dirasa awaliyya.* Khartoum: Wizarat al-Tarbiya wa'l-Tawjih, al-Shu'un al-diniyya wa'l-awqaf, 1979.

Negash, Tekeste. *Italian Colonialism in Eritrea, 1882–1914: Policies, Praxis, and Impact.* Stockholm: Almqvist and Wiksell, 1987.

Nelson, Harold D., et al. *Area Handbook for the Democratic Republic of the Sudan.* Washington, D.C.: U.S. Government Printing Office, 1973.

Niblock, Tim. *Class and Power in the Sudan: The Dynamics of Sudanese Politics, 1898–1985.* Houndsmills, U.K.: Macmillan Press, 1987.

Norton, Augustus Richard, ed. *Civil Society in the Middle East.* 2 vols. Leiden: E. J. Brill, 1995.

*Nur, Mu'awiya. *Mu'allafat.* 2 vols. Khartoum: Qism al-Ta'lif wa'l-Nashr, Jami'at al-Khartum, 1970.

al-Nuwayhi, Muhammad. *Muhadarat an al-ittijahat al-shi'riyya fi al-Sudan.* Cairo: Matba'at Nahdat Misr, 1957.

O'Fahey, R. S., ed. *Arabic Literature of Africa.* Vol. 1, *The Writings of Eastern Sudanic Africa to c. 1900.* Leiden: E. J. Brill, 1994.

*Okier, Abdel Gader. "Education Amongst the Beja." *Oversea Education* 23 (1951): 194–96.

O'Malley, L. S. S. *The Indian Civil Service, 1601–1930.* London: John Murray, 1931.

Ong, Walter J. *Orality and Literacy: The Technologizing of the Word.* London: Routledge, 1991.

Orwell, George. "Shooting an Elephant." In *Shooting an Elephant and Other Essays,* 3–12. New York: Harcourt, Brace and World, 1950.

Osman, Khalid H. A. "The Effendia and Concepts of Nationalism in the Sudan." Ph.D. diss., University of Reading, 1987.

Osman, Mohammed K. "The Rise and Decline of the People's (*Ahlia*) Education in the Northern Sudan (1927–1957)," *Paedagogica Historica* 18, no. 2 (1979): 355–71.

Osterhammel, Jürgen. *Colonialism: A Theoretical Overview.* Translated by Shelley Frisch. Princeton, N.J.: Markus Wiener, 1997.

Permanent Committee on Geographic Names for British Official Use. *First List of Names in the Anglo-Egyptian Sudan.* London: Royal Geographic Society, 1927.

Potter, David C. *India's Political Administrators, 1919–1983*. Oxford: Clarendon Press, 1986.

Powell, Eve Troutt. "Brothers along the Nile: Egyptian Concepts of Race and Ethnicity, 1895–1910." In *The Nile: Histories, Cultures, Myths*, edited by Haggai Erlich and Israel Gershoni, 171–81. Boulder, Colo.: Lynne Rienner Publishers, 2000.

Powell, Eve Marie Troutt. "Colonized Colonizers: Egyptian Nationalists and the Issue of the Sudan, 1875 to 1919." Ph.D. diss., Harvard University, 1995.

Prakash, Gyan. "Subaltern Studies as Postcolonial Criticism." *American Historical Review* 99, no. 5 (1994): 1475–90.

Rakha, Hasan Ali. *Al'ab sudaniyya*. Khartoum: al-Matba'a al-Hukumiyya, 1964.

Ranger, Terence. "Connexions between 'Primary Resistance' Movements and Modern Mass Nationalism in East and Central Africa." *Journal of African History* 9 (1968): 437–53, 631–41.

———. "Making Northern Rhodesia Imperial: Variations on a Royal Theme, 1924–1938." *African Affairs* 79, no. 316 (1980): 349–73.

———. "The Inventing of Tradition in Colonial Africa." In *The Invention of Tradition*, edited by Eric Hobsbawm and Terence Ranger, 211–62. Cambridge: Cambridge University Press, 1983.

Ravindiran, V. "Discourses of Empowerment: Missionary Orientalism in the Development of Dravidian Nationalism." In *Nation Work: Asian Elites and National Identities*, edited by Timothy Brook and André Schmid, 51–82. Ann Arbor: University of Michigan Press, 2000.

Reid, Donald Malcolm. *Cairo University and the Making of Modern Egypt*. Cambridge: Cambridge University Press, 1990.

Renan, Ernest. "What Is a Nation?" In *Becoming National: A Reader*, edited by Geoff Eley and Ronald Grigor Suny, 41–55. New York: Oxford University Press, 1996.

Rizq, Yunan Labib. *Al-Sudan fi ahd al-hukm al-thuna'i al-awwal, 1899–1924*. Cairo: Dar Nafi' lil-Tiba'a, 1986.

Roberts, A. D., ed. *The Colonial Moment in Africa: Essays on the Movement of Minds and Materials, 1900–1940*. Cambridge: Cambridge University Press, 1990.

*Robertson, James. *Transition in Africa: From Direct Rule to Independence*. London: C. Hurst and Co., 1974.

Robinson, Ronald. "Non-European Foundations of European Imperialism: A Sketch for a Theory of Collaboration." In *Studies in the Theory of Imperialism*, edited by Roger Owen and Bob Sutcliffe, 117–42. London: Longman, 1972.

Rodney, Walter. *How Europe Underdeveloped Africa*. Washington, D.C.: Howard University Press, 1974.

Roy, Naresh Chandra. *The Civil Service in India*. 2d ed. Calcutta: Firma K. L. Mukhopadhyay, 1960.

Ruay, Deng D. Akol. *The Politics of Two Sudans: The South and North, 1821–1969*. Uppsala, Sweden: Nordiska Afrikainstitutet, 1994.

Rushdie, Salman. *Midnight's Children*. New York: Everyman's Library, 1995.

Ryan, James R. *Picturing Empire: Photography and the Visualization of the British Empire*. London: Reaktion Books, 1997.

Said, Edward. *Culture and Imperialism*. London: Chatto and Windus, 1993.

Said, Edward W. *Orientalism*. New York: Vintage Books, 1978.

———. *Representations of the Intellectual*. New York: Pantheon Books, 1994.

Sa'id, Bashir Muhammad. "Min iftitah khazzan Sinnar ila nash'at al-sihafa al-sudaniyya." Vol. 1, pt. 3 of *Al-Sudan min al-hukm al-thuna'i ila intifadat Rajab*. Khartoum: Sharikat al-Ayyam lil-Adawat al-Maktabiyya al-Mahduda, 1986.

Salih, Kamal el-Din Osman. "The British Administration in the Nuba Mountains Region of the Sudan, 1900–1956." Ph.D. diss., University of London (SOAS), 1982.

Salih, Mahjub Muhammad. *Al-Sihafa al-sudaniyya fi nisf qarn, 1903–1953*. Khartoum: Khartoum University Press, 1971.

Sami, Ahmad Abd Allah. *Al-Sha'ir al-sudani Muhammad Sa'id al-Abbasi*. Khartoum: Dar al-Irshad, 1968.

Sandell, Liza. *English Language in Sudan: A History of Its Teaching and Politics*. London: Ithaca Press, 1982.

Sanderson, G. N. Introduction to *The Memoirs of Babikr Bedri*, by Babikr Bedri. Vol. 2. Translated and edited by Yusuf Bedri and Peter Hogg. London: Ithaca Press, 1980.

Sanderson, Lilian. "The Development of Girls' Education in the Northern Sudan, 1898–1960." *Paedagogica Historica* 8, no. 1 (1968): 120–52.

Sanderson, Lilian Passmore, and Neville Sanderson. *Education, Religion, and Politics in Southern Sudan, 1899–1964*. London: Ithaca Press, 1981.

*Santandrea, Stefano. *A Popular History of Wau: From Its Foundation to about 1940, including The Story of Wau Mission Schools*. Khartoum: Encounter, 1989.

Sarkar, Sumit. *Writing Social History*. Delhi: Oxford University Press, 1997.

*Sarsfield-Hall, E. G. *From Cork to Khartoum: Memoirs of Southern Ireland and the Anglo-Egyptian Sudan, 1866–1936*. Foreword by Viscount Rochdale. Keswick, U.K.: n.p., 1975.

Schmid, André. "Decentering the 'Middle Kingdom': The Problem of China in Korean Nationalist Thought, 1895–1910." In *Nation Work: Asian Elites and National Identities*, edited by Timothy Brook and André Schmid, 83–107. Ann Arbor: University of Michigan Press, 2000.

*Schuster, George. *Private Work and Public Causes: A Personal Record, 1881–1978*. Cowbridge, U.K.: D. Brown and Sons, 1979.

Seton-Watson, Hugh. "Old and New Nations." In *Nationalism*, edited by John Hutchinson and Anthony D. Smith, 134–37. Oxford: Oxford University Press, 1994.

Shafiq, Ahmad. *Hawliyyat Misr al-siyasiyya: Al-hawliyyat al-ula, sanat 1925*. Cairo: Matba'at Hawliyyat Misr, 1925.

al-Shahi, Ahmed S. "Proverbs and Social Values in a Northern Sudanese Village." In *Essays in Sudan Ethnography (Presented to Sir Edward Evans-Pritchard)*, edited by Ian Cunnison and Wendy James, 87–104. London: C. Hurst and Co., 1972.

Sharkey, Heather. "Domestic Slavery in the Nineteenth- and Early Twentieth-Century Northern Sudan." M.Phil. thesis, University of Durham, 1992.

———. "*Tabaqat* of the Twentieth-Century Sudan: Arabic Biographical Dictionaries as a Source for Colonial History, 1898–1956." *Sudanic Africa* 6 (1995): 17–34.

———. "Two Sudanese Midwives," Part 1: "Congenital Syphilis: A Sudanese Midwife's Report," and Part 2: "Batul Muhammad Isa: Biography of a Sudanese Midwife." *Sudanic Africa* 9 (1998): 19–38.

———. "Arabic Literature and the Nationalist Imagination in Kordofan." In *Kordofan Invaded: Peripheral Incorporation and Social Transformation in Islamic Africa*, edited by Endre Stiansen and Michael Kevane, 165–79. Leiden: Brill, 1998.

———. "Colonialism and the Culture of Nationalism in the Northern Sudan, 1898–1956." 2 vols. Ph.D. diss., Princeton University, 1998.

———. "A Century in Print: Arabic Journalism and Nationalism in the Sudan, 1899–1999." *International Journal of Middle East Studies* 31, no. 4 (1999): 531–49.

———. "Articulating the Nation: Arabic Literary Landscapes from the Sudan and North Africa." To appear in a volume of essays from a conference on Literature and Nationalism in the Middle East and North Africa, held at Edinburgh University in July 2000.

———. "Christians among Muslims: The Church Missionary Society in the Northern Sudan." *Journal of African History* 43, no. 1 (2001): 51–75.

Sharkey-Balasubramanian, Heather. "The Egyptian Colonial Presence in the Anglo-Egyptian Sudan, 1898–1932." In *White Nile, Black Blood: War, Leadership, and Ethnicity from Khartoum to Kampala*, edited by Jay Spaulding and Stephanie Beswick, 279–314. Lawrenceville, N.J.: Red Sea Press, 2000.

*Shibayka, Makki. *Al-Sudan abra al-qurun*. Cairo: Matba'at Lajnat al-Ta'lif wa'l-Tarjama wa'l-Nashr, 1964.

*Shields, Ried F. *Behind the Garden of Allah*. Philadelphia: United Presbyterian Board of Foreign Missions, 1937.

Shin, Gi-Wook, and Michael Robinson, eds. *Colonial Modernity in Korea*. Cambridge, Mass.: Harvard University Asia Center, 1999.

Shukla, J. D. *Indianisation of All-India Services and Its Impact on Administration*. New Delhi: Allied Publishers Private Limited, 1982.

*Shuqayr, Na'um. *Tarikh al-Sudan al-qadim wa'l-hadith wa-jughrafiyatuhu*. Cairo: n.p., 1903.

al-Shush, Muhammad Ibrahim. *Al-Shi'r al-hadith fi al-Sudan*. Vol. 1, *Al-shi'r al-taqlidi wa-bidayat al-tajdid*. 2d ed. Khartoum: Dar al-Tiba'a, Jami'at al-Khartum, 1971.

———. Introduction to *Al-Adab al-sudani wa-ma yajibu an yakuna alayhi*, by Hamza al-Malik Tambal, 3–19. 2d ed. Beirut: Dar al-Fikr, 1972.

Sidahmed, Abdel Salam. *Politics and Islam in Contemporary Sudan.* New York: St. Martin's Press, 1996.

Sikainga, Ahmed Alawad. *Slaves into Workers: Emancipation and Labor in Colonial Sudan.* Austin: University of Texas Press, 1996.

Sikka, Ram Parkash. *The Civil Service in India: Europeanisation and Indianisation under the East India Company (1765–1857).* New Delhi: Uppal Publishing House, 1984.

Simon, Reeva S. "The Imposition of Nationalism on a Non-Nation State: The Case of Iraq during the Interwar Period, 1921–1941." In *Rethinking Nationalism in the Arab Middle East,* edited by James Jankowski and Israel Gershoni, 87–104. New York: Columbia University Press, 1997.

Singh, Chadrahas. *The Civil Service in India (1858–1947).* Delhi: Atma Ram and Sons, 1989.

Sinha, Mrinalini. *Colonial Masculinity: The 'Manly Englishman' and the 'Effeminate Bengali' in the Late Nineteenth Century.* Manchester: Manchester University Press, 1995.

Sivan, Emmanuel. "Arab Nationalism in the Age of the Islamic Resurgence." In *Rethinking Nationalism in the Arab Middle East,* edited by James Jankowski and Israel Gershoni, 207–28. New York: Columbia University Press, 1997.

Smith, Anthony D. *State and Nation in the Third World: The Western State and African Nationalism.* New York: St. Martin's Press, 1983.

Sontag, Susan. *On Photography.* New York: Farrar, Straus and Giroux, 1978.

Spaulding, Jay. "Slavery, Land Tenure, and Social Class in the Northern Turkish Sudan." *The International Journal of African Historical Studies* 15, no. 1 (1982): 1–20.

———. *The Heroic Age in Sinnar.* East Lansing: Michigan State University Press, 1985.

Spaulding, Jay, and Lidwien Kapteijns. "The Orientalist Paradigm in the Historiography of the Late Precolonial Sudan." In *Golden Ages, Dark Ages: Imagining the Past in Anthropology and History,* edited by Jay O'Brien and William Roseberry, 139–51. Berkeley: University of California Press, 1991.

Spivak, Gayatri Chakravorty. "Can the Subaltern Speak?" In *Marxism and Interpretation of Culture,* edited by Cary Nelson and Lawrence Grossberg, 271–313. Urbana: University of Illinois Press, 1988.

*Squires, H. C. *The Sudan Medical Service: An Experiment in Social Medicine.* London: William Heinemann, 1958.

Sraïeb, Noureddine. *Le Collège Sadiki de Tunis, 1875–1956: Enseignement et nationalisme.* Paris: CNRS Éditions, 1995.

*Staniforth, Arthur. *Imperial Echoes: The Sudan—People, History, and Agriculture.* Oxford: WorldView Publishing, 2000.

*Stanton, E. A. "The Anglo-Egyptian Sudan." *Journal of the Royal Asiatic Society* 11, no. 43 (1912): 261–74.

*Stanton, Edward A. "Khartoum." In vol. 2 of *The Story of the Cape to Cairo Railway and River Route, from 1887 to 1922,* edited by Leo Weinthal, 282–87. London: The Pioneer Publishing Company, 1923.

*Symes, Stewart. *Tour of Duty.* London: Collins, 1946.
*Taha, Abd al-Rahman Ali. *Al-Sudan lil-Sudaniyyin: Tama' fa-niza' wa-wathba fa-jihad,* edited by Fadwa Abd al-Rahman Ali Taha. 2d ed. Khartoum: Khartoum University Press, 1992.
Taha, Fadwa Abd al-Rahman Ali. Introduction to *Al-Sudan lil-Sudaniyyin: Tama' fa-niza' wa-wathba fa-jihad,* by Abd al-Rahman Ali Taha. 2d ed. Khartoum: Khartoum University Press, 1992.
*Tambal [a.k.a. Tanbal], Hamza al-Malik. *Al-Adab al-sudani wa-ma yajibu an yakuna alayhi.* 2d ed. Beirut: Dar al-Fikr, 1972.
*Tanbal [a.k.a. Tambal], Hamza al-Malik. *Al-Adab al-sudani wa-ma yajibu an yakuna alayhi.* Cairo: n.p., 1927.
———. *Diwan al-Tabi'a.* Cairo: N.p., 1931.
*al-Tayyib, Abd Allah. *Muhadarat fi al-ittijjahat al-haditha fi al-nathr al-arabi.* Cairo: Matba'at Nahdat Misr, 1959.
*Thomas, Graham. *Sudan: Death of a Dream.* London: Darf Publishers, 1990.
*Thomas, Graham F. *Far from the Valleys.* Lewes, U.K.: Book Guild, 1995.
Thompson, E. P. *The Making of the English Working Class.* New York: Vintage Books, 1966.
Thompson, Elizabeth. *Colonial Citizens: Republican Rights, Paternal Privilege, and Gender in French Syria and Lebanon.* New York: Columbia University Press, 2000.
Tignor, Robert L. *Modernization and British Colonial Rule in Egypt, 1882–1914.* Princeton, N.J.: Princeton University Press, 1966.
Tilly, Charles. "How Empires End." In *After Empire: Multiethnic Societies and Nation-Building (The Soviet Union and the Russian, Ottoman, and Habsburg Empires),* edited by Karen Barkey and Mark von Hagen, 1–11. Boulder, Colo.: Westview Press, 1997.
Tosh, John. *The Pursuit of History.* London: Longman, 1984.
*al-Tum, Amin. *Dhikrayat wa-mawaqif fi tariq al-haraka al-wataniyya al-sudaniyya, 1914–1969.* Khartoum: Khartoum University Press, 1987.
*"Two Murder Trials in Kordofan." *Sudan Notes and Records* 3 (1920): 245–59.
*Udal, N. R. *Education in the Northern Sudan.* Rome: Reale Accademia D'Italia, 1938.
U.S. Committee for Refugees. *World Refugee Survey 1998.* Washington, D.C.: U.S. Committee for Refugees, 1998.
———. "Country Report: Sudan." <http://www.refugees.org/world/countryrpt/africa/sudan.htm>. Accessed 29 December 1999.
*Uthman, al-Dardiri Muhammad. *Mudhakkirati, 1914–1958.* Khartoum: Matba'at al-Tamaddun, n.d.
Vatikiotis, P. J. *The History of Modern Egypt.* 4th ed. Baltimore: Johns Hopkins University Press, 1991.
Viswanathan, Gauri. *Masks of Conquest: Literary Study and British Rule in India.* New York: Columbia University Press, 1989.
Warburg, Gabriel. *The Sudan under Wingate: Administration in the Anglo-Egyptian Sudan, 1899–1916.* London: Frank Cass, 1971.

————. "Religious Policy in the Northern Sudan: Ulama and Sufism, 1899–1918." *Asian and African Studies* 7 (1971): 89–119.

————. *Islam, Nationalism, and Communism in a Traditional Society: The Case of Sudan.* London: Frank Cass, 1978.

Warburg, Gabriel R. *Historical Discord in the Nile Valley.* London: Hurst and Co., 1992.

Warren, Allen. "Citizens of the Empire: Baden-Powell, Scouts and Guides and an Imperial Ideal." In *Imperialism and Popular Culture*, edited by John M. MacKenzie, 232–56. Manchester: Manchester University Press, 1986.

Weber, Eugen. *Peasants into Frenchmen: The Modernization of Rural France, 1870–1914.* Stanford, Calif.: Stanford University Press, 1976.

Wehr, Hans. *A Dictionary of Modern Written Arabic*, edited by J. Milton Cowan. 3d ed. Ithaca, N.Y.: Spoken Language Services, 1976.

*Willis, C. A., comp. *The Upper Nile Province Handbook: A Report on Peoples and Government in the Southern Sudan, 1931.* Edited by Douglas H. Johnson. Oxford: Oxford University Press, 1995.

Willis, John Ralph, ed. *Slaves and Slavery in Muslim Africa.* Vol. 1. London: Frank Cass, 1985.

*Wingate, Francis Reginald. "The Story of the Gordon College and Its Work." In vol. 1 of *The Story of the Cape to Cairo Railway and River Route from 1887 to 1922*, edited by Leo Weinthal, 563–611. London: Pioneer Publishing, 1923.

*Wingate, Reginald. "Sir James Currie's Life and Work." *East Africa and Rhodesia* 25 (1937): 894–95, 897.

Wolpert, Stanley. *A New History of India.* 4th ed. Oxford: Oxford University Press, 1993.

Wöndu, Steven, and Ann Lesch. *Battle for Peace in Sudan: An Analysis of the Abuja Conferences, 1992–1993.* Lanham, Md.: University Press of America, 2000.

Woodruff, Philip. *The Men Who Ruled India: The Founders.* London: Jonathan Cape, 1953.

Woodward, Peter. *Sudan: The Unstable State, 1898–1989.* Boulder, Colo.: Lynne Rienner, 1990.

Ya'qub, Muhammad Salih. *Sudaniyyat fi salunat al-adab.* Khartoum: Khartoum University Press, 1991.

Yasin, Muhammad Uthman. *Al-Sha'ir Tawfiq Salih Jibril: Dhikrayat wa-ahadith.* Beirut: Dar al-Thaqafa, 1971.

Young, Crawford. *The Politics of Cultural Pluralism.* Madison: University of Wisconsin Press, 1976.

————. *The African Colonial State in Comparative Perspective.* New Haven, Conn.: Yale University Press, 1994.

*Yunis, Nagib. "The Kuku and Other Minor Tribes of the Kajo Kaji District." *Sudan Notes and Records* 7 (1924): 1–41.

Zartman, William I., ed. *Elites in the Middle East.* New York: Praeger, 1980.

Zerubavel, Yael. *Recovered Roots: Collective Memory and the Making of Israeli National Tradition.* Chicago: University of Chicago Press, 1995.

Zulfo, Ismat Hasan. *Karari: The Sudanese Account of the Battle of Omdurman.* Translated by Peter Clark. London: Frederick Warne, 1980.

Index

al-Abbasi, Muhammad Sa'id, 188n48
Abboud, General Ibrahim, 126
Abd Allah, Abd al-Salam, 90
Abd Allah, Arafat Muhammad, 103–4,
    106, 181n67
Abd al-Latif, Ali, 38, 78, 104
Abd al-Qadir, Salih, 106
Abd al-Rahim, Muhammad, 109, 118,
    152n61, 170n41
Abd al-Raziq, Ibrahim, 102–3
Abdullahi, al-Khalifa. See al-Khalifa
    Abdullahi
Abu'l-Azayim, Mahmud, 111, 113,
    166n134
Abu'l-Rish, Muhammad Abbas, 108,
    181n66
Abu Rawf literary society, 37–38
Abu Shahin, George, 83
Acculturation, 20, 40–42, 121–22, 134.
    See also Westernized "natives"
Addis Ababa Agreement of 1972, 135
Ahfad University for Women, 55
Ahmad, Ibrahim, 90
Ahmad, Jamal Muhammad, 100
Ahmad, Muhammad (al-Mahdi), 5
Algeria, 16
Ali, Mirghani, 119
Ali, Muhammad, 4
American Presbyterian missionaries, 23
al-Amin, Ubayd Hajj, 106
Anderson, Benedict, 123–24

Anglo-Egyptian Agreement of 1899, 18
Anglo-Egyptian Agreement of 1936, 73
Anglo-Egyptian "Condominium," 5–6,
    21, 70–71
Anti-colonialism. See Colonial
    resistance
Arab League, 136
Arab/Black classification system, 21
Arabic as lingua franca, 7, 11, 131–32
Arabic literature, 10, 51–52, 104–11,
    123, 127–31
Arabism, 52, 127–33
Archer, Geoffrey, 49
Arkell, A. J., 81
Arslan, Shakib, 64
Ashri al-Siddiq, Abd Allah, 38–39
Ashri al-Siddiq, Muhammad, 38–39
al-Asil (journal), 108
al-Atabani, Isma'il, 54, 89, 166n134
Atiyah, Edward, 90
Atlantic Charter of 1941, 91
Autocracy, 81, 125–26
al-Ayyubi, Salah al-Din, 188n46
al-Azhar (school), 27

Babikr, Khalaf Allah, 114
Babus. See Westernized "natives"
Baden-Powell, Robert, 46
Badri, Ali, 90
Badri, Babikr, 21, 26, 79, 80, 114,
    155n49, 184n93